ADVENTURES
with
OLD VINES

ADVENTURES
with
OLD VINES

A BEGINNER'S GUIDE TO BEING A WINE CONNOISSEUR

RICHARD L. CHILTON JR.

ROWMAN & LITTLEFIELD
LANHAM • BOULDER • NEW YORK • LONDON

Published by Rowman & Littlefield
A wholly owned subsidiary of The Rowman & Littlefield Publishing Group, Inc.
4501 Forbes Boulevard, Suite 200, Lanham, Maryland 20706
www.rowman.com

Unit A, Whitacre Mews, 26-34 Stannary Street, London SE11 4AB, United Kingdom

Distributed by NATIONAL BOOK NETWORK

British Library Cataloguing in Publication Information Available

Library of Congress Cataloging-in-Publication Data
Names: Chilton, Richard L., 1958– author.
Title: Adventures with old vines : a beginner's guide to being a wine connoisseur / Richard L. Chilton Jr.
Description: Lanham : Rowman & Littlefield, 2017. I Includes index.
Identifiers: LCCN 2017023127 (print) I LCCN 2017023639 (ebook) I ISBN 9781538106143 (electronic) I ISBN 9781538106136 (hardback : alk. paper)
Subjects: LCSH: Wine tasting. I Wine and wine making.
Classification: LCC TP548.5.A5 (ebook) I LCC TP548.5.A5 C49 2017 (print) I DDC 641.2/2—dc23
LC record available at https://lccn.loc.gov/2017023127

♾™ The paper used in this publication meets the minimum requirements of American National Standard for Information Sciences—Permanence of Paper for Printed Library Materials, ANSI/NISO Z39.48-1992.

Printed in the United States of America

To Mom, Dad, Maureen, Ricky, Sarah, Charlotte, and Hope,
your enduring love and support make me tick.

To Bill Kavanagh, whose passion for everything was truly inspiring,
but his love of Saint-Emilion was wicked.

CONTENTS

ACKNOWLEDGMENTS

As with anything in life, writing a book is not a singular pursuit. Many people provided me much-needed help and counsel. For that I am deeply thankful. My best friend and wife, Maureen, who for thirty-six years has put up with a lot of swirling, tasting, and lugging wine home after our many vineyard trips. Her enthusiasm for my passion is great and her palate is even better. Many thanks go to my dad, Richard Sr., who after a distinguished career in advertising has published eight books on baseball and football. He showed me the value and power of the printed word, a real gift. Gabby Stone's help with the research and writing of the wine profiles was invaluable, as was her counsel with editing and making sure I was on point. She is a great friend and true lover of wine. Lacy Kiernan, a very talented young photographer, who agreed to work with me and provide navigational skills in obtaining the rights to our photographs and taking many of the pictures for this book. Her skills are great and I am sure you will be hearing about her in the future. Jessica Murphy, my very dedicated and exceptional assistant, was nearly flawless in her typing and understanding my written word. She never wavered, draft upon draft. Jeff Smith, my co-partner at Hourglass, and our very talented winemaker, Tony

Biagi, who made sure that my description of how wine is really made was as crisp as a good Sauvignon Blanc. Susan McEachern and Rebeccah Shumaker, my editor and her assistant, who were steadfast and patient with their advice for me on how to turn this book into a reality. Many thanks to the late Al Hotchin and his colleague Geraldine Tashjian from the Burgundy Wine Company for introducing and teaching a young guy the seductive pleasures of Burgundies. Many thanks to all the vineyards from around the world that provided pictures for this book.

INTRODUCTION

⌇

My wine journey started in 1976. I was living with my family in Ho-Ho-Kus, New Jersey, in an old house that, like many houses of that era, had to be retrofitted with a bomb shelter and equipped with three weeks of food, water, and provisions in case of a nuclear attack. Once the threat had diminished, these shelters fell into disuse, so my dad lobbed out the question, "What should we do with ours?" It was a dark, dank space that housed a good many spiderwebs and much mold. In the past it had been used as a darkroom for photography, but I immediately shot back, "Let's turn it into a wine cellar." My dad, largely a spirits drinker, agreed under duress from both myself and my brother Chip, who was working at a well-known local wine shop (as a part-time job) and who had suggested that he was eligible for great employee discounts. We immediately started filling the cellar and tasting wines from all different wine regions. I felt it would be important for future success if I knew my way around the wine industry, so I plunged in and immersed myself in the myriad of information that was around in those pre-Internet days. Robert Parker's *Wine Advocate* was just starting up, and his in-depth analysis of wine regions was a big help. I tasted and studied, tasted and studied, starting with Bordeaux, then the Rhône,

Burgundy, and other French regions. With every tasting and bottle of wine that I tried, I discovered how much I loved the experience but also how little I knew. At that moment, I realized that wine connoisseurship was not just an open-and-shut wine book but rather a wine journey—an endless stream of vintages, wine varietals, bottle variation, and marriage with different kinds of foods. No two wines are the same, just as no two palates are identical. That is what makes the experience so much fun and immensely rich to share with others.

In 2006, I had the good fortune to co-found the Hourglass Wine Company, when my partners Jeff Smith, Michael Clark, and I purchased a significant yet unbranded fifty-eight-acre vineyard in St. Helena (Napa Valley), California. We subsequently merged with Jeff Smith's small, four-acre, super-premium Cabernet Sauvignon estate vineyard, Hourglass. Over time we created one of the leading multiple varietal vineyards in Napa Valley. Once I took the plunge from wine lover to wine producer, my journey started reaching new heights.

This book, which is a compilation of my wine experiences over the past forty years, is a primer for all those just starting on their wine journeys. The vineyards that I highlight as benchmark wines are listed not necessarily because they are the most expensive, most prestigious, or most popular, but rather for their unique places within the wine world, and the fact that no wine connoisseur could fully enjoy his or her journey without tasting these wines and having a memory marker as to their distinctive styles. Some are very expensive; some are not . . . the expensive wines should be shared with a group of other wine connoisseurs in much the same fashion as people get together in book clubs to enjoy the stories. You really need only one glass of each of these wines to record the style and taste for your scholarship. Taste and study, taste and study, go region by region enjoying and experiencing the true excitement and joy that wine can bring. You have started a lifelong journey that will bring marvelous pleasure and satisfaction. I hope this book helps to demystify the process and stimulate your interest.

Good luck, and always remember to pull the cork.

1

GETTING STARTED
AND BUYING WINE

How to buy and build a wine cellar is probably the most commonly asked question for wine lovers, particularly newcomers who are starting their wine journey. In other words, what to buy and when? Most people buy wine for an immediate need—they have a party to go to or they are hosting a dinner. They visit their local wine store and say, "I need a wine that I would like to serve tonight." This is potentially the most expensive way to buy. Either they are getting wines at a very high price or most often a young wine not ready to drink. Wine consumers in the United States drink their fine wines much too young compared to other parts of the world, particularly in Europe and Great Britain. (Although everyday wines, forming the majority of what's on the market, are meant to be drunk soon after purchase.) Sophisticated wine lovers would never drink a claret (a common term for red Bordeaux wines) before its tenth birthday and for especially robust vintages, like 1990, they would prefer to enjoy a fifteen- to twenty-year-old bottle.

When you are starting out, it takes foresight and planning to understand that developing a first-class cellar is a long-term proposition. There are few things more gratifying than buying a wine, cellaring it until it reaches maturity, then pulling that wine out many years later and finding that it's a masterpiece. Wine needs to age. It needs to shed its tannins and evolve in the bottle, not only in the oak casks. So you'll need to allocate a realistic amount of money to start your cellar, buy your wine, and then have the discipline to wait until it's truly ready.

Wine buying shouldn't be that complicated, particularly in light of all the wine-rating publications and websites that have proliferated over the years. The better ones, like Robert Parker's *Wine Advocate*, Allen Meadows's Burghound, Antonio Galloni's Vinous, and the *Wine Spectator*, coupled with advice from writers such as Lettie Teague and Masters of Wine like Clive Coates, Michael Broadbent, and Serena Sutcliffe, can be enormously helpful.

When buying wine you must first establish what type of wine you like. Do you prefer the more tannic wines typical of Bordeaux or the Rhône, for instance, versus California, Burgundy, or Italy, whose wines feature different varietals and blending styles?

An important discipline is to focus on buying and tasting the very good vintages. For example, in 2005 both Bordeaux and Burgundy made one of the great vintages of our lifetimes. A good rule of thumb is that in these special, highly acclaimed vintages most every reputable producer will make great wines, so you can decide what you want to spend or how much you want to allocate to a region like Burgundy and then buy what you can afford. The Grand or Premier Crus might be too expensive for you but there are many lovely wines from Burgundy and Bordeaux in these great years to fit everybody's pocketbook. If price is a concern, look for the second labels from the top vineyards, the *petits châteaux* and the Village Burgundies, for affordable good wine. Once you understand that principle, you can allocate your resources accordingly.

Off years are tricky, and even though it's important to experience some of the best wines of these vintages you might want to consider saving your resources for the better years.

I remember in 1982, when virtually everyone made great wines in Bordeaux, you could have bought the truly great first growths for $400 a case—wines like Lafite, Margaux, Latour, and Mouton—but you might not have been able to afford them. But wines like the super seconds Pichon Baron, Léoville Las Cases, Cos d'Estournel, Lynch Bages, or Léoville Barton—also made incredibly good wines that might have been a little bit easier on your pocketbook. The *petits châteaux* like Meyney and Simard also offer tremendously good values in great years. The super seconds are still drinking exquisitely well and you could enjoy the *petits châteaux* for ten to fifteen years. In fact, I recently had the 1982, 1983, and 1986 Gruaud-Larose Saint-Julien in a mini vertical tasting and they were as exquisite as anything you could dream about. I had purchased each bottle for less than $20, but the secret was not to drink these incredibly long-lived wines too early. A few of my fellow wine lovers were younger than the wines, and it was great fun to see people experience the magic of tasting wine made before they were born. Having a developed cellar and the willpower not to drink too early can provide you with this memorable experience.

So the first rule of thumb is to choose an excellent vintage and buy the best that you can afford within that vintage. Second, in some years, mainly due to weather variation, some regions or appellations produce better wine than others. In Bordeaux, for instance, the subtle but distinctive nuances between the Left Bank (Pauillac, Saint-Julien, Margaux, and Saint-Estèphe) and the Right Bank (Pomerol, Saint-Emilion) can be a factor in your selection. And so you can go deeper and buy in a year that's spotty by using wine publications to determine where the best values for your money can be found. But the most important element is to begin by identifying, from a stylistic point of view, which wines appeal to your senses. Many new wine lovers seem to start their journey in Bordeaux or California, where a more rigid ownership structure makes the wines easier to understand and group.

The Bordeaux region of France, with its territorial appellations and rigid classification systems that date back to 1855, is easier to understand and master than the complex world of Burgundy. Burgundy largely resembles a patchwork quilt of domaine owners who might have ownership of vineyards as small as 0.5 hectare (about 1.2 acres) in several different areas of the Côte de Nuits or Côte de Beaune. Burgundy is not only very small it still, has a very fragmented ownership structure—for example, the 50.6-hectare (120-acre) Clos de Vougeot vineyard is divided among eighty proprietors. Most vineyards are really just centuries-old farms with a laid-back agrarian culture of winemaking. In contrast, Bordeaux, with its high-style châteaux, large-volume production, and corporate ownership, is a big business that has taken on luxury-brand cachet worldwide. This has not proven, however, to be detrimental to the quality of the wine. New winemaking techniques, viticulture equipment, and genetically enhanced vine stocks have improved the consistency of the product much to the benefit of the serious wine lover. Don't be alarmed when I say genetically enhanced vine stocks. These aren't designed to make a super grape that tastes magnificent, but are rather vines that are resistant to fungus, root-boring insects, and droughts. They have, however, had an effect on a wine lover's urgency to buy the latest so-called Wine of the Decade because with this consistency, the wine trade seems to be making many, many Wines of the Decade. In past days a heralded vintage was cause for great celebration and a dramatic upward adjustment in prices. In addition to it being truly excellent, one of the reasons the 1982 vintage caused such tremendous excitement was that a great vintage was really long overdue after so many lackluster years during the 1970s. In fact, the most heralded vintage of the 1970s was the tannic vintage of 1975, but after forty-one years, in the case of many châteaux, the fruit is gone and the tannins never left, making it a huge disappointment. Thus by 1982, the pent-up demand was enormous. Today it seems different; if you don't buy the 2008, you always have the 2009 and 2010 to choose from. Not worse, just different.

When starting out in Bordeaux it is easy to notice the difference between the Right and the Left Bank wines: the Right Bank wines (meaning the Pomerol and Saint-Emilion appellations) are predominantly Merlot, while the Left Bank appellations (Pauillac, Saint-Julien, Margaux, and Saint-Estèphe) are more Cabernet Sauvignon–based. This has to do with the terroir and the wine lover's appetite for tannins and structure in a wine. The different types of wine that people enjoy largely come down to personal preference. Everybody's palate is different and often changes over the years. I feel that my mood, environment, and food pairing will often dictate what type of wine I want to enjoy. Is it a cold day when I am having a stew? I'll reach for a Rhône or a claret. Pasta Bolognese and a Gaja Barbaresco are iconic together. Burgundy, though, is just special and in a league of its own. Once you experience the supple power of the Pinot Noir grape you'll likely be hooked for life.

Yet the wines of Burgundy remain a mystery to many wine lovers. The structure of the landholdings and the appellations goes back to the fourteenth century and really hasn't changed since. The system of the landholdings and the impact of the terroir make it very difficult to understand Burgundy without making a trip to witness the charm and magnificence of the wines in their home setting. The wines of Burgundy are predominately Pinot Noir for the Côte de Nuits and Chardonnay and Pinot Noir for the Côte de Beaune; in fact, laws were enacted in 1395 by Duke Philip the Bold to prevent blending of any other varietal with the Pinot Noir grape. Napoléon (being Napoléon) cheated on this when he blended more tannic grapes like Syrah into his prized Chambertin to quasi-fortify his bottles during his extended military campaigns. The Pinot Noir grape is the most seductive and romantic grape of them all. Thin-skinned and easily bruised, it is incredibly hard to ferment, but when done right it produces the most regal wines in the world.

Burgundy is essentially set up into two distinct areas, the northerly slope of the Côte de Nuits and the southernmost slope the Côte de Beaune. Within the Côte de Nuits lie many appellations that contain areas within areas. In Gevrey-Chambertin, for example, there are different subareas each making distinctly different wines but all using the same grape varietal, Pinot Noir. How can this be? The answer lies in the soil, or as the French call it, the "terroir."

Burgundy sits atop a prehistoric limestone formation that has evolved over thousands of years. It runs from the northernmost section of Chablis to the southernmost area of the Mâconnais. In between is the Côte d'Or (Golden Slope), which comprises both the Côte de Nuits (mostly Pinot Noir grapes, plus 5 percent Chardonnay) and the Côte de Beaune (Chardonnay and Pinot Noir grapes). It should be noted that even though Beaujolais is technically in Burgundy, the purist would consider it a different area. In Beaujolais, the predominant grape varietal is the Gamay grape and the terroir is more granite-based as opposed to the limestone foundation of Burgundy. Within the Cote d'Or it is this dramatically varied terroir that allows for the remarkably diverse styles of wine all using the same grape. Look at a map and you will see that all the vineyards are west of the Route Nationale 74, which is the major north-south highway through the region. There is one exception, Flagey Echézeaux. The only vineyard area on the other side of the highway, its terroir makes their wine distinctively different.

The ownership structure within Burgundy is also very complicated. The Cistercian monks were among the first to aggressively dedicate themselves to winemaking in Burgundy and in 1336 created a walled vineyard, the Clos de Vougeot, which still produces some of the greatest Burgundy wines. During the next four centuries the region was controlled by the dukes of Burgundy and later was annexed to the Kingdom of France. It wasn't until after the French Revolution and the change to the Napoleonic code of inheritance that the large plots were sold and broken up to satisfy taxes. This is the predominant reason for the small plot holdings of many family producers. Ownership, which is often passed down generation to generation, can be as small as 0.5 hectare (1.2 acres) to much larger. As a result of these small landholdings, the need for an essential marketing cooperative or *négociant* arose. The *négociant* would buy grapes from local growers, vinify them together, and market the wine with his own label. The *négociants* gained tremendous power and, while owning some of their own grapes and vines, they control approximately 70 percent of the planted area of Burgundy (30 percent is bottled by vineyard owners under their own labels). As a rule, most of the Grand Crus are owned by non-*négociants* but it is the wines made by the *négociants* that sometimes can be spotty. In the good years they are great and can represent value, but I would steer clear of their communal wines in lesser-quality years. Jadot, Latour, Drouhin, and Faiveley are all leading *négociant* firms.

Much like Bordeaux in 1855, a rating system was adopted to classify the Burgundy vineyards—in 1861, the Beaune committee of agriculture started the current system of rating vineyards by the Grand Cru, Premier Cru, and Village designations. The Grand Cru rating, which is the highest and best, not surprisingly has the smallest number of acres. The Premier Cru, which isn't quite as good but still wonderful, has more, and the Village designation represents the largest area of the vineyards. The Grand Cru and Premier Cru wines must be from their designated area but the Village wines can be an amalgamation of grapes from the whole village, leading to the dilution of the pedigree. The true Burgundian's heart might be with the Grand Cru, still the true benchmark wines, but his or her pocketbook might be with the Village wines. There is no shame in this.

The Côte de Nuits is the king of the red wines while the Côte de Beaune is the queen of the whites, with the exception of the subtly stylistic Volnays, the rich wines of Aloxe-Corton, the powerful Pommards, and the lighter, more supple wines from Santenay, Savigny-lès-Beaune, and Pernand-Vergelesses. In the end, however, it is the excellent soils or terroir that make Burgundian wines stand truly apart from the pack. To try these wines is to fall in love. To pay a visit and learn the nuance of the area is to have your heart stolen.

Over the last ten years the financial appreciation of fine wine has probably made it the best performing asset class. I have wines in my cellar today from the 1982, 1985, and 1990 vintages that have $10, $15, $20 price tags still on the bottles. As I mentioned previously, a first growth in 1982 that initially sold for $400 a case today commands as much as or more than $2,500 a bottle. An incredible appreciation from $400 a case to $30,000 a case. This is because of worldwide demand, the stellar quality of the wine, and the fact that it is very scarce.

So that begs the question: collecting versus speculating. I think true lovers of wine are not speculators; they are drinkers, tasters, and enjoyers of wine. I have never purchased a case of wine in order to resell it, but rather to have it in my cellar to enjoy over the many years that it will last. I know a few people who will buy wine and then sell a portion of their collection once it matures, to fund future purchases. Buying wine to speculate is a practice for the investor, not for the true wine lover.

I've often had people say to me, "I can't drink this wine. It's now worth $1,000 a bottle, when will there ever be an occasion good enough to drink this wine?" That is a very dangerous precedent to establish. A true wine lover thinks of wine in terms of not what the appreciated price of the wine is but rather what you initially paid for it. And feel comfortable in knowing that if you really want to appreciate wine you must pull the cork, taste the wine, and enjoy it. If you have that mind-set you'll be better able to appreciate the wine rather than wait for the ideal moment that may never come. Remember that the most expensive wine in your cellar is not the wine that costs the most, but the wine that goes bad.

In the early days the use of futures or *en primeur* for buying wines was a very good method to obtain really terrific vintages, because you were generally getting a wine with an established provenance at a lower price. The practice began in Bordeaux as a way for château owners to sell some of their wines earlier than usual as a way to generate cash flow for their businesses. They needed the money, so it was a way for them, in essence, to factor wines out early. With the surge in wine prices and the many good vintages over the last twenty years, a lot of producers are in much better financial shape than they were in the past. In fact the trend now is for the well-capitalized vineyards to sell less *en primeur* and hold wines in their library (inventory) for release at auction five to ten years later at market prices. Look for these estate offerings because, although they are expensive, you'll have a firm grasp on the wines' provenance. The bargains on futures, therefore, are not as great; but they still can be a good opportunity to buy large quantities of fine wines at pre-established prices.

When you're buying through futures, it's most important to focus on the quality and the reputation of the retail establishment you are buying from. You must develop a rapport with the wine merchant that you feel comfortable with—it should be a well-capitalized establishment with trustworthy people. Do they have a long history of being able to make good on their commitments? Buying wine *en primeur* is basically an unsecured contract that you have with that wine merchant. Keep your eyes open because there have been horror stories in the past of merchants collecting large amounts of money then reneging or filing bankruptcy, leaving the wine lover high and dry. Well-regarded wine dealers, however, are usually very honorable merchants.

Over the last ten years the auction market for fine wine has really exploded, making it a viable option for rounding out your cellar. The wine that flows through the auction market includes not only mature wines ready to drink but also some very rare and hard-to-find older wines. Sometimes bargains abound, but don't expect a steal because auction house premiums and taxes must be added in. In addition, you have to be very careful with respect to the quality of the wines and how they were stored, or any vagaries in how they were shipped. In addition, some auction houses do a better job than others of vetting the provenance of the wine. Counterfeit wine is a big business so you have to understand which auction houses take the time to verify the provenance, conditions, and storage of their offerings. This information is often recorded within the catalog, and is a very useful tool for the wine lover who wants to round out a collection and taste some wines that might have been missed when released.

As noted above, there is significant and growing wine fraud. Counterfeit wine existed for centuries, ranging from the vineyard level, as with the Georges Duboeuf Beaujolais scandal, to the auction or secondary market. The most famous case of wine fraud occurred in 2012 when an Indonesian man by the name of Rudy Kurniawan supposedly assembled the greatest cellar in the world and then began selling off his collection via the auction market. What he was doing was buying dramatically lesser quality wines and affixing fake labels to the bottles from some of the most expensive and well-known vineyards in the world. A series of sales raised suspicion but it wasn't until he put up for auction several bottles of Domaine Ponsot's Clos Saint Denis from 1945 to 1971 that the heir Laurent Ponsot sounded the alarm. Domaine Ponsot, one of the oldest and most respected vineyards in Burgundy, didn't start producing their Clos Saint Denis until 1982. When the Federal Bureau of Investigation raided Kurniawan's home they found scores of old bottles, fake labels, and average wine. He was arrested, found guilty, and is in prison for a very long time. The esteemed *Wine Spectator* magazine notes that as much as 5 percent of the world's wines sold in the secondary market could be counterfeit. This gives further credence to buying wines *en primeur* or upon release, as knowing provenance in wine buying is essential.

STORING WINES
Establishing a Cellar

Wine needs to be stored at constant temperature and humidity. However, the great myth is that every wine has to be stored at 55 degrees Fahrenheit with 75 to 80 percent humidity forever. That's not the case, although it's certainly very helpful. The key component of wine storage is first and foremost humidity, which affects the corks. If bottles are stored in a dry environment, air can seep through the corks, which will oxidize and ruin the wine. The two elements most responsible for killing wine are oxidation through cork disintegration, and rapid or extreme fluctuations in temperature. One of the reasons why most people won't ship wines in the summer is that they generally travel in storage bins that can reach 120 degrees for extended periods of time, effectively ruining the wines. Unless you see the visual effects of protruding corks or seepage around corks, you might never know. It's always important to check the corks and tops to see if there's any stickiness, or if the cork protrudes above the bottle rim. Often that indicates wine seepage and exposure to high temperature.

Some young collectors or those living in urban areas might not have the space for dedicated wine storage. I remember when I was just out of college and stored my wines in a closet in my New York City apartment. As the seasons changed and the temperatures in the apartment moved up or down a little bit, it didn't affect the wine as much as dryness or lack of humidity would. It might make them mature faster, therefore if you have wine at 65 degrees it will mature faster than a wine stored at 55 degrees. Cooler temperatures retard the development of the wines. However, storage can be too cold as well as too hot, so wine stored at 40 degrees could suffer. It's really about minimizing the movement of the temperature: Some gradual movement, either up or down, is perfectly acceptable for the wines' development.

Wines also need to be kept in dark places; so, if you have a cellar, keep the lights off. Also, try not to move your wine or play with it. If you envision the great cellars at historic vineyards, wherever they may be, whether in France, Germany, or California, oftentimes they are underground, they're dark and dank, and the bottles don't get touched for decades—the perfect environment for storing wine.

The great debate that has raged in the wine industry since 1995 has been the continued use of cork as a stopper for wine versus other forms of closure, such as plastic resins or screw caps. Natural cork stoppers, which are used in 64 percent of the eighteen billion wine bottles produced annually worldwide, are harvested from the *Quercus suber* or cork oak. The bark is stripped in an environmentally sound way that ensures that the oak, which generally lives for upward of three hundred years, remains healthy. Portugal and Spain provide approximately 80 percent of the worldwide production of natural cork stoppers used in the wine industry. The debate has lingered as to whether the cork is the best and most efficient closure mechanism to prevent air from penetrating the bottle and damaging the wine. The industry had quality problems during the 1970s and 1980s and poor cork was harvested. Since cork is a natural material, it is susceptible to decay and contamination if quality isn't properly checked. (Cork can contain molds and during the cork-cleaning process a chlorine called trichloroanisole [TCA] is used. A cork becomes tainted when the TCA reacts with the mold. It is estimated that 1 percent of wines using natural cork stoppers are affected by tainted corks.) In addition, cork needs a certain amount of moisture to preserve itself. Even a good-quality cork will disintegrate if exposed to a dry environment, so it's important to provide the right humidity during storage. Corks are expensive, so poor quality and high costs impelled the wine industry to experiment with other forms of stoppers. Plastic resins and screw tops were introduced in the hope that they would provide a more reliable form of closure. Scientifically, they are more reliable in forming a better seal but the question lingers as to whether their density allows for the slight aeration that cork provides, which over time naturally aids in the maturing process of long-lived wines. In addition, the use of plastic resins and screw tops for more expensive wines can diminish their prestige in the eyes of consumers, regardless of wine-preservation issues. It appears that the cork industry has taken note and quality has improved dramatically. Currently you will see non-cork stoppers used in lower-priced mass-produced wines, such as early-drinking white wines from Australia, New Zealand, and the United States. For wines that don't have aging potential it is a suitable alternative, but the romance of popping a cork is lost.

CHOOSING A STORAGE SYSTEM

Many of the storage systems that you can buy through magazines look very elaborate. Typically organized as double-bottle bins, they often have space for only one or two bottles deep in each slot. In my opinion they are very dangerous to use. I've never liked them as much as bins that will hold anywhere from twelve to thirty-six bottles that you can clearly see. Individual bins are very hard to access. You have to put your arm through these racking systems, and often you'll misplace bottles back there because you don't know what you have. And so, if you're going to build a storage facility, open shelves are best. Indeed, if you were to visit those historic cellars in France, you'll see the open bin system used almost exclusively.

So larger open bins where you can see what you have and take a proper inventory offer the best storage system. What should they be made of? I've always liked storage facilities that are composed of brick and slate, in large part because they retain coolness and dampness and maintain a good constant temperature. Wood and steel are good alternatives but the bins must be very sturdy, well constructed, and, most important, be able to withstand the tremendous weight of your stored bottles over a long period of time.

Once your cellar is built and you have accumulated the start of a proper wine collection, it will be important to catalog where you have stored wines from different regions and years. I have two central wine-storage locations, one off-premise for very young wines and one for wines that have neared drinkability. When you have a robust cellar it is vital that you maintain an account of the age and maturity of your collection, or else you will suffer lost bottles or cases that go bad. Remember my motto, "The most expensive bottle of wine in your cellar is the one that goes bad."

DECANTING YOUR WINE

When is it appropriate to decant wine and what is the best way to decant and serve wine? Not all wine needs to be decanted but most older wines benefit. Decanting wines serves two distinctly different missions. First, when you decant wine it allows oxygen to mix with the wine so as to open the wine and make it more approachable; second, it separates the wine from any tannin sediment that has precipitated out during the maturation process. All wines have tannins, but certain red wine varietals have a more noticeable amount, notably Cabernet Sauvignon, Syrah, and the Nebbiolo grape from Italy. They are going to throw off more tannins and the older the wine, the more pronounced the sediment. So decanting wines and eliminating the sediment will not only make your wine-drinking experience more pleasurable, it will also tend to save you from a far worse hangover once you have finished drinking your wine. Young wine from Burgundy or Merlot-based wines generally don't need to be decanted until they are older, perhaps ten years or more, as they are not very tannic grape varietals. If you choose to decant these younger wines, they will still benefit from the aeration that the process provides.

As I previously discussed, decanting wine serves two purposes: the elimination of tannin sediments and providing proper aeration. The secret of decanting wine is finding a proper funnel. The best is a wide-mouth silver or porcelain funnel, although if you don't have an elaborate one a typical plastic kitchen funnel is acceptable (although not preferable). Wine connoisseurship does lend itself to some forms of pageantry and ritual, and the implements that you use are an integral and deeply satisfying part of the process. Great gift items for the serious wine lover abound, from old sterling silver funnels to elaborate bone-handle corkscrews. One modern improvement that contributes to the ritual is the use of a Mr. Coffee filter instead of the old hopsack fabric. The coffee filters will catch more of the sediment and are easier to use.

Once you start the decanting process and are pouring the wine slowly through the funnel, you will see how much sediment these older bottles of wine will throw off. I can't help but think every time after I have decanted a wine how badly my head would have hurt the next day had I not chosen to decant the wine.

What's important about decanting is not only the elimination of the sediment, but that it will also help in the aeration of the wine, which will soften it up. Understand, though, that if you're drinking an older wine like a 1961 Lafite Rothschild or a 1945 Mouton, once the wine hits the air, it sometimes can maderize in a matter of minutes. And so you have to be very careful when decanting older bottles. Once you open an older bottle and you decant it, replace the stopper in the decanter until you're ready to start drinking the wine. If it's a very old bottle, say from the 1940s or 1950s, don't decant it immediately but keep the bottle upright for twenty-four hours before opening. All the sediment will fall to the base, then you can uncork the wine and gently put the cork back until serving.

I remember drinking a 1947 Lafite Rothschild that turned or maderized within a matter of minutes after we decanted it. So you have to be very careful with very old wines and their exposure to air. Young, tannic wines, however, need at least one to two hours or more, open and exposed to as much air as possible. That is one of the problems of ordering big, tannic red wines at restaurants. By the time they start to open up and be approachable, you have finished the meal. Try to order the wine in advance and have it opened before your arrival or ask the sommelier to pour it into your glass after decanting even if you aren't ready for it as it will open up faster in your glass than in the bottle. The bigger the mouth of the carafe, the more air that circulates, making your wine more approachable in a shorter period of time.

3

THE ART OF TASTING
How to Appreciate Wine

TASTING AND JUDGING WINE

The number-one priority for wine collectors is pulling the cork and tasting the wine. It's enjoying wines, and building a knowledge base and reservoir of information about different years, varietals, and regions. One of the ways that Master of Wine connoisseurs can judge a bottle of wine so expertly—you've all heard about or seen someone in a blind tasting sampling a wine and immediately declaring "Ah, that's a 1961 Cheval Blanc"—is to taste several thousand bottles of wine over the years and understand the nuances of the types of grape and the characteristics of the vineyards. The master can identify the different aspects and the permutations of the wine. What is the region? Where is it from? What is the texture? What are the characteristics of the varietal, the scents and texture of the nose? Additionally, what are the characteristics of the vintage? One of the most important characteristics of a successful wine taster and of understanding the difference between wines is the concept of *typicity*. The Oxford English Dictionary defines typicity as the quality or fact of a wine being typical of its geographical provenance and of the grape variety from which it is made. In essence we are asking, does the wine reflect its varietal type and does the true character of the grape emerge? Does a French red Burgundy taste like a Pinot Noir or does a Saint-Emilion taste the way a Merlot and Cabernet Franc blend should? There are very distinct differences between wines, varietals, and regions, which you'll only begin to identify through proper tastings and understanding each individual typicity. This aspect of tasting wine is what I call "benchmarking," the central theme of this book. It is an absolutely essential part of the wine journey.

So tasting is vital. Don't be afraid to open a bottle with your spouse or friends and taste, record the smell, the characteristics of the fruit, the body, and the complexity of the structure. According to studies, smell accounts for up to 90 percent of what one perceives to be the taste. So take the time to smell the wine's aroma and try to record the memory. The brain has a tremendous ability to memorize scents and flavors, so use this ability to remember the nuances of the nose before moving on to tasting the wine.

One of the most important rituals during your wine journey should be the recording of good tasting notes. Almost all serious wine connoisseurs record their wine experiences in notebooks that over time will provide a living history of their journey. By recording the names of the producers, the year the grapes were harvested, the vineyards and regions, and your impressions about the color, nose, and complexity of the wine, you will create a snapshot of your experience that will allow you to taste the same wine years later and consider its evolution, either real or imagined.

VERTICAL AND HORIZONTAL TASTINGS

There are many ways to taste wine. You can taste one bottle or a myriad of bottles. You can do a vertical tasting versus a horizontal tasting. In a vertical tasting you taste the same wine from different years. For instance, Mouton Rothschild from 1982 to 1995. A horizontal tasting is when you taste, for example, the different châteaux from the appellation of Pauillac made in the 1982 vintage.

You might select several different Pauillacs to understand the nuances and complexities of the different wines and who made the best wines that year and why. So whether it be vertical or horizontal, each tasting method is extremely valuable in your wine education and journey. In addition, it can be great fun to assemble your collection to provide wines specifically for these kinds of tastings.

One memorable tasting that I assembled is a good example of this: Back in 1988, I was thinking about all the great wines that had been produced during the 1980s, and I decided to put together a group of wines that epitomized the best that the 1980s had to offer.

I called it "the wine trust," and got five wine friends to kick in $200 each. We agreed to cellar the wines until 2000, when we would celebrate the millennium with a two-day tasting. We bought twelve bottles, all of which turned out to be legendary. We tasted the 1982 and 1986 from Château Margaux, Château Mouton Rothschild, and Léoville Las Cases, the 1985 La Tâche and Grand Echézeaux from Domaine de la Romanée-Conti, the 1985 Taylor's Port and the 1986 Château d'Yquem (in my opinion the best sweet wine in the world and one of the best wines period). I assembled the collection to taste together at a specific tasting. These specific tastings can be very fun and rewarding and if you and some fellow wine lovers pool your resources, you can put together six great Burgundies from 2005 or eight clarets from the magic decade of the 1990s and return to taste them in ten to fifteen years. Whether it be a horizontal or vertical tasting, both are fun and enjoyable. If you want to dig deeper into a certain vineyard, then do a vertical tasting. Sometimes it takes a while to assemble the appropriate wines from each of the different years in order to get a true comparison. I have known examples of collectors searching for ten to fifteen years to collect a comprehensive vertical tasting of, say, Château Margaux. A horizontal tasting is more common and easier to assemble, and it is also one of the best ways to develop knowledge about a region or an appellation.

Generally, most people taste wine via a transparent tasting. In this tasting, whether it be a vertical or horizontal tasting, participants see the bottles to be tasted and have full transparency from the start. The other way to taste and judge wine is a blind tasting, which is rarer but can produce some amazingly honest results. The blind tasting can be both powerful and surprising because the wines being tasted are hidden from view (hence blind), and the participants maintain no preconceived ideas about the quality related to brand name, vintage year, or price. It is really interesting how many people are prejudiced by labels, high price per bottle, or the fact that it is a Grand Cru or first growth.

THE JUDGMENT OF PARIS

The most famous blind tasting of all time was the event held at the Intercontinental Hotel in Paris on May 24, 1976, by Steven Spurrier, the British owner of Caves de la Madeleine, and the Académie du Vin. The nascent and undiscovered wines of Napa Valley were tasted side by side with the very best wines from France. Nine of France's leading wine experts judged the blind tasting and after much deliberation, Mike Grgich's 1973 Chateau Montelena, a leading Napa Valley Chardonnay, beat out a 1973 Meursault Charmes from Burgundy and was declared the winner in the white wine category. In the red wine category, Warren Winiarski's, 1973 Stag's Leap was declared the winner over a 1970 Château Mouton Rothschild. All bedlam broke out—to the French, there was no way that wines from Napa Valley could dethrone the kings of Bordeaux and Burgundy. On that particular day in the fall of 1976, Chateau Montelena and Stag's Leap Wine Cellars, up against some of the greatest names in French wine history, were in fact the kings of the hill. Would Chateau Montelena and Stag's Leap have succeeded if the tasting had been transparent? No chance . . . the wine judges would have been prejudiced by the French wines' stature and legacy. This tasting, with its victory for Napa Valley, was chiefly instrumental in the discovery and popularization of the American wine industry. As the great wine writer Robert Parker said about the Judgment of Paris, "The Paris tasting destroyed the myth of French supremacy and marked the democratization of the wine world. It was a watershed event in the history of wine." Wines from the New World were suddenly on the map.

I remember a tasting that I organized many years ago, when Chilean wines were coming into their own. I bought the Chilean Concha y Toro Cabernet Sauvignon in 1980 for about $5 or $6 a bottle. I bought several cases and I really enjoyed it. Several years ago, I was rummaging through my odds and ends bin and found a couple of bottles that were properly stored but left over from the early 1980s. My first thought was, wow . . . let's give it a go and see how well the wine has held up. I decided to serve it blind in a casual tasting that included some second growth Bordeaux. Well, it was still a superb wine and the relatively new wine lovers I shared the wine with couldn't believe how complex it still was. After I told them what they'd tasted they responded, "Wow, this is amazing. I never would have ranked it as high if I had known it was a $5 or $6 Concha y Toro." So the decision of blind versus transparent tastings can influence whether tasters judge a wine or a label.

DEVELOPING YOUR PALATE

If you are developing your palate try tasting some distinctly different wines that have very nuanced and identifiable characteristics. Château Cos d'Estournel, which is the preeminent wine from the Left Bank appellation of Saint-Estèphe, has a distinctly different taste, nose, and complexity from most other Bordeaux wines. In France, as in the wine industry all over the world, the top wines are all about the terroir or soil. In Saint-Estèphe the soil has high clay content and less gravel. Because of the poor drainage and the cooler soil, the grapes have a higher acidity that results in a very distinctive style that is often more austere than other Left Bank appellations.

Wines from Australia (such as Penfolds), the Malbec-dominated wines from Argentina, or the wines from the northern Rhône Valley (which are distinctly different from their southern counterparts because of their terroir and Syrah grapes), when tasted are uniquely different from each other and bring with them a different set of nuances and styles, and perceiving these differences is an important aspect of a wine lover's tasting education and journey.

WHEN TO DRINK

How long do you keep a wine and when is the right time to drink it? Clearly there is no universal timetable. Many factors go into the decision: the type of wine or grape varietal; climate and producer style; the tannins, acidity, and sugar content; how a winemaker makes his wine (whether he destems; if he blends different grape varieties; declassifies his inferior grapes and uses only heartier grapes; whether it was a smaller vintage with more robust grapes or it was a bigger vintage). As I mentioned previously, the varietal type plays an important role in a wine's aging process due to the grape's varying tannic makeup. Cabernet Sauvignon, Syrah, and Nebbiolo tend to produce longer-lived wines. But I think aging is probably one of the biggest misconceptions in wine collecting and wine appreciation. Most wine lovers, especially Americans, drink their wine way too early. If you're able to buy wine by the case, instead of just a few bottles at a time, you can experiment with how the wine matures. Wine evolves over time, especially in the bottle; the better wines will soften and retain their fruit, thus reaching perfection. If you drank them young you would never experience their magic. An important point to remember is that tasting is really the only way that you can develop an appreciation and an encyclopedic knowledge of wine through experiencing its nose and taste, remembering its nuances, and writing notes for the future.

WHEN WINE IS READY

When is a wine ready and when is it not? There is a certain point when wine stops improving in the bottle, and then will plateau, and eventually there's a downward progression. Wine after it's bottled can go into a dumb period. So don't be fooled if you buy a wine and find it robust, and wonderful and earthy, and then you try that wine a year later and it's hard, closed, and lacking fruit or finesse. It's not because of your storage, but wine goes into a dumb phase and then comes back as it matures within the bottle. So it's important to try wine over a cycle, over a longer period of time. Also, when you're tasting a wine, don't drink it all at once. Leave a little in the bottle to see how it evolves later in the evening. Try the wine when you're pouring, then let it sit. Drink a little bit and then put it aside and come back to it a half hour or an hour later if you can, as you rotate through the tastings. You'll appreciate how much more it has opened up, and because of the interaction with air it will have different complexities that will be differently nuanced. Remember that for the big, young wines, you generally need to have them opened up for an hour or more before you taste them. You will need less time for the softer grape varietals like Pinot Noir and Merlot. But every wine, even the bigger wines from Bordeaux's Pauillac region (in the Left Bank region of Bordeaux) there is no one standard. Generally, the more tannic the wine, the longer it will take to open or mature, but not every vintage is going to be the same. The better vintages and the bigger wines will tend to evolve more slowly. But when you experience a bigger wine like Château Latour, Léoville Las Cases, Lynch Bages, or wines from the house of Cordier (Gruaud-Larose or Talbot), they will take a long time to evolve in the bottle; the gift is that they can last as long as forty or fifty years.

AGING WHITE WINES

The aging of white wines is probably one of wine's biggest mysteries. You can age white wines if they have higher acidity and are properly stored at lower temperatures. Remember that white wines typically need a lower temperature if you are going to age them so if you're optimally at 55 degrees Fahrenheit for red wines, then 52 degrees would be your optimal storage temperature for white wines. White wines can be cellared, and the better white wines from great appellations like Bâtard-Montrachet or Corton-Charlemagne can be cellared if they are stored properly, then you can enjoy them for twenty or more years. Properly stored great wines from good vintages can last a good while and are a treat to drink.

FORTIFIED WINES

Fortified wines such as ports, madeira, and the nonfortified king of sweet white wines, Sauternes, can last a long time and evolve for decades in the bottle. I would not even think about drinking a vintage port before its twentieth birthday and most likely its mid-life at age thirty. These wines are revered for their ability to age for sixty to eighty years, or in the case of madeira, even longer. New evidence shows that vintage Champagne can evolve for decades in the bottle. Previously, the general belief has been that Champagnes generally do not last for a long period of time. But it's now known that the better vintages of Champagne, properly stored, can last up to forty years. It is worth noting that as Champagne ages, it loses its fizz and resembles a mature white wine, such as a Burgundy. This is generally the case for all white wines—as they age, they become less about the crisp, primary fruit and take on an array of deeper, nuttier characteristics. Too many wine lovers will discard an older bottle of properly stored Champagne and say it's bad because the fizz is gone when it is still a terrific wine. It becomes all about expectation and your knowledge of how white wines mature and age. All must be properly stored at the lower temperature of 52 degrees. Don't forget: lower temperature, but also higher humidity. As with all wine, seepage of oxygen through the cork is the most common cause of wine going bad.

SAVING FOR LATER

A lot of people ask about these nitrate filters that suck the air out of the bottle if you haven't finished the whole thing. Do they work? Perhaps, but I'm a bit of a purist about wine gadgets. One trick I've always used, which I find to be very appealing, is to always keep some half bottles (375 milliliters) around. If you are drinking a wine and only finish half, grab the 375-milliliter bottle and make sure it's properly cleaned out. And when I say cleaned out, I mean rinsed with cold water and no soap. Make sure that the bottle is dry and then take the rest of the wine that's left and pour it into the half bottle. Insert the cork so that the cork is touching the wine. You will be able to come back to that wine in several weeks' time and it will be fine. If you want to hold it for a longer period of time, say a year, just run some wax around the top of the cork, which will properly store the wine. If the cork meets the wine, then no air can intrude. Just a little trick to be able to store a bottle of wine that you've opened and only half finished.

4

COLLECTING VERSUS CONNOISSEURSHIP

REASONS TO COLLECT

I've seen many fancy wine cellars lavishly furnished with couches, elaborate storage racks, and tasting implements. The owners keep their most expensive bottles or cases up front for all to see. When I ask them whether they have even tasted their priceless bottles, like maybe a 1982 Lafite Rothschild, they reply, "Absolutely not! That bottle cost me $1,000 and I could never taste a bottle that expensive. I have it out just for show."

People collect wines for many different reasons, whether as a status symbol, an investment return, or a special treat to enjoy with friends. They are entitled to approach wine collecting in any way they wish, but in my humble opinion the wine experience or journey is about connoisseurship: the art and enjoyment of tasting the differences, both conspicuous and subtle, between different terroirs, years, and grape varietals. In that vein, the sport of fishing and wine tasting have one thing in common. I remember in my youth, my family used to go deep-sea fishing with an old sea captain named Charlie Ridgway. Captain Ridgway was very crusty and despite losing an arm in the war could bait a hook as fast as anyone. As Captain

Ridgway told me at age ten, "Son, if you don't put your line in the water . . . you have no chance to catch a fish." The same is true for wine. If all you do is look at that 1982 Château Lafite Rothschild, you will never enjoy the wine or learn about all the complexities that open up on your palate.

CONNOISSEURSHIP

Connoisseurship is the art of tasting wine: pulling the cork, savoring the delight, recording the experience, and comparing the differences between wines of different regions, varietals, and countries. That fancy bottle with the unplugged cork will never give you that pleasure.

I do subscribe to the theory of setting aside unique bottles for special occasions like twenty-first, fortieth, fiftieth, or sixty-fifth birthdays or anniversaries. This can be a delightful way to enjoy wine, particularly because the buildup is so full of excitement and anticipation. My wife, Maureen, who has many great wine stories after being with me for thirty-five years, had just turned forty and we had a birthday dinner and a tasting of Burgundies to mark the occasion. Shortly after her dinner, my thoughts started to drift to her big birthday in ten years. For that celebration something special would be required. I checked my cellar and even though I have a bunch of 1961 Bordeaux, I didn't have the multiple bottles needed, so for the next two years I intently followed the wine auctions until at last I found a jeroboam of 1961 Château Lafite Rothschild that was in excellent shape, showing a good fill level. I carefully stored the wine for eight years, we opened it up at her fiftieth birthday celebration, and it was everything you could have asked for in a 1961—the nose was rich and powerful, and the subtle expression of blackberries and spicy pepper lingered for much longer than anyone would have expected. It was symbolic that everybody at the party got a chance to drink a great wine made in the same year as my wife's birth. Wine has that ability to celebrate life as it takes on the myriad of complexities as it matures through its own life.

SELLING WINE AS A CONNOISSEUR

We will discuss in later chapters the art of selling wine, but it is fair to say that the difference between wine collectors and wine connoisseurs is that wine connoisseurs never sell wine with profit as their main goal. Sometimes connoisseurs with very deep and large collections need to cull a region or vintage because they realized that they might have overbought and will probably not be able to enjoy certain wines before they mature. Remember my motto, "The most expensive wine in your cellar is the one that goes bad." Selling wine to cull your collection is quite normal, but to sell a prized wine to reap financial gain, even if it is to buy more wine, is not in the spirit of connoisseurship. Here's an example: Say you are lucky enough to have bought a case of 1982 Petrus as a future in February 1983. The first growths were all released at the now unbelievable price of $400 per case. Petrus, if my memory serves me, sold at the premium price of $440 per case; so for $440 per case you now have a call option on one of the greatest wines ever. A good connoisseur should have been tasting this wine and recording the results all through the last thirty-plus years as the wine has evolved. How wine matures in the bottle and over time is an important lesson in understanding and appreciating wine. As the wine's potential was discovered, its price escalated as well and now I believe it sells for over $30,000 per case at auction. If you were to have sold this wine and received the financial gain, my bet is that the former owner would never go back and try a bottle or two of the 1982 Petrus, thus robbing him of a very special tasting experience.

Sometimes wine collectors will buy a case of famous wine and over time drink half and sell the other half to defray the cost, or perhaps replenish their treasury for new purchases. This experience is acceptable because, first, the wine connoisseur had/has the tasting experience over the life of the wine. Second, not all wine connoisseurs have the same amount in their treasury, so a sale will allow you to taste a broader array of fine wines (which should be your goal).

This in fact happened to me recently. Way back in 1983, when I was going crazy over the 1982 Bordeaux vintage, I did in fact buy several wines through futures, including the 1982 Château Lafite Rothschild.

After some lean years in Bordeaux during the 1970s, the excitement over the 1982s was electric. In addition to the quality of the wine, it was the real start of famed wine writer and critic Robert Parker's career, and his pronouncement that the 1982 Bordeaux were the wines of the century very much added to the excitement. I couldn't contain myself and told several friends and business colleagues that the 1982 futures were not to be missed. One business acquaintance responded, "Great, but I don't know how to do it." My eagerness to spread the message and wine love made me reply, "No problem, I will take care of everything—you just send the check." So I bought him two cases of the 1982 Château Lafite Rothschild for $400 per case. He received the wines and was delighted. We stayed in touch a while but after five years, we drifted and didn't communicate until about one year ago. I then received a call from him asking if I remembered the wine purchase, and that even though he had thoroughly enjoyed one case he was selling the second at auction to finance further wine purchases. I am not sure of the final price that he received at auction, although 1982 Château Lafite Rothschild in original wood cases is approximately $30,000 per case.

So in summary, a wine connoisseur has the experience of drinking his or her purchase, savoring each bottle with an eye to discovery, scholarship, and enjoyment, whereas the wine collector buys and maintains wine to look at, impress others, and trade for profit.

5

HOW TO READ A WINE LIST

For many people a wine list represents:

1. High anxiety.
2. Inadequacy—some sommeliers make you feel inadequate.
3. Insecurity—you don't want to look foolish.
4. Confusion—so many selections and price points.

Confronted by a wine list at a nice restaurant, diners can feel a bolt of anxiety as they face the daunting prospect of selecting the correct bottle. This is coupled with the fact that some (but certainly not all) sommeliers make their customers feel inadequate and intimidated about their selection, but reading a wine list and selecting the best bottle, whether it be the best value or the best wine overall, is not as hard as people think.

KNOWING VINTAGES AND PRODUCERS

When I read a wine list, I can always pick out the best bottle for the money even if I have never heard of the château or producer. It's important to remember that in truly excellent vintage years pretty much all wine producers make great wine. In Bordeaux, for instance, most châteaux whether large or small, famous or obscure, made great wine in 1990, 2000, 2005, and 2010, so if your wallet can't stretch to a 2005 Cheval Blanc but you can afford a 2005 *petit château* like Meyney or Simard, go for the year 2005 even from an unknown château. Knowing the best vintage years for each wine region will greatly help your wine selection (most mobile devices now have wine apps for vintage years). One of the most important aspects of understanding and making good choices from a wine list is getting to know the best and most consistent producers from the different regions. Even though this will take some research, it is important to understand which winemakers are the most consistent in their approach, their focus on quality, and how rigorous they are in declassifying grapes in off years so as to produce wines of good quality even in subpar vintages. In Burgundy it is names like Dujac, Jadot, Rousseau, Roumier, D'Angerville, and Lafarge. In Bordeaux certainly the first growths, but also names like Léoville Las Cases, Rauzan Segla, Pichon Baron, Pichon Lalande, Angélus, Lynch Bages, Cos d'Estournel, Trotanoy, and La Conseillante are a guarantee of quality. It is also important to take note of the vintages that might not be blockbusters but are still attractive. These vintages, which can be quite approachable while young, are often less expensive. Red Burgundies from the years 2011, 2008, 2006, 2003, and 2002 are good examples of this.

In addition, in Burgundy, where the classification is very rigid with respect to quality, wines that are classified as Village wines can be purchased at attractive prices. If you are on a budget, look for these wines because in good years they can be superb. If the Grand and Premier Cru wines are designated to a specific vineyard, the grapes must be grown in that vineyard to gain that classification. With Village wines the grapes can be an amalgamation of grapes from the town all commingled into one cuvée. This leads to lower prestige, lower prices, and in the good to great years some fabulous wines that are very approachable while young.

Armed with this knowledge of both vintage years and quality producers, you can now hunt for the best bargains.

DECIPHERING THE WINE LIST

Most of the good wine lists are tiered, with prominent wines in great vintage years at crazy prices, prominent wines in off years at high prices, and value wines from good vintages at affordable prices. There is always something for everybody.

The sucker play that you always need to be watchful of is the prominent wine in an off year. I have heard lots of people say, "Oh, I have always wanted to try a Château Cheval Blanc and look, the 1993 is not as expensive as the 2005 vintage." This is perfectly OK as long as the price has been adjusted for the subpar vintage and the wine is not sold at a high price because of its premium brand. Keep in mind, some restaurants with very large wine lists, like the 21 Club and Gramercy Tavern in New York City or Bern's Steakhouse in Tampa, offer very good value with older wines in part to stimulate wine consumers to come to the restaurant and order multiple bottles to enjoy. Having a large inventory of older wines and selling them at attractive prices is an important feature of their dining and wine experience and true wine connoisseurs should seek out these restaurants in order to facilitate their education and journey into older wines.

Many times in my wine journey I have experienced what I like to call the "two bottle rule." Here's how it works: You and a few friends go into a nice restaurant and study the wine list. You zero in on the best bargain, which has either been mispriced or just not updated, but when you make your selection the sommelier says, "Oh, very nice, but you have just picked the last bottle, or we only have two left." This is very annoying because had you picked the most expensive bottle of wine on the list, you could have all that you wanted. Sommeliers do this to protect their wine list and balance out supply for future customers. That might be good business for the restaurant but it is annoying for the customer, and staff should be more transparent up front.

PLANNING AHEAD

One of the biggest problems with ordering wine at a restaurant is that it never really has the appropriate amount of time to breathe and open up. Say you want to enjoy a 2005 Léoville Las Cases. The sommelier will bring the wine and open the bottle, you will be asked to try it, and he will let it breathe for maybe fifteen minutes versus the forty-five to sixty minutes that is really needed. Inevitably the wine is closed and tannic, disappointing the consumer. It's ideal if you can order your wine earlier and have it fully ready to drink by the time you arrive. This may be hard to pull off with newer restaurants but not at old favorites where you have an intimate knowledge of the wine list and sommelier. (Note that many restaurants now post wine lists on their websites, which facilitates advance study or advance ordering of a particular wine. For the serious wine lover, I encourage spending time to review the list. It will lead to a more fulfilling wine experience.) This problem is magnified by the many wine lists today that contain very few older bottles and a lot of new wines from current vintages. These lists can be tough to choose from, but stick with your discipline of the best years and the producers whom you know and trust. If you are still having a tough time choosing your selection, remember that not all grapes are the same. Use your knowledge of grape varietals to help in your selection process. Looking for a Bordeaux and all that you see are wines from 2010 and 2011? Well, the 2010 is a super year and nowhere ready yet, but the 2011 is a good not great vintage that produced low yields and ripe, lower-alcohol wines in both the Right and Left Banks. The secret to picking which wines from the 2011 vintage are ready today versus five years from now, however, is that the Left Bank wines (Saint-Julien, Pauillac, Margaux, and Saint-Estèphe) are predominantly Cabernet Sauvignon and therefore much more tannic and longer lived. The Right Bank wines (Pomerol and Saint-Emilion) are more Merlot-based, softer, and more approachable early. Your selection of a Right Bank 2011 would be correct as they are starting to drink well now. Varietals such as Pinot Noir, Merlot, Gamay, Chardonnay, and Sauvignon Blanc are all grapes that can be enjoyed earlier than their bigger, mostly red counterparts like Cabernet Sauvignon, Cabernet Franc, and Syrah.

As a note of caution, some of the older vintages, particularly in the older whites, might be past their peak drinking period and thus it would be advisable to check a vintage chart, such as the one at the end of this book, before buying or ordering.

The purpose of including this summary of great vintages is not only to give the wine connoisseur a framework for the vintages to seek out or to avoid but also to illustrate how much great wine has been made over the last twenty-five years. The consistency of wine production due to modern viticulture techniques has improved product quality dramatically. Weather still plays a dominant role in deciding off years, but this chart shows the consistency of quality for those countries where the weather isn't as volatile. Climate and grape varietals go hand and hand. The more fragile grapes, like Pinot Noir (which tends to be grown in cooler regions where the risk of extreme weather is higher) and Chardonnay, are highly susceptible to volatile weather patterns, whereas the thicker-skinned grapes, like Cabernet Sauvignon, Syrah, and Nebbiolo, are more durable. The non-great vintages from competent growers are still good and it is important that the wine connoisseur not be snobbish about only drinking great vintages. These good but not great vintages will offer ample pleasure and enjoyment but should provide a framework and control mechanism for what the wine enthusiast should pay for these wines.

6

THE HISTORY AND ROLE
OF THE SOMMELIER

THE ORIGINS OF THE SOMMELIER

In "A Turn of the Corkscrew," Michael Steinberger wrote, "Many French sommeliers came to the job not by choice but by conscription, and the position has usually been a life sentence. In France, the sommelier was often someone who entered the restaurant trade as a barely pubescent teen with dreams of becoming a chef (and no prospect of attending university). Then deemed unworthy of a place at the stove, our man (and it always was a man) got shunted off to the wine cellar, where he was condemned to spend the rest of his working days in the shadow of the egomaniacal prick who beat him out of the kitchen." As a result, the reputation of French sommeliers as being arrogant and rude has a basis in truth. "Condescension and humorlessness have long been defining features of French wine service."

According to British master sommelier David Johnson, the word "sommelier" evolved from the French *sommier*, which further derives from the old Provençal word *saumalier*, which meant a pack animal driver. In Middle French *soumelier* was an "official charged with transportation of supplies," and from there the word has eventually come to mean wine waiter.

Since that time, however, the image of the sommelier has softened and changed. The modern-day sommelier is now a multifaceted wine expert who is in charge of managing the wine list, buying and selecting the wine, and training the restaurant staff on the importance of excellent wine service and the marriage of food and wine. They are there to make your experience a pleasant one but also to sell wine. The role of advising the customer and selling wine is in tandem and it's important to feel out your sommelier's credibility. Is he steering you to the most expensive wine or is he listening to your budget and wishes? At well-established Michelin-star restaurants, the sommelier often has obtained a sommelier certification or in the case of a few, the Master of Wine distinction, which in today's world is a rare feat. Some of these über-sommeliers have obtained rock-star status and grown into wine celebrities in their own right.

The über-sommelier Aldo Sohm, of New York's Le Bernardin, sums up the role: "We are expected to provide a positive wine experience. If a restaurant is ambitious enough to even have a wine cellar and employ a sommelier, we must pair the wine and serve it perfectly, and the customer must always be happy. When you take it all together, it's a big job."

ESTABLISHING A WORKING RELATIONSHIP WITH A SOMMELIER

Many new wine connoisseurs have a hard time understanding and appreciating the role of the sommelier, even when the sommelier is eager to help. Navigating through a large and complicated wine list is hard and often very intimidating for the new connoisseur. Sommeliers are there to help and make the process less painful. Sometimes, however, they come off as arrogant and condescending. This is unfortunate and several steps can be taken to minimize the friction. It is important when dealing with a sommelier to set your own timetable for choosing the wine. Too often they will hover, making you feel rushed and implying that only they know which wine to pick. Politely say, "Thank you very much; please give me a minute to review the list." They will get the hint and disappear, giving you valuable time alone to look at the list and formulate your strategy or any question you may have. Not all sommeliers are arrogant. Many are finely schooled scholars of wine who are immensely helpful given the number of wines they taste on a regular basis, but unfortunately the poor ones give the rest a bad rap. Feel out your sommelier and get a sense of his experience and after your selection talk wine with him. He will respond to your level of knowledge, sincerity, and interest. If you are in the mood to try new wines, in the hands of a good sommelier you have the opportunity to discover sensational bottles you might have otherwise overlooked.

PRE-TASTING

If I have developed a rapport with my sommelier and I have purchased a great bottle of wine, I usually invite him to taste the wine with me so he can enjoy and make a mental note of how the wine is evolving. Be aware, though, that some restaurants employ the pre-tasting method by the sommelier. This is really old school, and don't be shocked when the sommelier opens the bottle (usually out of your sightline) and pours a small taste to sample the wine before allowing you to try it. This was once a widespread and important ritual for the sommelier in order to catch any corked or bad bottle before it gets to the customer. I have sent back wine many times in the past but no matter how often you do it, it is always tough. One story I will always remember was from 1991 when my wife and I were tasting in the cellar of the then-young Burgundy winemaker Jacques Frédéric Mugnier, who had just taken over from his father with his first vintage, the 1985s. We were tasting the 1988 Chambolle Musigny from the bottle. The excitement was high as he poured my wife and me a glass. I smelled the nose and immediately noticed the wine was corked. A vague stare was all I could muster as he asked me how I liked the wine before he had even tried it. He poured himself a glass and immediately said, "It's terrible, it's corked." As he poured it out, I was relieved knowing that I had the same impression but I was saved the embarrassing moment of being wrong. So the pre-tasting is a useful ritual to avoid the awkwardness of a bad bottle. Beware, however, of the heavy-handed sommelier who, when handling a fabulous bottle, pours more than a simple taste. If they have any wine in the glass after tasting, that is too much. I have witnessed sommeliers who have poured almost half a glass when I have purchased an important wine like Burgundy's famed La Tâche. I never hesitate to call them on this when they take advantage of the situation. It doesn't happen all that often, but the situation can be tense when it does.

7

VINES, GRAPES, AND CLIMATE . . . AFTER ALL, IT'S JUST FARMING

The image of richly bunched grapes hanging from sturdy vines under a broad canopy of leaves that seemingly acts as a natural umbrella to the sun and wind is a very romantic impression for many wine lovers. Many new wine enthusiasts think of wine as a product, rather than as a perishable item that we are blessed to enjoy. Oftentimes as things change, they do tend to stay the same. Grape cultivation has been around for many thousands of years; new technology has enabled it to improve manyfold but the essence is the same. The growing of grapes is still at heart a farming business. Sure, new techniques like canopy pruning, drip lines, and high-powered fans and heaters have been introduced, along with new, genetically enhanced vine stocks that are resistant to droughts, beetles, and rot. But weather and changing climate have been constants and are *the* major factors in whether a vintage is to be successful or simply *vin ordinaire*.

THE SEASONS OF THE GRAPE

In this chapter we will explore the myriad roles that weather plays in determining the outcome of those luscious grapes that produce great wines. Since grapes are an organic material, they need sunshine to grow and reach their required ripeness and maturity. Grapes are grown all over the world but different weather patterns (sunshine and heat) play a deciding role in which varietal is successful in any given region. The thin-skinned Pinot Noir, for instance, needs cooler climates without overpowering heat in which to flourish, while the thicker-skinned Cabernet Sauvignon grape needs heat to elevate its natural sugar and ripeness. Generally speaking, put a Pinot Noir in central Spain, Napa Valley, or Australia, and you will have a hard time producing consistently great wines. The same would be true with Cabernet Sauvignon in Burgundy.

Weather patterns play a big factor in which years are truly great. During the winter months, well after the harvest when the vines are dormant due to the cold weather, the process starts for the new year. Since vines are really just plants, they need a good amount of rainfall to renourish the soil. The dormant period of winter is when the winemaker prunes the vines to concentrate the new growth on the stronger, richer canes. Spring weather is especially important as the newly developing buds are very susceptible to frost, hail, and heavy rain, which can cause mildew and disease.

Summer, both early and late, really sets the stage, starting with the early summer months of late May and June when flowering takes place. As the buds start to flower, ideally weather should stay sunny and moderately warm but not exceptionally hot, as vines in dramatic heat at this time will shut down. Grape development will thus be retarded, and fruit quality and quantity will suffer.

After flowering, the grapes remain very fragile and susceptible to adverse weather conditions. *Coulure* (poor fruit set, or as Americans call it, shatter) is driven by extreme weather conditions right after flowering, which causes the new grapes not to develop. Merlot is highly susceptible to this condition, which can result in dramatic loss of grapes and reduced overall production. As we move into the high summer months the grapes start to ripen and (depending on the varietal) need a long warm summer. This is where weather patterns are the trickiest. Too much rain and the fruit can become diseased, too little rain and extreme heat and the vines shut down. Since the grapes are growing and ripening as the summer progresses, it is important that the nights become cooler to allow the grapes to rest and maintain acidity. In addition, in the more climatically unstable regions like Burgundy, Bordeaux, Alsace, Champagne, and Germany, storms can produce hail the size of golf balls. Highly localized hailstorms can dramatically destroy maturing fruit, and can occur in the Côte de Beaune but not the Côte de Nuits, or vice versa, and have plagued Burgundy in 2012, 2013, 2014, and 2016. These hailstorms are the fear of all wine growers who devoutly hope they are random acts of nature and not the product of a permanently changing weather pattern.

As the summer starts to wane and the days get shorter, the winemakers start to think about the harvest. There is no set time to pick the grapes as different varietals in different regions need to be picked earlier than others. The general rule is that harvest should take place one hundred days after flowering, though Mother Nature can always interfere with that. Ample sunshine and cooler nights with the absence of rain is the best. An Indian summer of high temperatures in early fall will elevate sugar levels and cause grapes to be picked earlier than normal. This depends of course on the grapes and the producer's style. Once the winemaker decides that the grapes have reached the desired ripeness (the optimum balance of sugar and acidity), the harvest begins with an all-out frenzy to bring in the fruit. In the hotter climates, picking generally begins in late afternoon on through dark to avoid the most extreme heat of the day.

Allowing the grapes to remain on the vines for a longer period can sometimes make up for a cooler summer, but in the end it's about picking the grapes at their moment of optimal ripeness. I was fortunate to experience this phenomenon when I was asked to pick during the 1994 harvest in Burgundy for Jean Pierre de Smet's Domaine de l'Arlot. I entered the vineyard and experienced the backbreaking work of bringing home the harvest. At the time, Domaine de l'Arlot declassified their grapes in the field, which means that the pickers got to choose which grapes would be discarded or kept for production. This process has largely but not entirely been eliminated as it leads to quality-control issues and too much variability in grape selection. Today most of this sorting process is carried out later in the winery either by hand or, at the larger wineries, by an optical grape scanner.

By the end of my stay, my back was sore, my hands were gnarled, my French was better, and I gained much valuable knowledge of the complex effects that weather can have on the grapes' development.

For an ideal vintage every element has to go smoothly and even though good winemakers can make up for slight differences, they cannot overcome the wrath of Mother Nature.

8

FROM THE GRAPE
TO THE BOTTLE
How Is Wine Really Made?

The art (or should that be science?) of transforming grapes into wine is hardly a new phenomenon. At its essence, it is a simple process: Throw some bunches of grapes into a jar, seal it shut, and wait a few months. Over the last century, however, technical advancements have opened up an array of refinements for today's highly qualified winemaker to draw upon, from optical sorting tables to exhaustive catalogues of different yeast strains and barrel specifications. None of these options, it should be noted, guarantee a better wine. Indeed, many of the world's great wines are made in alarmingly low-tech facilities, a fact that should by no means be confused with a lack of care or attention to detail. In an era when so much is possible, it is important to remember that good winemaking is as much about what you don't do, resisting the temptation to interfere and, for those producers who chase the holy grail of terroir expression, ensuring that the delicate voice of the vineyard is not drowned out by heavy-handed vinification.

While certain winemaking practices are determined by style, for example, the secondary fermentation of sparkling wine or addition of grape spirit to fortified wine, the premise of modern winemak-

ing is broadly similar wherever you are in the world. This chapter is an easy-to-understand guide that outlines the key stages and most important decisions that need to be made once the grape has left the vineyard until the finished product is bottled.

SORTING THE GRAPES

On arrival into the winery, ideally in small crates to protect the fruit and as soon after harvesting as possible, the bunches of grapes are placed on a sorting table. Here, any damaged berries, leaves, and other vineyard debris can be removed. This "triage" is often a labor-intensive job carried out by hand, although the modern winemaker can now deploy vibrating or even optical sorting tables capable of identifying and removing less-than-perfect fruit. Some argue that the pursuit of such uniformity can strip character from the finished product; advocates praise the consistently high quality of the resulting juice.

DESTEMMING

Often carried out in tandem with the sorting process, this removal of berries from the stalk is today common practice for most wines, both red and white. As well as reducing astringency, the absence of these tannic, diluting stems can help the wine achieve a deeper color and slightly higher alcohol level. Meanwhile, the fermentation is likely to be marginally slower, cooler, and therefore more controlled without stems, whose irregular shape gives the crushed grapes (or "must") greater contact with oxygen. Destemming is usually carried out by machine, a rotating cylindrical colander, although a small number of old-school producers feel they can justify the time-consuming but ultimately gentler option of doing this by hand.

Some wine makers choose to skip this step for some or all of their crops. This occurs either in the case of carbonic maceration, a technique typically used with light-bodied, fruity red wines, or for whole-bunch fermentation, an approach most famously seen but by no means universally adopted in Burgundy. The Cabernet Sauvignon of Bordeaux, with its inherent varietal tendency toward "green" flavors, is the most obvious beneficiary of destemming.

CRUSHING

Once any undesirable elements have been removed, the grapes will be crushed in order to break open the berries and thereby encourage fermentation. Traditionally this process was done by foot; indeed, many of the Douro's most prestigious port producers still swear by this laborious approach for their top wines. Far cheaper, quicker, and more reliably thorough is the almost ubiquitous use of machines. These are calibrated to tread the crucial line between crushing the berries without smashing the grape seeds, which would release bitter tannins and unpleasant oils into the must. In an ideal world, the time span between harvest and crush will be as short as possible so that the key stage of fermentation can proceed in an orderly fashion.

As with other stages of the winemaking process, oxygen exposure needs to be carefully managed, especially for white wines, which are particularly vulnerable to becoming brown and spoiled by excessive oxidation. As ever, however, there is a fine balance to tread, with some oxygen required to kickstart the fermentation process and controlled oxidation used as a tool by winemakers to broaden the flavor spectrum beyond primary fruits. Without oxidation, there would be no sherry (oloroso or amontillado), madeira, tawny port or, at the less extreme end of the spectrum, Gran Reserva Rioja as we know it. In short, oxygen is not the enemy, but a valuable ally that requires careful monitoring.

FERMENTATION

This is the moment when the grapes' natural sugar is converted into alcohol and carbon dioxide. The alchemy is carried out by yeast, which is found naturally in the vineyard (often referred to as "wild yeast") and will be brought into the winery on the grape skins. Many winemakers, especially those responsible for bigger-volume brands where consistency is vital, will choose to inoculate their must with carefully selected cultivated yeast. Not only will this encourage a more regular, even fermentation, but certain strains of yeast offer different attributes. Some of these may relate to the character of the end product, creating wines with higher alcohol, enhanced fruit

character, or deeper color; others may concern the winemaking process, offering improved tolerance to temperature extremes or the sulfur dioxide that is widely used in wine as a disinfectant and preservative. The time frame for fermentation can be as short as a day or two for port, where the process is halted by adding spirits to fortify the wine (even though plenty of sugar still remains), right through to many months for those highly concentrated grapes used to make the intensely sweet Trockenbeerenauslese of Germany and Austria. For most winemakers, however, this closely monitored period lasts inside a week for red wines and perhaps two or three weeks for whites, which tend to be fermented at a cooler temperature. During this period red wines will require the cap of grape skins that floats to the surface to be submerged regularly (*pigeage* or "punching down"), with juice pumped over the top in order to achieve, hopefully, just the right level of extraction.

The fermentation process can take place in any number of different vessels, from large stainless steel tanks complete with state-of-the-art temperature control and laboratory-grade hygiene, to prized old wooden vats whose heat-retaining properties can help maximize the amount of color extracted from the grape skins. Other producers prefer inert, cheap concrete vessels, while recent years have witnessed a trend for these to be molded into egg-shaped vats. Fans such as Pontet-Canet in Pauillac praise the greater circulation of the liquid, usually achieved manually by regular stirring (*battonage*) and enhanced surface-area contact with lees (the mix of dead yeast cells and grape skins), both of which can bring greater complexity and texture to the finished wine. The other vessel commonly used for fermentation is the barrel, especially in the case of richer or sweet white wines destined for oak maturation, where this earlier introduction can enhance and harmonize the fuller style and, if well managed, improve the integration of oak flavor in the wine.

PRESSING

For white wines this stage will often happen prior to fermentation, but red wines benefit from extended skin contact, which is the source of their color; squeeze a red grape berry and, with very few

exceptions, the juice will be almost colorless. In some wineries the technology involved has changed very little since the Middle Ages but, depending on budget and desired style, modern equipment can now achieve precise control over how much pressure is exerted and therefore the level of phenolic extraction.

RACKING

Once fermentation and pressing are complete, the wine needs to be separated from the sediment now lying at the bottom of its vessel. This process, carried out several times during the *elevage* period between fermentation and bottling, helps to clarify the wine and, for red wines especially, is another opportunity for controlled oxidation. A number of wineries pride themselves on a gravity-fed layout, which means that for stages such as this their wine can be spared the aggression of a pump and instead drain more gently downhill into the next empty vat. For many white wines this is the end of the road: They will probably undergo additional filtration before being bottled and released for immediate consumption. Where richer styles of white and red wines are concerned, however, there remains more work to be done.

MALOLACTIC FERMENTATION

Most red wines and some white wines, especially Chardonnay, will now undergo a phase referred to variously as malolactic fermentation ("malo"), or perhaps most properly, malolactic conversion, since this is not strictly a second fermentation, although the bubbles of carbon dioxide given off in the process can make it appear that way. A useful way to tone down high acidity, stabilize the wine, and add greater complexity, malolactic fermentation sees the hard malic acid, which is found naturally in grapes and other fruit such as apples (whose Latin name, *malum*, is behind the term), transformed by ambient bacteria into the far milder, buttery lactic acid (derived from *lactis*, the Latin word for milk). Winemakers in warmer regions, where acidity is likely to be naturally low, may wish to avoid this step by adding sulfur dioxide or keeping the wine at a low temperature. The

other notable exception is Riesling which, despite its naturally high acidity, does not appear to respond well to this process, making a virtue of its crispness.

BARREL MATURATION

Many, although certainly not all, of the world's great wines will spend some time maturing in barrels. While newer barrels in particular will impart an element of toast, hazelnut, or vanilla flavor, the primary purpose of the barrel is usually to allow controlled oxidation, a process that in itself brings added complexity. The barrel also provides a natural, gentle way to stabilize the wine, deepen its color, and soften any rough tannins. Meanwhile its naturally porous nature means that during extended maturation, usually between one and two years, as much as 2 to 8 percent of the wine may evaporate (the "angels' share" as whisky producers call it), thereby helping to concentrate the flavor of what remains. For winemakers the barrel, especially if it's new, is a major expense. Then there's the size, the level of toast, the type of oak, and even which cooper you choose. Barrels made by French coopers are often highly prized for their fine grain but carry a cost to match. American oak is often half the price but can bring sweeter, more overt vanilla character to the wine. That doesn't stop it playing a role in some of the world's most admired wines, with California's Ridge and many great Riojas standing as prime examples. Hungarian or Slavonian oak can prove a handy compromise, bringing a grain and character similar to French oak at a far friendlier price.

With age, the amount of character imparted by the barrel will diminish. Again, different producers in different regions will prize extreme ends of this spectrum. While a winemaker in Bordeaux or Napa might buy significant quantities of new barrels each year, traditional producers in Austria or Piedmont can be found painstakingly repairing large, decades-old casks. Meanwhile no self-respecting sherry or port producer would be caught dead using new barrels. It is perhaps here more than at any other stage of the winemaking process that the producer should stop to consider what sort of barrel, if indeed any, is most suitable for his particular wine rather than his ego. Putting poor-quality fruit into a new barrel will not transform it into Château Lafite, any more than putting a couch potato in tennis whites will make him Roger Federer.

BLENDING

Behind many great wines lies immensely skillful blending. In fact, for a winemaker, it's where the rubber meets the road. This is not simply about marrying the likes of Cabernet Sauvignon, Cabernet Franc, Merlot, and Petit Verdot, as you might see in a classic Bordeaux blend. In this region as with many others, producers may well have vinified certain parcels of vineyard separately to preserve their distinct character. Of these micro-vinifications, some will have been matured in new barrels, a proportion in second fill barrels, and perhaps even another batch in something more radical such as concrete eggs. Nor is there just the one wine to consider: It is now standard practice for the big names in Bordeaux to produce a second- and perhaps even third-tier wine, saving poorer-quality fruit or grapes from younger vines from sullying their flagship wines. Then there's the decision of when to blend: After malolactic fermentation may be standard practice for many red wines, but the traditional "field blends" that still feature strongly in port's Douro Valley vineyards can see multiple varieties harvested together and co-fermented. The picture becomes still more complex in Champagne, where a nonvintage expression such as Louis Roederer's Brut Premier may comprise as many as six hundred different blending components, including reserve wine from previous harvests. To achieve consistent character from year to year is a real testament to the winemaker's skill.

FILTRATION

Almost every wine will undergo some form of fining and filtration in order to clarify the end product by removing particles left over after fermentation. These range from yeast cells and grape cellulose to bacteria, proteins, and pectins, which may leave undesirable haze, aromas, or flavors in the wine if left unchecked. The practice tends to be most rigorous for larger-scale, everyday wines whose production process is more rapid. At the fine-wine end of the spectrum, the longer vinification period allows time for a more natural, less involved approach that sees these particles gradually drop out during barrel maturation and get removed in the racking process. Modern-day filtration draws on a variety of high-tech membrane options, while fining agents may be derived from unlikely sources such as egg white, fish bladders, and bentonite clay.

BOTTLING

And so, finally, after months or even years resting in barrel, the wine is ready to be bottled. Until the last few decades of the twentieth century this job would often have been carried out by merchants, with the wine shipped from the winery while still in barrel. Today, however, the vast majority of high-quality producers prefer the control of bottling in house, with those who can afford the outlay having their own bottling line. This is a precarious moment for the wine, which can be exposed to bacteria or damaging amounts of oxygen if due care is not taken.

Once bottled, the wine may well be cellared at the winery for a further period, especially those styles built to age, in order for it to reach the end consumer as close to its optimal drinking as cellar space and cash flow allow. In Rioja this period of bottle aging is dictated by law, with a Gran Reserva required to spend at least two years in barrel and a further three in bottle before it can be released. As provenance becomes ever more vital for the most desirable fine wines, Château Latour has shunned the *en primeur* system in favor of holding back stock for a decade or longer. In 2016, Château Latour released the last of its 2000 vintage with the perfect provenance and cellaring that allowed the estate to set its price at a notable premium over that commanded by bottles of precisely the same wine already on the market. It serves as an extreme example of the level of control that winemakers can now exert over their grapes. Once the bottle leaves the winery, of course, it's a different story altogether.

9

LET THE JOURNEY BEGIN . . . THE BENCHMARK WINES

The purpose of this book is to share some of my observations and lessons learned during my forty-one-year journey loving and appreciating wines. The love and scholarship of my wine journey has been an important aspect of my life and the friendship and continued curiosity of the industry has been rewarding. If you are serious about wine or just getting started, it is important to recognize that it's a journey. Very enriching, yes, but a long-term journey that will take you to all corners of the globe. To become a true wine connoisseur, you must realize the difference between varietals, regions, and countries and use this benchmarking as a way to memorize the difference between quality, years, and styles. The only way to accomplish this is to taste and document the best of the best in order to realize style differences. The wines that I have provided as benchmark wines are listed not because they are the most expensive, highest prestige, or most popular, but rather because of the unique place they hold within the wine world and the fact that no wine connoisseur could enjoy their journey without tasting these wines and having a memory marker as to their distinctive styles. Some are very expensive; some are not . . . the expensive wines should be shared within a group of other wine connoisseurs much in the same fashion as people get together in book clubs to enjoy their stories. You only really need one glass of each of these wines to record their style and taste for your scholarship. I wanted to write this book for the serious new wine connoisseur, not the expert, although I am sure they will enjoy it and recognize many of the things I have experienced. I can't imagine the serious wine connoisseur going through his journey never having experienced the unbelievable subtlety and finesse of a Château Petrus, the overwhelming power and structure of a Latour, the pure seduction and mind-blowing richness of a great Burgundy, or the distinct style of a great Gaja Barbaresco.

The main reason for benchmarking these wine experiences is to have a dedicated memory for comparison when tasting wines of lesser quality. I don't expect that everybody has the pocketbook to enjoy these wines on a regular basis. That isn't the goal . . . but as you enjoy wines of lesser stature you will appreciate and draw conclusions about which wines you want to experience over time. There are many, many great Burgundies available and over time you will have a basis for comparison and know which ones to enjoy on a regular basis. To know and appreciate the best will enable you to appreciate wines of lesser quality, but also wines from different regions and countries. If you go through life just tasting wines from California or France, your wine journey will never be truly complete.

The most important thing, however, is to taste and study, taste and study, go region by region and pull the cork, thus experiencing the true excitement and joy that wine can bring. You have started a life-long journey that will bring wonderful pleasure and satisfaction. I hope this book helps to demystify the process and excite your interest. Let's get started . . . on to the benchmark wines.

VINEYARD PROFILES

CHÂTEAU ANGÉLUS

Angélus's recent promotion in the Saint-Emilion reclassification marked the culmination of more than two decades of ambitious vineyard, winery, and marketing work by its family owners.

Château Angélus, which takes its name from the prayer that is traditionally recited three times daily, and its wine are both easily distinguished by the symbolic bell used to call the faithful to their devotions. While this estate at the foot of the Saint-Emilion plateau dates back to 1782, its owners, the de Boüard family, trace their Bordeaux roots back over seven hundred years. In more recent times, sharp-eyed James Bond fans may have spotted Angélus's distinctive label in a *Casino Royale* cameo. Such canny marketing is typical of Hubert de Boüard, who has led this property with cousin Jean-Bernard Grenié since the late 1980s. One of his earliest moves was to change its name from L'Angélus to Angélus for the simple reason that it enabled the estate to appear at the top of alphabetical lists. That is far from the limit of the owners' ambitions for Angélus, whose postwar image has been steadily rebuilt via a mix of modern technical know-how and

strict yield control. In 1996, Angélus was promoted to Premier Grand Cru Classé status, and 2012 saw Angélus further elevated to the elite ranks of Premier Grand Cru Classé "A." Despite the legal dispute over this reclassification launched by several demoted châteaux, Angélus saw an

CHÂTEAU ANGÉLUS CO-OWNER AND MANAGER HUBERT DE BOÜARD.

immediate flurry of trading on the secondary market and added a celebratory 30 percent markup to its 2012 release—a controversial move at a time when other Bordeaux estates were facing pressure to hold or drop prices to reflect diminished demand. Today Angélus has welcomed the next generation, with Stéphanie de Boüard promising to continue her father's track record for innovation.

TOP VINTAGES

"Rich, dense, and unctuous" is how Angélus's owners describe its style, although the almost 50 percent dose of Cabernet Franc imparts an important elegant pedigree to this wine. Angélus is certainly a powerful wine and its big, extracted style can prove a bit much for Bordeaux purists, although it is certainly built with long-term aging in mind.

The following vintages are particularly noteworthy from this estate:

2010   A big, lavish wine that made quite an impression, even if some tasting notes could be describing a port rather than a Bordeaux.

2009   A showy expression that for some showed Angélus at the top of its game, although others found the concentration too much.

2005   Decadent in style with no shortage of complexity, even if the real drinking pleasure will have to wait for its tannins to soften.

2003 57 percent Cabernet Franc was used for freshness in this hot year. Upgraded by Parker a decade on, others remained less convinced.

2000 A year when Angélus's ripe, extracted style was at its most flattering and harmonious.

1990 Widely hailed as a return to form for Angélus, this flamboyant wine has been shining through a long drinking window.

1985 The first vintage with de Boüard in charge, this good year for Merlot adds a sumptuous quality, even if the wine is now fading.

Dream vintage: 1953 A year that offers great charm from Bordeaux, but whose wines are understandably now fading gently with age. Nevertheless, Angelus picks out this vintage as a particular star of its back catalogue, albeit from a very different winemaking era.

CHÂTEAU AUSONE

The Right Bank's classification system may be rather more fluid—and legally contested—than that of the Médoc, but this Saint-Emilion château sets an undisputed benchmark.

Rising both literally and figuratively above its peers, Château Ausone perches on the southern edge of the medieval hilltop town of Saint-Emilion. The estate is named after fourth century AD *vigneron* and poet Decimus Magnus Ausonius, the site of whose villa forms part of today's Ausone. Despite this link, the château as we know it today was founded far more recently by Jean Cantenat in the eighteenth century. After passing through the hands of the Lafargue family, it was inherited by Edouard Dubois, in whose family Ausone stayed until the mid-1990s. For all this apparent continuity, Ausone endured an unsettled period for much of the twentieth century due to tensions

At a Glance

ADDRESS
33330 Saint-Emilion, France
Tel: +33 (0)5 57 24 24 57

PEOPLE
The Vauthier family (owners)
Alain Vauthier (manager)

SIZE
7.3 hectares of vineyard, producing around two thousand cases a year of the *grand vin* and an even smaller quantity of the second wine.

KEY WINES
Château Ausone
Chapelle d'Ausone

GRAPE VARIETIES
Cabernet Franc (around 55 percent of the *grand vin*)
Merlot (45 percent)
Cabernet Sauvignon (a minority proportion is used in the second wine)

between the various family members involved in its running. Until winemaker Pascal Delbeck arrived in 1976, the wines struggled to live up to the potential of their outstanding terroir.

Planted on a steep, southeast-facing slope, the top part of the vineyard sits on the limestone plateau that must surely play a role in the pure, mineral character of a wine that shows a deep connection to its site. Also of note is the age of the estate's Cabernet Franc vines, the oldest of which were planted in 1906. As well as helping to explain the low yields at Ausone, these old vines no doubt contribute to the striking intensity of the fruit in these highly expressive, slow-maturing wines. These attributes and more have emerged ever more strongly since 1996, when the estate became fully owned by the Vauthier family, long involved with the management of Ausone through a link by marriage to the Dubois family. Under the guidance of Alain Vauthier and more recently his daughter Pauline, Ausone's star has risen once more.

SAINT-EMILION

Boasting by far the most attractive town in the Bordeaux region, Saint-Emilion is one of the area's largest appellations. The major-

ity of top estates here are located either on or around the base of the limestone plateau that rises from the sandy plain stretching to the Dordogne River. Adding further to the complexity of this appellation is the gravelly soil on its northeastern border with Pomerol. In contrast to the Médoc, where Cabernet Sauvignon is king, the Right Bank is Merlot country. Cabernet Franc also has an important role to play here, although this early-ripening variety's fragrant, lighter character creates a rather different style to that of its famously structured genetic offspring Cabernet Sauvignon.

TOP VINTAGES

Today's Ausone stands as prime evidence for the argument that a mark of truly great terroir is its ability—in the right hands, of course—to transcend the vagaries of vintage.

The following vintages are particularly noteworthy from this estate:

2010   A Saint-Emilion star in a year of stiff competition. Dense but not heavy, explosive but tightly knit fruit; "extraordinary," says Parker.

2005   It was top scores and effusive praise all around for Ausone in this highly regarded year. Built for the long term.

2003   An estate that retained freshness in a year when many wines toppled over from the sheer ripeness of this famously hot vintage.

2000   In a year that lent itself to wines of great structure, Ausone looks set to offer immense reward for those with patience.

1995   A vintage for the Right Bank and an important moment for Ausone, which came under Alain Vauthier's full control this year.

Dream vintage: 1983   Given the challenges faced by Ausone during much of the twentieth century, anyone venturing back into venerable vintages should proceed with caution. Although largely overshadowed by the previous 1982 vintage, 1983 was particularly rewarding on the Right Bank

and, despite challenges posed by heat and rot, both were more than overcome by Ausone thanks to its prime hillside positioning.

CHÂTEAU CHEVAL BLANC

Beloved by James Bond and owned by a luxury powerhouse, Cheval Blanc's distinctly glamorous image is underpinned by its seat at the very top of the Saint-Emilion classification.

Just a stone's throw from Pomerol, Cheval Blanc shares some of that appellation's voluptuous qualities. However, while Pomerol's Merlot does still have an important role to play here, the balance of gravel alongside clay and sand has nudged this estate into becoming perhaps the world's most famous source of Cabernet Franc. Indeed, before it acquired its present form and title, the vineyard was known as "Le Barrail des Cailloux," or "barrel of small stones."

Cheval Blanc was one of a number of Saint-Emilion properties created in 1832 when Comtesse Félicité de Carle Trajet decided to downsize her two-hundred-hectare Figeac estate by selling off land to a number of interested parties. New owners the Ducasse family gradually expanded their holdings until 1871 when, passed via marriage into the Laussac-

At a Glance

ADDRESS
33330 Saint-Emilion, France
Tel: +33 (0)5 57 55 55 55

PEOPLE
Pierre Lurton (estate manager)

SIZE
Forty-one hectares, divided between Cabernet Franc (58 percent) and Merlot (42 percent). Around 6,500 cases of the *grand vin* are produced annually.

KEY WINES
Château Cheval Blanc
Le Petit Cheval

GRAPE VARIETIES
Cabernet Franc
Merlot
In most years the *grand vin* is dominated by this estate's famous Cabernet Franc, although a few vintages such as 2000 and 1999 have in fact been Merlot-led.

Fourcaud family, Cheval Blanc reached its current forty-one-hectare form. Together with Ausone, the estate was placed at the very top of the Saint-Emilion hierarchy, Premier Grand Cru Classé "A," with the creation of this appellation's first official classification in 1955. Unlike Ausone, however, Cheval Blanc enjoyed more consistent management during the twentieth century. Even when sold out of family ownership in 1998 to LVMH chairman Bernard Arnault, the installation of respected winemaker Pierre Lurton as estate manager ensured that quality remained at a standard befitting a member of this luxury group. As a finishing touch, 2011 saw the unveiling of its sleek new cellar, a striking modernist addition to the traditional Saint-Emilion landscape.

PIERRE LURTON

You don't need to spend much time in Bordeaux before coming across the Lurton name. Between them, the family members manage about 1,300 hectares across twenty-seven properties. However, it is Pierre Lurton who holds the most high-profile job of all as estate manager at Cheval Blanc for the last two decades. As if this were not responsibility enough, LVMH has also handed him the reins of the world's most famous sweet wine, Château d'Yquem. In addition to his winemaking skills, honed at family estate Clos Fourtet under the guidance of revered consultant Emile Peynaud, Lurton has demonstrated considerable commercial acumen. In 1998, a year that favored the Right Bank, he raised eyebrows by releasing Cheval Blanc at a higher price than the Left Bank first growths. Backed by glowing critical reviews, the wines were eagerly snapped up by consumers and made a bold statement about the prestige of this jewel in the Saint-Emilion crown.

TOP VINTAGES

So consistent has Cheval Blanc proved under Lurton's management that, having survived Bordeaux's trio of highly forgettable years in the early 1990s (in 1991 there was no *grand vin* at all), it is difficult to detect a disappointing vintage.

The following vintages are particularly noteworthy from this estate:

2011   Not a year of widespread acclaim but the Cabernet Franc here delivered an aromatic wine of great delicacy and restraint.

2010   A wine of structure and intensity, with an enticing Cabernet Franc–led aroma at the start and immense length on the finish.

2000   Although apparently in no rush to fully reveal itself, this wine is taunting tasters with enticing glimpses of the pleasure to come.

1998   Hailed by Lurton as the greatest Cheval Blanc in the second half of the twentieth century, this was a pivotal year for the estate's image.

1990   The richness of this vintage is tempered by Cabernet Franc, which injects vital freshness to create a highly seductive result.

Dream vintage: 1947   Even among those who have never tasted it, Cheval Blanc 1947's reputation alone makes it likely to rank high on most lists of the world's all-time legendary wines. For those who have been fortunate enough to encounter a bottle, the superlatives speak for themselves. "I honestly don't expect ever to taste a wine better than this," says Jancis Robinson MW.

CHÂTEAU FIGEAC

Favoring delicacy over concentration and sometimes taking a few years to reveal its true charm, Figeac may officially rank as only a second-tier Saint-Emilion but it attracts loyal fans.

You would be forgiven for placing this Saint-Emilion estate on the Left Bank in a blind tasting: The gravelly soils of Figeac mean that it contains an unusually high dose of Cabernet Sauvignon. The estate shares this gravel with famous neighbor Cheval Blanc, which was indeed created from one of several parcels of land sold off by Figeac in the nineteenth century. The name Figeac may in fact trace its roots not to anything grape-related, but from the Latin word *ficus*, in French *figue*, meaning fig tree. Founded on the site of a second-century Roman villa, by the fourteenth century "Figeacus" covered about five hundred hectares. After Henry of Navarre destroyed its medieval château in 1590, the Cazes

At a Glance

ADDRESS
33330 Saint-Emilion, France
Tel: +33 (0)5 57 24 72 26

PEOPLE
The Manoncourt family (owners)
Frédéric Faye (estate director)

SIZE
Forty hectares of vineyard. Annual production of the *grand vin* is about ten thousand cases, with around one thousand cases of the second wine.

KEY WINES
Château Figeac
Petit-Figeac (called La Grange Neuve de Figeac until 2012)

GRAPE VARIETIES
Cabernet Sauvignon (35 percent of total plantings)
Cabernet Franc (35 percent)
Merlot (30 percent)
The grape proportions of the *grand vin* are similar to those of the vineyard plantings.

family built a Renaissance replacement, parts of which still feature in the eighteenth-century successor that stands today. Figeac
stayed with the Cazes and their descendants until it was sold to
a Parisian in 1838. This marked the start of a turbulent era, with
further ownership changes, vineyard sales, and absentee landlords.
Stability returned with Thierry Manoncourt, who took over from
his father and grandfather, but unlike them he chose to live on
site. For sixty-four years until his death in 2010, this agronomist
made consistently high-quality wines in a very classic, unflashy
style. Manoncourt was initially succeeded by son-in-law Comte
Eric d'Aramon, but 2013 saw gossip fly as Jean-Valmy Nicolas
from La Conseillante was brought in and former vineyard manager
Frédéric Faye took charge. With modernizing consultant Michel
Rolland now employed, Figeac fans are watching nervously for
signs of a style change.

FIGEAC OFFSPRING

A casual scan through Saint-Emilion's estates will throw up a number
of châteaux bearing the Figeac name. This is no coincidence: These
and others were once part of the original five-hundred-hectare Figeac property, which, until the nineteenth century, stretched from the

edge of the village of
Saint-Emilion to the
outskirts of Libourne.
In addition to giving
its name to Yôn-Figeac,
La Tour Figeac, Croix-
Figeac, and La Tour du
Pin Figeac, among the
more illustrious prop-
erties to have bene-
fited from vineyard parcels sold off by Château Figeac over the years
are Pomerol's La Conseillante and top-flight Saint-Emilion estate
Cheval Blanc. Indeed, it was a strongly held and regularly voiced
belief of Figeac's long-term custodian, the late Thierry Manoncourt,
that, despite their "B" grade classification, his wines were very much
the equal of this thoroughbred neighbor.

TOP VINTAGES

There seems to be a recurring trend with Château Figeac that its wines do not always shine when tasted *en primeur*, with the inevi-table result that initial scores and reviews rarely make this a headline property. However, once bottled the wines seem to emerge from their shell to provide plenty of sophisticated, unflashy drinking pleasure, justi-fying its reputation as a leading member of the Premier Grand Cru Classé "B" châteaux.

The following vintages are particularly noteworthy from this estate:

2010   Shunning the huge concentration that characterized many wines from this vintage, Figeac offers a vibrant, fresh Cabernet style.

2009   Bringing welcome restraint to a year of great ripeness, this was initially austere compared to its peers but is now very inviting.

2005   As with many estates this year, critics hailed this show of fine tannins and bright fruit as Figeac's most exciting wine for a decade.

2000   In true Figeac style, this shunned the blockbuster punch of many wines from this vintage in favor of fragrance and elegance.

1990   A beautifully textured and balanced wine that has flourished with age and still has some distance to run.

1983   For some critics this edged out the highly regarded 1982 with its delicate but textbook example of a classic, mature claret.

1982   Greater richness and concentration than the 1983, offering aromatic, sweet fruit and immense pleasure.

Dream vintage: 1959   It is difficult—and perhaps unnecessary—to choose between this great vintage and the more famous year of 1961 that followed soon after. However, the seductive combination of richness and vitality that is still recognizably Figeac makes this a wine to look out for.

CHÂTEAU HAUT-BRION

A vineyard oasis in the modern-day suburban sprawl of Bordeaux, first growth Haut-Brion and its top wine have been winning admiration from as early as the sixteenth century.

Is this the world's oldest luxury brand? A recent dig into the local archives unearthed a contract from 1521 involving wine from "the place known as Aubrion." However, Haut-Brion's formal birth as a wine estate dates to 1533, when Jean de Pontac bought the property, whose name derives from a Gascon description of its location on a plot of high ground in the gravelly— hence Graves—region to the south of Bordeaux.

It was de Pontac who built a château on the estate, later enlarged during the seventeenth century by Arnaud III de Pontac, who can also claim credit for building Haut-Brion's international reputation. This early prestige can be seen in the 1660 cellar book of English king Charles II. Over a two-year period his court served visitors a total of 169 bottles of "wine of Hobriono." The English diarist Samuel Pepys was also a fan, noting an outing in 1663 where he drank "a sort of French wine called Ho Bryan that hath a good and most particular taste that I never met with."

We then fast-forward through three changes in family ownership, each of which added fresh improvements to the estate, to 1935 when Haut-Brion was bought by US financier and neighbor Clarence Dillon. Following the marriage of his granddaughter

At a Glance

ADDRESS
135, avenue Jean Jaurès
33608 Pessac, France
Tel: +33 (0)5 56 00 29 30

PEOPLE
Prince Robert of Luxembourg
(president)
Jean-Philippe Delmas (estate manager)

SIZE
Fifty-one-hectare estate, of which over forty-eight hectares are planted with red grape varieties and just under three hectares with white. Annual production is around twenty thousand cases, of which the *grand vin* is ten to twelve thousand.

KEY WINES
Château Haut-Brion
Le Clarence de Haut-Brion (called Bahans-Haut-Brion until 2007)
Château Haut-Brion Blanc
La Clarté de Haut-Brion

GRAPE VARIETIES
Merlot (45.4 percent of red plantings)
Cabernet Sauvignon (43.9 percent)
Cabernet Franc (9.7 percent)
Petit Verdot (1 percent)
Semillon (52.6 percent of white plantings)
Sauvignon Blanc (47.4 percent)

Joan to Prince Charles of Luxembourg, the estate today—together with La Mission Haut-Brion and Quintus in St Emilion—is presided over by their son Prince Robert. However, much of the credit for Haut-Brion's notably consistent performance goes to the three generations of the Delmas family who have overseen its vineyards and winemaking.

GRAVES

Located to the south of the city of Bordeaux and on the left bank of the Garonne River, Graves is a large appellation encompassing high-quality subregions such as Sauternes and Pessac-Léognan, where

PRINCE ROBERT OF LUXEMBOURG.

Haut-Brion is located. Indeed, before the Dutch drained the Médoc in the seventeenth century, it was this corner of the region that formed the cornerstone of Bordeaux's international reputation.

Graves takes its name from the gravelly soil that characterizes much of this appellation. Among other distinguishing features is the milder climate here, which means that harvest can often be as much as two weeks ahead of the more northerly Médoc. Unusually for Bordeaux,

Graves also stands out for the quality of its white wines, although these remain small in production compared to red styles.

Other top Graves estates to look out for include Haut-Brion's sister château La Mission Haut-Brion, as well as Pape Clément, Haut Bailly, and Domaine de Chevalier.

TOP VINTAGES

Haut-Brion is admired for its consistent performance over the last twenty years. This is often attributed at least in part to its superb terroir, which both imparts a distinctive character and seems capable of overcoming the challenges posed by Bordeaux's Atlantic climate.

The following vintages are particularly noteworthy from this estate:

2010   A flurry of top scores in a top vintage for this distinctly aristocratic, elegantly defined wine.

2009   An uncharacteristically rich, concentrated Haut-Brion, but keeping a suppleness and balance that bodes well for the future.

2005   Delicacy and power enrobed with a velvety texture that looks set for a glorious evolution.

1996   A year that will reward the more patient fans of long-lived, classic Bordeaux.

1989   Hailed by Parker as his "desert island wine," this vintage of Haut-Brion attracted top scores for both its red and white.

1982   The Bordeaux vintage that thrilled critics and continues to provoke superlatives as it matures. Haut-Brion proved no exception.

Dream vintage: 1961   One of the undisputed stellar Bordeaux vintages of the last century, at Haut-Brion this year also marked the beginning of a transformative decade. Estate manager Georges Delmas handed the reins to his son Jean-Bernard in 1961, starting a period of renovation that, among other developments, saw Haut-Brion become first of the first growths to install stainless steel tanks.

CHÂTEAU LA MISSION HAUT-BRION

A stone's throw from Haut-Brion, La Mission may not share its sibling's first growth status but in some years has been known to match or even surpass it in quality.

Despite the similarity of name and position just across the road from Haut-Brion, La Mission Haut-Brion retained its own distinct history until the two estates were formally joined by the Dillon family in 1983. Even so, when the château was bought in 1540 by Marie-Arnaud de Lestonnac, the reputation of the wines made by his neighbor—and, in fact, brother-in-law—no doubt encouraged him to plant vines.

The religious "La Mission" element links to 1664, when de Lestonnac's pious granddaughter Olive left the estate to a religious order. For the century that the château then known as Haut-La Mission remained in their control, the Lazarite friars carried out major improvements to the buildings, vineyard, and wine. Confiscated in 1792 after the French Revolution, the estate was bought at auction by Martial-Victor Vaillant, but his only daughter sold it in 1821 to New Orleans–born Célestin Chiapella. This

At a Glance

ADDRESS
67, rue Peybouquey
33400 Talence, France
Tel: +33 (0)5 56 00 29 30

PEOPLE
Prince Robert of Luxembourg
(president)
Jean-Philippe Delmas (estate manager)

SIZE
Twenty-nine hectares of vineyard, of which almost twenty-seven are planted with red varieties. Average annual production of the *grand vin* is six to seven thousand cases and five to seven hundred for the white.

KEY WINES
Château La Mission Haut-Brion
La Chapelle de La Mission Haut-Brion
Château La Mission Haut-Brion Blanc
(known as Château Laville Haut-Brion
before 2009)
La Clarté de Haut-Brion—a blend of white grapes from both Haut-Brion and La Mission Haut-Brion

GRAPE VARIETIES
Merlot (42.7 percent of
vineyard plantings)
Cabernet Sauvignon (47 percent)
Cabernet Franc (10.3 percent)
Semillon (85 percent)
Sauvignon Blanc (14 percent)
Muscadelle (1 percent)

forged a strong US following for the wine, adding to its prestige so that by the time the estate had passed via the ownership of several merchants into the hands of the Woltner family in 1919, a bottle of La Mission Haut-Brion sold for more than any other Bordeaux wine except its nearest neighbor.

It was the Woltners who carried out much-needed moderniza-

tion of the estate and added a white wine. For all these advances, later generations struggled to agree on how their estate should be managed, so it was put up for sale and found a natural new owner in the Dillon family. Their care and investment is leading La Mission Haut-Brion into a bright new era.

GRAVES CLASSIFICATION

The Médoc's prestige today masks the fact that it was the Graves that first established Bordeaux's winemaking reputation. This gulf wid-

ened with the 1855 classification, whose commercial influence persists today, but which excluded every Graves estate with the sole exception of Haut-Brion. In a bid to restore pride—and with it profit—to the appellation, 1953 saw the creation of an official Graves classification. However, despite the 1959 addition of four more whites and two reds, the move struggled to achieve anything more than symbolic success. Little more than 10 percent of the vineyard area is included, with the single-tier structure offering consumers no quality hierarchy. Nor does the "cru classé" designation give much sense of distinction.

A more useful move was the 1987 creation of an appellation called Pessac-Léognan. With almost half its area made up from these classed-growth estates, this subregion is a helpful starting point for those in search of top-quality Graves.

TOP VINTAGES

La Mission Haut-Brion is regarded as a more masculine, gutsier counterpart to its grander sibling Haut-Brion, and the extreme proximity of these estates leads to inevitable similarities in the gravel-rich terroir that lends both such style, longevity, and an uncanny ability to shine in difficult years.

The following vintages are particularly noteworthy from this estate:

2010 Since 2007 the estate has shifted emphasis from Merlot to Cabernet, whose character shines through in this ageworthy vintage.

2009 Despite the warmth of this year, the wine managed to retain the dusty, warm-brick character that it shares with Haut-Brion.

2005 A stellar year for La Mission, even if that concentration and structure require some patience; a mere 5,600 cases were made.

2000 Super savory, mineral, and dense, with the energy to propel this wine forward in style for many decades to come.

1990 Although not attracting quite the same levels of admiration as its previous vintage, this dense, persistent style made a real impact.

1989   Full marks from Parker and exhilarating tasting notes from other critics, this vintage wowed with its vitality and opulence.

1982   A great wine from a great vintage that continues to impress with its length, liveliness, and elusive mix of richness with subtlety.

Dream vintage: 1959   La Mission is one of several estates to see this year widely acknowledged as surpassing its—still superlative—effort with the legendary 1961 vintage. Both stand as a great tribute to Henri Woltner, who oversaw an impressive fifty vintages at the château.

CHÂTEAU LAFITE ROTHSCHILD

Of all Bordeaux's prestigious châteaux, it was this Pauillac estate that captivated a new tidal wave of Chinese buyers, sparking the recent—now rapidly deflating—price bubble.

Bordeaux vintners have collectively undergone a series of peaks and troughs in recent centuries, but the name Château Lafite stands out for its particularly influential, symbolic role in the region's latest chapter. The name Lafite enters the history books in the twelfth century thanks to a monastic connection with this site on a raised area of land to the north of Pauillac; however, it was the Ségur family in the seventeenth century who really established the estate's winemaking reputation. Its popularity at the court of Louis XV, in the eighteenth century, helped to secure Lafite's domestic prestige, and by the 1800s British prime minister Robert Walpole was a regular customer. The estate was also a well-known favorite of US president Thomas Jefferson.

At a Glance

ADDRESS
33250 Pauillac, France
Tel: +33 (0)5 56 59 26 83

PEOPLE
Baron Eric de Rothschild (owner)
Charles Chevallier (technical director)

SIZE
112 hectares spread across three main plots. Average annual production stands at sixteen thousand cases of the *grand vin* and twenty thousand cases for Carruades.

KEY WINES
Château Lafite Rothschild
Carruades de Lafite

GRAPE VARIETIES
Cabernet Sauvignon
Merlot
Petit Verdot
Cabernet Franc
Typical composition of the *grand vin*: 80 to 95 percent Cabernet Sauvignon, 5 to 20 percent Merlot, zero to 5 percent Cabernet Franc and Petit Verdot. Carruades typically contains a higher proportion of Merlot.

With the French Revolution and subsequent Reign of Terror, Lafite changed owners a number of times. Despite this upheaval, its prestige remained, as proved by the estate's inclusion at the top of the hierarchy in the Left Bank's 1855 classification. Since 1868, the first growth has been owned by the Rothschild family, who have steered Lafite through the trials of phylloxera, world wars, and various recessions, with intervening periods when prices soared. As the Chinese joined the fine-wine market, Lafite caught their attention above all. Commentators noted a winning blend of prestige, high volume, and distinctive etched label, which cannily featured a Chinese symbol in the "lucky" 2008 vintage. Fraud and volatile prices were the flip side of this success, but represented only a small blemish on the luster of an estate that continues to blaze brightly.

PAUILLAC

No other commune can claim the same concentration of big names as this section of the Médoc, where three of the Left Bank's five first growths are located and no less than 84 percent of production comes from classed growths. Much of this reputation for quality stems from the deep, gravelly soils that characterize Pauillac and imbue its best wines with a cool, mineral edge, pure cassis fruit, and cedar wood flavors in a structured, ageworthy style: in short, wines that encapsulate what, for many wine lovers, Bordeaux is all about.

Lafite lies at the northern edge of Pauillac, right on the commune's Saint-Estèphe border, and is one of the largest estates in this appellation. Other top-quality Pauillac names to look out for include fellow first growths Mouton Rothschild and Latour, as well as Duhart-Milon, Lynch-Bages, Grand-Puy-Lacoste, Pichon Baron, Pichon Lalande, and Pontet-Canet.

TOP VINTAGES

In comparison with its fellow Pauillac first growths, the Lafite style is generally viewed as more perfumed and elegant than the masculine power of Latour or Mouton Rothschild's exotic, often flamboyant personality. Although the twentieth century saw Lafite sometimes fall short of expectations, since 1994 it has achieved greater consistency under the management of Charles Chevallier.

The following vintages are particularly noteworthy from this estate:

2010 This vintage captivated critics in the west but was eagerly snapped up by the Far East at the height of Lafite mania.

2009 Capturing all the sumptuousness of this vintage, this wine proved vibrantly attractive in youth but with plenty more to come.

2005 Complex and fine-boned, this was widely hailed as a classic, demonstrating more restraint than the blockbuster 2003 or 2000 vintages.

2003 Opulent but with the acidity to keep this exuberant vintage neatly in check, although still dancing.

2000 Polished and well put together but taking its time to relax and show off that depth. Set to be magnificent once it does unwind.

1996 A classic vintage for Bordeaux and Lafite was no exception, with this perfumed, refined expression epitomizing the house style.

1982 Another great Bordeaux year that enhanced rather than overwhelmed Lafite's fêted perfume and elegance.

Dream vintage: 1953 As Bordeaux picked itself up after the ravages of World War II, it was helped by a string of strong vintages in the late 1940s, but for Lafite 1953 marked a particular return to form. In a warm year, September rain extended the growing season and resulted in wines that appear to have been attractive young and evolved into a delicate, elegant maturity. Pauillac and Lafite in particular have been acknowledged as the stars of this vintage.

CHÂTEAU LATOUR

One of the three Pauillac first growths, Château Latour was once a sister estate of Lafite, but its famously powerful, structured style could hardly be more different.

It is somehow fitting that Château Latour is so immediately identifiable not by a grand château as is the case with Margaux or Lafite, but by the tower from which it takes its name. Despite being rebuilt in the 1620s, La Tour de Saint Maubert predates the estate's winemaking history by several centuries, having been first erected during the fourteenth century to defend the Gironde estuary against English forces during the Hundred Years' War.

Latour's wine-related prestige took off in the late seventeenth century when it came under the aegis of Alexandre de Ségur, a man whose extensive holdings included Lafite, Calon Ségur, and another château, known at that time simply as Mouton. Despite some challenging moments, Latour remained in Ségur family control until 1963, when it

At a Glance

ADDRESS
Saint-Lambert
33250 Pauillac, France
Tel: +33 (0)5 56 73 19 80

PEOPLE
Frédéric Engerer (president)

SIZE
Seventy-eight hectares, of which forty-seven hectares lie immediately around the château in a collective known as "L'Enclos," from which the *grand vin* is traditionally made. Annual production of this top wine is sixteen to twenty thousand cases, with a further ten to twelve thousand cases made of Les Forts de Latour.

KEY WINES
Château Latour
Les Forts de Latour
Pauillac de Latour

GRAPE VARIETIES
Cabernet Sauvignon
(80 percent of plantings)
Merlot (18 percent)
Cabernet Franc and Petit Verdot
(2 percent combined)

was taken over by the UK financial group Pearson in tandem with wine merchant Harveys of Bristol. Day-to-day running of the estate was placed in the hands of local broker Jean-Paul Gardère, who is largely credited for restoring Latour's by this time rather dog-eared fortunes. The *chai* was renovated, stainless steel vats—a rarity in the region at that time—were installed, and a major planting program took place, with the fruit of these young vines ushering in the creation of sec-

ond wine Les Forts de Latour. In 1993, after Allied Lyons, by this time owner of Harveys, bought out Pearson's share in 1989, the estate passed back into French ownership when it was bought by businessman François Pinault's Groupe Artemis. Under the management of Frédéric Engerer, Latour is forging a glorious new era.

A BREAK WITH TRADITION

As the world's wine trade made its annual pilgrimage to taste the 2011 Bordeaux vintage, Latour rattled the region's cast-iron commercial convention by announcing that this would be the last year its wines would be offered *en primeur*. Instead, the estate confirmed a plan that many had suspected for a while: to mature the wine in its own

capacious cellars until it was "ready to drink." Although revolutionary for Bordeaux, where the *négociant* network has traditionally taken control of sales and distribution once the wine is bottled, Latour's new approach is no different from established practice among many top producers in Champagne or Rioja. At a time when the *en primeur* system has been facing criticism in any case, this move allows the château to release its wines closer to maturity, as well as guarding more closely against fraud and perhaps, some commentators have suggested, allowing Latour to gain greater control over sales than is possible under the *négociant* system.

TOP VINTAGES

Regarded as one of the most consistently impressive first growth per-
formers over the last century, Latour has reinforced this reputation
in its two decades under Engerer's care. This class has not only seen
the estate shine out from the pack in acclaimed vintages, but appears
to be carrying it effortlessly through more contentious years.

The following vintages are particularly noteworthy from this estate:

2010   Dark and dense but supple and refreshing, this impressed
with its trademark Latour power in an energetic, refined package.

2009   The ripeness of this year complemented Latour's minerality
and structure to create a stunning wine.

2005   Intense, focused, savory, and with a
length on the palate that looks set to be matched
by its longevity over the decades to come.

2003   Latour handled the heat of this year with
impressive style, capturing its richness but without tipping into overripeness.

2001   In a year overshadowed by the millennium vintage, Latour produced a wine that
demands attention.

2000   For an estate that is known for its bold
style, this concentrated year produced an eyewa-
tering, commanding, impressive result.

1996   A classic, structured year for Bordeaux in
general, which Latour captures with an enticing
liveliness that lifts it another notch.

1990   Within a field of ageworthy, impressive
wines from this hot, dry year, Latour stands out
as a major star.

Dream vintage: 1961   Hardly a surprising vintage to feature in a roll
call of Bordeaux greats, but high-quality competition still sees this
Latour ride high as one of the great wines of the last century.

CHÂTEAU LÉOVILLE LAS CASES

Frozen by history into second growth status, such is the widespread admiration for the quality of Léoville Las Cases that it has been unofficially dubbed a "super second."

It is no coincidence that Saint-Julien is home to such a profusion of estates bearing the name "Léoville": until the early nineteenth century they existed as a single entity. Domaine de Léoville enjoyed a grand existence—under its original name of Mont-Moytié, it was one of the earliest wine producers in the Médoc—and by the end of the eighteenth century this 120-hectare property was the largest in the region. However, land redistribution and economic depression in the wake of the French Revolution forced the estate to be gradually split among the Las Cases, Barton, and Poyferré families. It was the first of this trio that kept hold of the largest portion of the original property.

At a Glance

ADDRESS
33250 Saint-Julien Beychevelle, France
Tel: +33 (0)5 56 73 25 26

PEOPLE
Jean-Hubert Delon (owner)

SIZE
Ninety-eight-hectare estate. Most of the grapes for the *grand vin* come from the sixty-hectare Clos Léoville Las Cases. Annual production of this wine stands at between nine and fifteen thousand cases.

KEY WINES
Grand Vin de Léoville du Marquis de Las Cases
Clos du Marquis
Le Petit Lion de Marquis de Las Cases

GRAPE VARIETIES
Cabernet Sauvignon (66 percent of vineyard plantings)
Merlot (24 percent)
Cabernet Franc (9 percent)
Petit Verdot (1 percent)

After passing through three generations of the Las Cases family, in 1902 the estate's general manager Théophile Skawinski acquired a share. This stake was gradually increased by his son-in-law André Delon and subsequent descendants up to the present day, which sees Skawinski's great-great-grandson Jean-Hubert Delon at the helm.

It was Skawinski who came up with what was at the time a novel idea of producing a second wine from the estate. Clos du Marquis is really a distinct wine from the *grand vin*, using grapes from a different plot called the Petit Clos. It is therefore more accurate to refer to a newer creation, Le Petit Lion, as the second wine of Las Cases. First made in 2007, it is made from younger vines within the same Clos Léoville Las Cases that is used for the flagship. In keeping with its more accessible style intended for earlier drinking, Le Petit Lion also contains a higher proportion of Merlot.

SAINT-JULIEN

It may lack the stardust of first growth estates, but Saint-Julien makes up for this with a clutch of truly first-class second growths, including each of the three Léoville châteaux, as well as Ducru-Beaucaillou and Gruaud-Larose.

Positioned between Margaux and Pauillac, Saint-Julien's close proximity to the Gironde makes for a wide variety of microclimates and soil structures between estates, although gravel dominates. To generalize, however, this appellation is widely viewed as a source of very classic claret, producing wines that balance power and longevity with a certain poise and subtlety.

TOP VINTAGES

The wines of Léoville Las Cases count among some of the most masculine, powerful expressions of Saint-Julien. This can make them challenging to approach when young, but in the best vintages the château is often seen as rivaling the Médoc's first growths for quality.

The following vintages are particularly noteworthy from this estate:

2010   Attracting admiration for its concentration and purity, this is a vintage to leave patiently in the cellar until the tannins soften.

2009   Sweet, lush, and voluptuous, but with tannins to hold it in check; another massive but harmonious wine from Las Cases.

2005   Another vintage that sparked enthusiastic comparison with the first growths, in particular the masculine style of Latour.

2000   Very much built for the long term, the drinking window for this vintage keeps being pushed back further and further.

1996   It has taken some time for this wine to come around, but each passing year appears to bring ever more favorable reviews.

1986   Given top marks by Parker, this concentrated style has raised questions of balance but the overall verdict falls firmly in its favor.

Dream vintage: 1955   For some critics this vintage of Las Cases outshone its performance in Bordeaux's fabled 1961. In a warm, dry year, like many of the top-rated vintages it enjoyed some welcome rain in September to reinvigorate the thirsty vines and encourage optimal ripeness.

CHÂTEAU L'EVANGILE

*It may not have the image—or prices—of its neighbor
Petrus, but L'Evangile's wines are among the most
sought after and consistent in Pomerol.*

Owned by the Lafite-owning branch of the Rothschild family since 1999, L'Evangile is enjoying an era of investment and expansion that is burnishing the halo of an already highly regarded estate.

Originally called Domaine de Fazilleau when it was established around 1741, this is one of Pomerol's oldest properties. In 1862 it was bought by Paul Chaperon, who built the château, expanded the vineyard area, and helped L'Évangile to become regarded as one of Pomerol's most prestigious wines.

Through Chaperon's descendants and then their relatives the Ducasse family, L'Evangile remained in essentially the same hands up until 1990, when a 70 percent stake was sold to Domaines Barons de Rothschild. When this group eventually bought the estate outright in 1999, it kick-

At a Glance

ADDRESS
33500 Pomerol, France
Tel: +33 (0)5 57 55 45 56

PEOPLE
Charles Chevallier (technical director for Domaines Barons de Rothschild in Bordeaux)
Jean Pascal Vazart
(operations manager)

SIZE
Twenty-two hectares. Annual production for L'Evangile and its second wine, Blason de L'Evangile, is around five thousand cases.

KEY WINES
Château L'Evangile
Blason de L'Evangile

GRAPE VARIETIES
Merlot (80 percent of total vineyard plantings)
Cabernet Franc (20 percent)

started a period of major investment. A new vat room and cellar were completed in 2004, with a further fifteen hectares of vineyard bought from fellow Pomerol property La Croix de Gay in 2012.

L'Evangile may be in Pomerol, but it counts Saint-Emilion superstar Cheval Blanc as its immediate neighbor across the road, while to the north lies another Right Bank celebrity in the form of Petrus. This proximity means that L'Évangile shares some of the blue clay that is unique to Pomerol and especially predominant at Petrus. Meanwhile the property also enjoys a strong element of the gravelly soils seen at Cheval Blanc, which help to add a freshness and elegance as a complement to rich, sensual pleasures created when Merlot is planted on this dense clay.

THE ROTHSCHILD TOUCH

Not to be confused with the Baron Philippe de Rothschild family branch that owns Mouton Rothschild, Clerc Milon, and d'Armailhac, L'Évangile forms part of the Domaines Barons de Rothschild stable, headed by Baron Eric de Rothschild, that is home to Lafite-Rothschild, Duhart Milon, and Sauternes estate Rieussec.

Just as the Baron Philippe de Rothschild arm has extended its reach well beyond Bordeaux to create Opus One in Napa Valley, Almaviva in Chile, and Domaine de Baronarques in the Languedoc, so too Eric de Rothschild has brought a touch of Bordeaux magic to other ventures. To date these include Bodegas Caro in Argentina, Viña Los Vascos in Chile, and Domaine d'Aussières in Corbières.

TOP VINTAGES

The expertise and backing of the Lafite team certainly hasn't done any harm, but L'Evangile's reputation for consistently high quality can primarily be attributed to its superb location on the clay-gravel soils of Pomerol's eastern border.

The following vintages are particularly noteworthy from this estate:

2010   Combining richness with restraint, this vintage produced a wine of great charm and with the prospect of exciting longevity.

2009   "The most profound L'Evangile ever made?" questioned Parker on tasting this "astonishing" wine. Others echoed his praise.

2005   L'Evangile succeeded in translating the ripeness and intensity of this acclaimed vintage into a wine of subtlety and charm.

2000   Another example of this estate's ability to translate a year of great concentration into a harmonious, complex, very classy wine.

1985   Not about power but a sleek, well-balanced, and fresh wine offering real drinking pleasure.

1982   A wine that has fulfilled the promise of this celebrated vintage, offering an abundance of spice, leather, and dried fruit.

Dream vintage: 1966   Buying a wine of this age always entails a considerable element of risk, but anyone able to track down a well-cellared bottle of L'Evangile from this vintage stands a decent chance of experiencing an excellent example of mature claret for a satisfyingly modest price.

CHÂTEAU MARGAUX

*One of the five famed first growths of Bordeaux's Left Bank,
Château Margaux is not one to rest on its laurels, with a
recent flurry of initiatives to keep it ahead of the pack.*

Inextricably linked to the appellation that shares its name, Château Margaux has a long history that predates the sixteenth-century shift to viticulture that transformed the fortunes of this reclaimed coastal marshland.

As the Médoc's prestige soared, Margaux emerged as one of the brightest stars, counting Thomas Jefferson and Sir Robert Walpole among its fan club. However, the French Revolution cast a temporary shadow on the estate's fortunes and in 1801 it was put up for auction. We have successful bidder Bertrand Douat to thank for the Palladian mansion that stands out among the many grand edifices of the Médoc. Fast-forward through its shoo-in as a founding first growth of the 1855 classification, then ownership changes through a series of wars and recessions,

At a Glance

ADDRESS
33460 Margaux, France
Tel: +33 (0)5 57 88 83 83

PEOPLE
Corinne Mentzelopoulos (owner)

SIZE
A 262-hectare estate, of which eighty hectares are planted with red grapes and twelve hectares of white. Annual production of the *grand vin* is about 10,800 cases.

KEY WINES
Château Margaux
Pavillon Rouge du Château Margaux
Pavillon Blanc du Château Margaux
Margaux du Château Margaux

GRAPE VARIETIES
Cabernet Sauvignon
Merlot
Petit Verdot
Cabernet Franc
Sauvignon Blanc
Typical composition of the *grand vin*:
75 percent Cabernet Sauvignon,
20 percent Merlot, 5 percent Cabernet
Franc and Petit Verdot

until 1977 when Margaux was bought by its present owners, the Mentzelopoulos family.

As Bordeaux entered a new golden age during the early twentieth century, Margaux implemented a string of important changes. In the vineyard, the estate's late technical director, Paul Pontallier, conducted extensive organic and biodynamic trials. Meanwhile, among the features of a new cellar designed by architect Norman Foster is an experimental zone for initiatives such as microvinification from the château's collection of Cabernet Franc clones.

One of the few Médoc estates to make a white wine, since 2009 Margaux has also offered a third wine tier in its range. The idea here is to ensure that the *grand vin* receives the A-grade treatment that will assure a future as illustrious as its past.

MARGAUX

Margaux forms part of the Médoc, a largely flat tongue of land that was drained by the Dutch in the sixteenth century and reaches

north from the city of Bordeaux along the left bank of the Gironde estuary.

Flanked by equally prestigious neighbors Saint-Julien, Pauillac, and Saint-Estèphe, Margaux represents the most southerly appellation of this group and its gravelly soil is traditionally viewed as producing the region's most perfumed wines.

While Château Margaux remains the unchallenged queen of the appellation that shares her name, no fewer than twenty-one classed-growth châteaux crowd into this pocket of the Médoc. Among the most highly regarded Margaux estates are Rauzan-Ségla, Brane-Cantenac, d'Issan, Giscours, and du Tertre.

TOP VINTAGES

Bordeaux's international reputation enjoyed a huge boost during the first decade of the twenty-first century. Alongside external economic factors, this resurgence was aided by a flush of highly acclaimed vintages.

The following vintages are particularly noteworthy from this estate:

2010   An unusually high proportion (90 percent) of Cabernet Sauvignon gave this wine immense presence that attracted superlative reviews.

2009   Lush and ripe but retaining Margaux's trademark finesse, the soft, open style of this wine gave pleasure even in its extreme youth.

2005   Another strongly Cabernet vintage that combines richness and density with purity and lightness to create a thrilling result.

2003   A vintage that showed the class of Margaux, which channeled the ripeness of this year into a complex, dense, charming package.

2001   A far more old-fashioned, delicate expression of Margaux than the blockbuster vintage that preceded it.

2000   "A monumental example of the elegance and power that symbolize this extraordinary vineyard," raved Parker: 100 points.

1996   Regarded as a classic year for the Left Bank, this vintage seems to have produced an equally benchmark Margaux.

1990   The culmination of a trio of strong Bordeaux vintages, the heat of this year did not mask the estate's trademark elegance.

1983   Opinions are divided over whether Margaux performed better in 1982 or 1983, but this first vintage under Paul Pontallier has the edge.

Dream vintage: 1945   A year that suggests nature decided to join in the celebrations to mark the end of the Second World War. As in 1961, spring frosts led to naturally low yields, which then flourished in the warm summer weather. However, it is the historical context of this wine that adds a unique aura to this rarefied drinking experience.

CHÂTEAU MOUTON ROTHSCHILD

Its delayed elevation to first growth status is testament to the powerful personalities who have shaped this charismatic château that bears their family name.

Having seen its fortunes rise alongside stablemates Lafite and Latour under Alexandre de Ségur, Mouton acquired its distinctive suffix after being bought by Baron Nathaniel de Rothschild in 1853. Whether it was a snub at this foreign ownership or the fact that Mouton prices had slipped during the mid-nineteenth century, the estate was famously denied first growth status by the creators of the 1855 classification. Not until 1973, thanks to the effort of Nathaniel's great-grandson Baron Philippe de Rothschild, was the estate admitted to its coveted place at the top of the Left Bank hierarchy. This was far from the only groundbreaking development instigated by Baron Philippe, who led Mouton from 1922 until 1988. Soon after taking over the estate he broke with the convention of selling wine in barrel, announcing in 1924 that bottling would now take place at the estate itself.

Following Philippe's death, his only child, Baroness Philippine de Rothschild, gave up her acting career to guide Mouton Rothschild into the twenty-first century. Her strong personality instigated the addition of white wine Aile d'Argent in 1991, followed by the creation of second wine Le Petit Mouton in 1993. The last major project overseen by Philippine was the construction of a

At a Glance

ADDRESS
33250 Pauillac, France
Tel: +33 (0)5 56 73 21 29

PEOPLE
Philippe Sereys de Rothschild (owner)
Philippe Dhalluin (technical director)

SIZE
Eighty-four hectares with total annual production of twenty-five to thirty thousand cases, split between the *grand vin* and second wine.

KEY WINES
Château Mouton Rothschild
Le Petit Mouton de Mouton Rothschild
Aile d'Argent

GRAPE VARIETIES
Cabernet Sauvignon
(80 percent of plantings)
Merlot (16 percent)
Cabernet Franc (3 percent)
Petit Verdot (1 percent)
There are also a few hectares of white grapes planted, of which 56 percent are Sauvignon Blanc and Sauvignon Gris, 43 percent Semillon, and 1 percent Muscadelle.

state-of-the-art vat room, completed in 2012, which allowed for precise vinification of different plots and a permanent display for the estate's famous collection of commissioned artwork that adorns its labels. Following Philippine's death in 2014, her son Philippe Sereys de Rothschild has taken on the family mantle.

BEHIND THE LABEL

Among the many decisive acts by Baron Philippe de Rothschild was his celebration of the Allied victory in 1945 by commissioning artist Philippe Jullian to design a commemorative label for Mouton Rothschild. This highly collectible tradition has remained ever since, with featured artists including high-profile figures such as Chagall, Dalí, Míro, Picasso, Kandinsky, Warhol, Francis Bacon, HRH the Prince of Wales, Lucian Freud, Anish Kapoor, and Jeff Koons. Just as Lafite acknowledged China's growing interest in Bordeaux with its label design for the "lucky" 2008 vintage, so too it was noteworthy that Mouton chose Chinese artist Xu Lei to be its creative influence that year.

TOP VINTAGES

"Flamboyant," "exotic," "opulent," Mouton is a wine as charismatic as the owners who have shaped its fortunes over the last century and a half. The introduction of a second wine in 1993 appears to have bolstered the *grand vin*'s quality still further.

The following vintages are particularly noteworthy from this estate:

2010   All the richly textured exoticism that you would expect from Mouton, marrying huge density with balance and finesse.

2009   It was the extraordinary perfume of this wine that seduced critics upon release, although some detected richness over finesse.

2006   Interestingly, Mouton appears to have hit the mark with greater accuracy and flair here than in the acclaimed 2005 vintage.

1989   Positioned right in the middle of a trio of top vintages, this year saw Mouton recognized as a particular star performer.

1986   Great Pauillac presence with a fruit concentration that led to New World comparisons, this is becoming friendlier with age.

1982   The seductive richness of Mouton has taken time to emerge from a wine whose structure was almost impenetrable in its youth.

Dream vintage: 1945   Mouton didn't just celebrate the end of the war with a special label; it created a wine with a richness, depth, and energy that are pure celebration.

PETRUS

Although a long-respected name in Bordeaux, Petrus's lofty prestige—with a price tag to match—is a relatively recent phenomenon. A small production only adds to this allure.

The absence of any classification system in Pomerol may have delayed the rise of Petrus, but it certainly presents no barrier to the estate today. Mentioned in the same breath as Left Bank first growths in terms of quality, Petrus's significantly smaller production means that demand and therefore prices for this estate are notably higher.

Named after St. Peter, Petrus made its debut in the history books in the 1750s, when Jacques Meyraud bought land of this name from the Gazin estate. For well over a century from 1770, the property was owned by the Arnaud family. A gold medal at the Paris Exposition Universelle in 1878 boosted Petrus's image to the extent that it became regarded as the top producer in Pomerol and was able to command prices equal to a Left Bank second growth.

At a Glance

ADDRESS
3, route de Lussac
33500 Pomerol, France
Tel: +33 (0)5 57 51 17 96

PEOPLE
Moueix family (owners)
Olivier Berrouet (enologist)

SIZE
A 11.4-hectare vineyard, producing around 2,500 cases annually.

KEY WINES
Petrus

GRAPE VARIETIES
Merlot (95 percent of vineyard plantings)
Cabernet Franc (5 percent)
In most years the final blend is 100 percent Merlot.

The early twentieth century saw Petrus pass into the ownership of its then manager M. Sabin-Douarre, who gradually sold his shares to local hotelier Madame Loubat. By 1949 she owned the estate outright, working closely with merchant Jean-Pierre Moueix. It was under the fastidious care of this duo that the quality of Petrus rose still further and the postwar years produced a string of its most celebrated wines. Following Madame Loubat's death in 1961, the Moueix family steadily increased its stake, taking full control in 1969 and extending the vineyards. The same family remains in charge today with Christian Moueix at the helm, while further continuity has come in the form of winemaker Jean-Claude Berrouet, who oversaw forty-five vintages at Petrus before handing the reins to his son Olivier in 2008.

POMEROL

The smallest of Bordeaux's top-flight appellations, Pomerol is notably unremarkable in terms of either picturesque châteaux or topography. Indeed, it was largely through the efforts of Petrus's Jean-Pierre Moueix that this clay-rich plateau and its typically small estates rose to the internationally celebrated status that they enjoy today. Much of this identity and appeal is closely linked to the Merlot grape, which thrives in the Pomerol blue clay. Together they lend these wines their distinctively rich, fleshy character that is approachable at a young age yet also capable of great longevity. The superb 1982 vintage combined with a strong US dollar and rise of critic Robert Parker won over a legion of Pomerol fans and set the region on course for global stardom.

Other estates in this appellation to look out for include Vieux Château Certan, La Conseillante, Trotanoy, La Fleur-Pétrus, L'Eglise Clinet, L'Évangile, and that famously small-scaled estate, Le Pin.

TOP VINTAGES

If Pomerol is known for the richness of its wines, then Petrus takes that to its opulent extreme, but allied with an exoticism and structure that is built to last.

The following vintages are particularly noteworthy from this estate:

2010   A great year on both sides of the Gironde, and Petrus excelled in its lush exoticism tempered by a mineral edge.

2009   Despite the ripeness of this year, Petrus maintained a welcome control and coolness that sets it up well for the future.

2001   A year that has gained fans over time, but Petrus's appeal was immediate and continues to bloom as a particularly seductive wine.

2000   A thrilling combination of richness and tannin that has managed to retain a refreshing quality at the same time.

1998   Another master class in how to achieve concentration without compromising on freshness.

1990   A ripe, opulent year in any case, so no surprise to see that Petrus takes this to a higher level of expression and harmony.

1989   Regarded by Christian Moueix as "one of the best vintages in the twentieth century."

1982   A near-perfect year hailed with a string of perfect scores. With age a leafy Cabernet Franc delicacy is tempering the gamey richness.

Dream vintage: 1947   A legendary year for Petrus as the estate enjoyed a golden period after the Second World War.

CHÂTEAU PICHON
LONGUEVILLE-BARON

Lying adjacent to Latour, Pichon Baron has flourished under the backing and expertise of its present owner to be counted firmly among the Médoc's "super second" estates.

As you drive north through the heart of Médoc wine country it is impossible to miss two rather grand châteaux facing each other across the road to Pauillac. As this proximity and the similarity of names suggest, these two Pichon estates were once a single entity. Pichon Longueville was established toward the end of the seventeenth century as Louis XIV led a boom in France's cultural and political power. Its name came from Baron Jacques Pichon Longueville, who received a plot of vineyards as a dowry from his father-in-law, Pierre Desmezures de Rauzan, the steward of Margaux and Latour. The division of the estate came in 1850, when Baron Raoul Pichon de Longueville inherited one part, known as Pichon Baron, while his three sisters received the other, which became known as Pichon Lalande. It was Raoul who built the turret-clad château that stands today, just a few years before both properties were listed as second growths in the 1855 classification. Having remained in family hands until 1933, Pichon Baron then endured a challenging period until 1987, when it joined the portfolio of insurance group subsidiary AXA Millésimes. This ushered in an era of cru-

At a Glance

ADDRESS
33250 Pauillac, France
Tel: +33 (0)5 56 73 17 17

PEOPLE
Christian Seely (managing director of AXA Millésimes)
Jean-René Matignon (technical director)

SIZE
Seventy-three hectares, of which thirty are used solely for the *grand vin*, whose annual production has been cut significantly under AXA's ownership to around 12,500 cases.

KEY WINES
Château Pichon-Longueville au Baron de Pichon-Longueville
Les Griffons de Pichon Baron (introduced in the 2012 vintage)
Les Tourelles de Longueville (made from the Merlot-dominant Sainte-Anne plot)

GRAPE VARIETIES
Cabernet Sauvignon (62 percent of total vineyard plantings)
Merlot (33 percent)
Cabernet Franc (3 percent)
Petit Verdot (2 percent)

cial investment, with new winemaking facilities and renovation of the château, which became mirrored in an ornamental pool positioned on top of the estate's underground cellar. By the end of the 1980s, quality was back on track, thanks largely to Pichon technical director Jean-René Matignon and capable caretaker Jean-Michel Cazes of Château Lynch-Bages, who handed over the reins to Christian Seely in 2000.

AXA MILLÉSIMES

Although Pichon Baron is by no means the only estate in the Médoc to be owned by a corporation, AXA Millésimes stands out from the crowd for its high-quality portfolio of exciting wine properties across

Europe. Pichon may be the jewel in its Bordeaux crown, but nearby Château Pibran benefits from the same expertise to offer fabulous value for money. There is also Château Petit-Village in Pomerol and Sauternes first growth Château Suduiraut. Beyond Bordeaux, wine fans can do far worse than look to AXA's Burgundian estate Domaine de l'Arlot, Languedoc property Mas Belles Eaux, Disznókő in Tokaj, and the Douro's Quinta do Noval, home to the historic Nacional vineyard.

TOP VINTAGES

It may sound like a lazy characterization, but the wines of Pichon Baron are usually thought of as being more masculine and muscular than those of its sister across the road.

The 1960s and 1970s were a difficult time for Pichon Baron, but AXA's investment and Seely's bold decision to slash production of the *grand vin* have paid significant dividends in terms of quality.

The following vintages are particularly noteworthy from this estate:

2010   All the cedary character and intensity combined with restraint that Bordeaux, and especially Pauillac, delivers at its most classic.

2009   A generous year when the estate's conscious decision to avoid overextraction paid off with a ripe but highly sophisticated result.

2005   A year when the best wines showed beautiful purity of fruit, Pichon Baron was no exception, adding a dose of elegant restraint.

2000   A fitting tribute to Seely's first year in charge and welcomed as a prime example of structured but beautifully balanced Pauillac.

1990   Praised for its polished structure, with sweet fruit character emerging in maturity. Reports suggest that it is now at its peak.

Dream vintage: 1989   A vintage that demonstrated the triumphant revival of Pichon Baron as the investment of its new owners began to pay off. This wine attracted widespread praise, with favorable first growth comparisons.

CHÂTEAU PICHON LONGUEVILLE COMTESSE DE LALANDE

One of the larger estates in the Médoc, Pichon Lalande has undergone a series of major renovations to the château, winery, and vineyards since changing hands in 2007.

Often unsung amid the suit-clad businessmen who invariably hold court at these Médoc châteaux, a strong thread of female influence can nevertheless be traced in the history of many estates. At Pichon Longueville Comtesse de Lalande, that feminine touch lies at the heart of its origin, name, recent fortunes, and even the style of these wines.

For almost two hundred years, this Pauillac producer shared a history with its neighbor Pichon Baron as a single estate called Pichon Longueville. Upon the death of Baron Joseph de Pichon Longueville in 1850, the land was divided in two between his son and daughters. One of these daughters, Virginie, who was married to the Comte de Lalande, managed the female portion on behalf of her siblings, built the château, and ultimately gave her name to the place she made home. When Bordeaux's economic troubles after World War I forced Pichon Lalande's sale to Edouard and Louis Miailhe, it paved the way for the château's second formative female influence: Edouard's daughter May Eliane de Lencquesaing. From 1978 until 2007 she ran the estate herself

At a Glance

ADDRESS
33250 Pauillac, France
Tel: +33 (0)5 56 59 19 40

PEOPLE
Frédéric Rouzaud (president and CEO of the Roederer Group)
Nicolas Glumineau (technical director)

SIZE
Eighty-nine hectares split into eight plots around the château and an eleven-hectare plot in Saint-Julien, which is sold under a different label. Annual production of the *grand vin* is around fifteen thousand cases.

KEY WINES
Château Pichon Longueville Comtesse de Lalande
Réserve de la Comtesse

GRAPE VARIETIES
A replanting program aims to increase the amount of Cabernet Sauvignon to 61 percent of the total vineyard area, followed by:
Merlot (32 percent)
Cabernet Franc (4 percent)
Petit Verdot (3 percent)
The Cabernet Sauvignon–led *grand vin* usually contains a 15 to 30 percent proportion of Merlot.

with huge energy, modernizing facilities at home and spreading the Pichon Lalande name worldwide.

Today the second growth belongs to Champagne's Louis Roederer Group. After brief stewardship by another Bordeaux grande dame, Sylvie Cazes, since 2012 Pichon has been run by Nicolas Glumineau. From vineyard mapping, replanting, and biodynamic trials to a new vat room for microvinification, the next chapter in Pichon's story is being shaped by minute attention to detail.

ROEDERER ESTATES

The descendants of Louis Roederer have not contented themselves with the responsibility of preserving the prestige of their family Champagne house, but have steadily built up a stable of thoroughbred estates around the world. Alongside Pichon Lalande, Roederer's Bordeaux interests cover Saint-Estèphe properties Haut-Beauséjour and de Pez, while Maison Delas in the Rhône and Domaines Ott in Provence complete the group's French interests. Farther afield, Roederer's financial backing and expertise can be found at Ramos Pinto in the Douro. Moving across the Atlantic, the group's sparkling wine roots push through at Roederer Estate and Scharffenberger Cellars, both located in Anderson Valley, California.

TOP VINTAGES

Although the replanting program carried out by Roederer is steadily increasing the proportion of Cabernet Sauvignon to a level more common among its Médoc neighbors, Pichon Lalande has long been known for its high Merlot component. This doubtless contributes significantly to the estate's reputation for a notably voluptuous, feminine expression of Pauillac's structured style. Pretty rather than powerful, its wines tend to attract consistently favorable scores while leaving the limelight to bigger personalities.

The following vintages are particularly noteworthy from this estate:

2015   This medium-bodied wine is a great expression of both Cabernet Sauvignon and Merlot, which produces a well-balanced wine that should go the distance.

2010   This full-bodied and tannic wine is a little out of character for Pichon Lalande. Blended with a larger amount of Cabernet Sauvignon than normal (66 percent), it should evolve beautifully over a long time.

2009   This wonderful wine is opulent, luscious, and well balanced, showing characteristics of mocha, black currants, and tobacco. One of the great Pichon Lalandes in the last twenty years.

2003   A great balance of black currants, cherries, and licorice, this full-bodied wine enjoys rich tannins.

2000   A dainty, lively, smooth example from a year that was widely characterized by more powerful expressions.

1995   The house's traditionally high Merlot element shines through here in a sweet, chocolate-edged style, maturing with gamy charm.

Dream vintage: 1982   The opulent, forward nature of this estate's wines tends to reveal their appeal faster than more densely structured peers. Although that doesn't necessarily diminish Pichon Lalande's ability to offer pleasure with significantly more mature expressions, this vintage appears to have perfectly captured the character of this Médoc lady and is busy showing it off with enormous charm.

CHÂTEAU D'YQUEM

*Bearing the unique title of Premier Cru Classé Supérieur,
historic Sauternes estate Château d'Yquem can safely claim
an undisputed place as one of the world's greatest wines.*

Firmly enthroned as king of sweet wines, Yquem has been honing its late-harvest expertise since at least the sixteenth century. The estate's history reaches back still further: Records show that it belonged to the king of England until the Hundred Years' War ended in 1453, when it passed back into French hands.

Yquem was tended by the Sauvage family from 1593 before passing via marriage into the hands of the Lur-Saluces in 1795. They in turn guided it through the French Revolution, steadily enhancing the quality and facilities, and building a global reputation for this wine, which by the nineteenth century was being enjoyed in Russia, the US, and Japan.

At a Glance

ADDRESS
33210 Sauternes, France
Tel: +33 (0)5 57 98 07 07

PEOPLE
Pierre Lurton (president)

SIZE
A 189-hectare estate with 113 hectares of vineyard. Production levels are very variable for the *grand vin* but could be up to about 8,300 cases in a big year. Dry wine "Y" is limited to a maximum of 830 cases.

KEY WINES
Château d'Yquem
"Y," pronounced "Ygrec"

GRAPE VARIETIES
Semillon (75 percent of total vineyard plantings)
Sauvignon Blanc (25 percent)
The *grand vin* blend is very similar to the proportion of each variety in the vineyard. Containing around 80 percent Sauvignon Blanc, the makeup of "Y" is the exact opposite.

The Lur-Saluces era finally closed in 2004, when shareholder LVMH took full control, installing its man from Cheval Blanc, Pierre Lurton, at the helm. The estate made headlines in 2011 when a bottle from the 1811 vintage—of which just ten barrels were produced—sold for a white wine record of $117,000. Although Yquem has made a dry wine since 1959, called simply "Y," the focus here remains firmly on its historic sweet wine. Nevertheless, the foggy microclimate responsible for this unique wine does not always deliver the specific conditions required for *Botrytis cinerea*, or noble rot. Yields can therefore vary greatly and in some years—1910, 1915, 1930, 1951, 1952, 1964, 1972, 1974, 1992, and 2012—no Yquem was produced at all. If the weather does deliver, Yquem's team of two hundred pickers will spend six weeks scrutinizing not just bunches but individual berries. The final yield will equate to a meager one glass of wine per vine.

SAUTERNES

Located in the southeast corner of the Bordeaux region, Sauternes's profound, ageworthy sweet wines are the product of its unique but unreliable climatic conditions. As the cold water of the Ciron River flows into the warmer Garonne, the vines become cloaked in mist.

If this is burned off by sunny conditions, it creates ideal conditions for noble rot to develop. This fungus dehydrates the berries to create a sweet, concentrated flavor. However, if the weather is too cold and wet, the vines will instead become infected by gray rot, when the grapes must be discarded. At the other end of the spectrum, if the conditions are too warm and sunny then there will be no rot at all. Sauternes contains the smaller but also prestigious Barsac appellation. Besides Yquem, top châteaux include Climens, Rieussec, Suduiraut, and Coutet.

TOP VINTAGES

The very specific conditions required to create these sweet wines of Sauternes mean that great vintages from this appellation by no means necessarily follow the reputation of Bordeaux's red regions. While there has been a general shift among Sauternes producers to create slightly lighter, fresher wines than in the past, Yquem stands out as especially intense, complex, and long-lived.

The following vintages are particularly noteworthy from this estate:

2009   The estate recorded "perfect" weather right up to the end of picking, an adjective that appears to apply equally to the wine itself.

2007   A lighter, mixed-quality year for red Bordeaux, for Yquem this was a great vintage of exuberant richness and persistence.

2005   An all-around great vintage for Bordeaux, Yquem produced a wine of great depth and liveliness, if lighter than some years.

2003   Record-breaking heat met September rain to create a thorough botrytis outbreak and a rich, nervy, if slightly atypical Yquem.

2001   A breathtaking year for Sauternes, with Yquem producing a benchmark wine of enormous concentration and purity.

1990   The culmination of a trio of excellent Yquem vintages, this expression offers a compelling combination of richness and acidity.

1989   A dry, warm year that resulted in a small crop that produced a wine of hedonistic sweetness yet great complexity.

1988 The most classic expression from this great three-year run for Yquem, intriguing all the way from nose to an extremely long finish.

1983 Exotic fruit with huge vibrancy that still endures, making this an exciting, invigorating wine for those lucky enough to taste it.

Dream vintage: 1945 With a wine as astonishing and long-lived as Yquem, special examples abound in just about any decade you care to imagine. But the mahogany-hued 1945 offers a prime example of the supremely exciting character and quality that this great white wine is able to deliver with maturity.

DOMAINE BONNEAU DU MARTRAY (CORTON-CHARLEMAGNE)

Tended by the same family since the French Revolution, Bonneau du Martray is not only the largest owner of Corton-Charlemagne vineyards, but also the most celebrated.

Emperor Charlemagne may have given his name to this famous Grand Cru slope of the Côte de Beaune, but its unrivaled ruler today is Bonneau du Martray, whose 9.5-hectare plot makes this estate by far the biggest owner in Corton-Charlemagne. Part of an exclusive Burgundian club able to boast exclusively Grand Cru vineyards, Bonneau du Martray does make a small amount of red wine under the Corton classification, but it is no coincidence that only the white wines of this hillside attract the imperial suffix, and it is this larger part of the domaine's output that is most highly prized.

Despite the estate's notable size, it has shrunk considerably since the Bonneau-Véry family acquired their twenty-four hectare portion of Corton as part of a widespread sale of church land during the Revolution. Forget the lauded Chardonnays of today: At that time Gamay and Pinot Blanc ruled, while it was red Corton that commanded the top prices. Over the years, the domaine was slowly eroded by a combination of inheritance splits, the pulling up of vines as phylloxera struck, and sale of land during the 1930s slump. A reversal of fortune came in 1969, when Comtesse Jean

At a Glance

ADDRESS
2, rue de Frétille
21420 Pernand-Vergelesses, France
Tel: +33 (0)3 80 21 50 64

PEOPLE
Comte Jean-Charles le Bault
de la Morinière (owner)

SIZE
11.09 contiguous hectares, of which 9.5 hectares are classified as Corton-Charlemagne and the rest Corton. Total average production is around 4,150 cases for the white Corton-Charlemagne and just under six hundred cases for the red Corton.

KEY WINES
The domaine produces just two wines, both Grand Crus: Corton-Charlemagne for the white and Corton for the red.

GRAPE VARIETIES
Pinot Noir
Chardonnay

le Bault de la Morinière inherited the estate from her uncle, René Bonneau du Martray. Husband Jean studied viticulture and enology to polish this historic family gem, bringing winemaking, bottling, and sales in-house. Since 1994 his son Comte Jean-Charles le Bault de la Morinière has continued this work, embracing biodynamics and replanting weaker red plots with the Chardonnay that sings so brightly here.

CORTON-CHARLEMAGNE

Just where the northern edge of the Côte de Beaune meets the southern tip of the Côte de Nuits lies the hill of Corton. While this wood-topped hill is also home to red grapes, its upper southwest-facing slopes house the exclusively white Grand Cru of Corton-Charlemagne.

Legend has it that as far back as the eighth century, Emperor Charlemagne's wife ordered that this area be planted solely with white grapes so that her husband would not stain his beard. At fifty-six hectares, Corton-Charlemagne is one of the larger Grand Cru sites in Burgundy, allowing some estates to hold relatively large parcels; equally, however, such scale means that the style and quality of wine from this appellation can vary. In addition to Bonneau du Martray, other prominent names with Corton-Charlemagne holdings are Bouchard Père & Fils, Louis Latour, Coche-Dury, and Louis Jadot.

TOP VINTAGES

In keeping with the emphasis on vineyard character encouraged by a switch this millennium to first organics, then biodynamics, the winemaking influence here is notably light with just 30 percent new oak. The domaine is one of a few in Burgundy to hold back a good amount of its wines for mature release.

The following vintages of Domaine Bonneau du Martray Corton-Charlemagne are particularly noteworthy:

2012 Notably ripe and weighty after the 2011 vintage, this packs Grand Cru punch, balanced by a floral nose and saline finish.

2010 Ruthless selection made this one of the domaine's smallest vintages, but one whose intensity makes it worth seeking out.

2009 This ripe, rather wild wine may have lacked its usual elegance in youth, but critics were confident it would refine with age.

2008 Full of energy and chiseled structure, the ferocious acidity here needs time to settle and reveal the considerable mass behind.

2006 "A study in harmony and grace," according to Burghound; "simply dazzling," said Galloni—this is benchmark Burgundy.

2005 Broad but tense and intense, this has plenty of attractive fruit to counterbalance its fine acidity, creating a harmonious whole.

2004 Less density than the great 2005, but no shortage of focus and freshness, with a floral, appley nose giving way to bright minerality.

1999 While lacking the purity of its 2000 counterpart, the density, texture, and power of this wine look set to propel it further forward.

1992 This cool harvest created a notably mineral style, but one that has blossomed with maturity to reveal a vibrant array of flavors.

Dream vintage: 1986 Pretty but certainly not underpowered, this wine has been enjoying a long, graceful plateau of maturity. Once opened it unfurls the full panoply of fruit, honey, nuts, and mushroom that makes mature white Burgundy such an experience.

DOMAINE COCHE-DURY (MEURSAULT PERRIÈRES, MEURSAULT GENEVRIÈRES, CORTON-CHARLEMAGNE)

The white wines in particular from this Burgundy domaine may be among the most sought after on the planet, but you could hardly accuse its owners of chasing such cult status.

If Bordeaux is a land of suit-clad businessmen occupying grand châteaux, then the Burgundians often seem to revel in the marked contrast of their low-key rustic idyll. Jean-François Coche is very much of this latter breed, famously difficult to distract from his vines and surely the last person you would be likely to see in some New York auction showroom watching his precious wines sell for thousands of dollars. The third generation of Coches to look after this domaine, which was set up by his grandfather Léon in the 1920s, Jean-François worked beside his father, Georges, before inheriting the estate in 1972. Shortly afterward he expanded the family holdings through his marriage in 1975 to Odile Dury,

At a Glance

ADDRESS
9, rue Charles Giraud
21190 Meursault, France
Tel: +33 (0)3 80 21 24 12

PEOPLE
Jean-François Coche (owner)
Raphaël Coche (winemaker)

SIZE
Around nine hectares spread across six different communes, although around half the vineyard holdings are in Meursault. Annual production is around 4,200 cases.

KEY WINES
Grand Cru: Corton-Charlemagne
Premier Cru: Meursault-Perrières, Les Caillerets, and Genevrières, as well as a red Premier Cru site in Volnay

GRAPE VARIETIES
Chardonnay
Pinot Noir
Aligoté

who added her name to the enlarged property. In 1999 their son Raphaël Coche began working alongside his father, officially taking over as winemaker in 2010, but with little discernible shift in style. Each generation of the family over the last century has steadily added to the estate's vineyard holdings. Among the most notable of these acquisitions was the 1986 purchase of 0.34 hectare of Grand Cru land in Corton-Charlemagne. Despite this star site and the handful of delicate Pinot Noirs it makes from around the Côte de Beaune, Coche-Dury is primarily known as a producer of white wines, especially Meursault. This village is not only home to the family, but also its winery and around half the estate's vineyards.

And the wines themselves? Long-lived and rich, but buoyed by nervous tension rather than great ripeness, these are among the most highly prized rarities in Burgundy.

THE "PREMOX" POX

As if there weren't enough pitfalls to watch out for when buying mature wine, the problem of premature oxidation, or "premox," has sparked ripples of consternation among lovers of white Burgundy. Debate has raged over the cause of this blight, which only attracted serious attention at the dawn of the new millennium as people began broaching bottles from the 1995 vintage. Subsequent years showed this was no one-off and, even more worrying, just about every big name in white Burgundy was affected to some extent. In-depth analysis by lawyer Don Cornwall (available at http://oxi dised-burgs.wikispaces.com) found that up to 20 percent of wines were affected in an apparently random manner. Modern pressing techniques, excessive lees stirring, and lowered sulfur dioxide levels have all shouldered blame for these brown, lifeless wines, but the issue is yet to be satisfactorily resolved. For now, buying white Burgundy from the mid-1990s onward, however smart its pedigree, is not an activity for the faint-hearted.

TOP VINTAGES

Fortunately, the wines of Coche-Dury appear to have been relatively unscathed by the plague of premature oxidation, leaving the loyal fans of this domaine to relish its characteristic combination of consistency, intensity, and energy.

For all the outstanding quality of Coche-Dury's Grand Cru offering from Corton-Charlemagne, so small is production that it makes sense to focus on this estate's (only slightly) more prolific output from Perrières, widely regarded as Meursault's top Premier Cru.

The following vintages of Coche-Dury Meursault Perrières are particularly noteworthy:

2012   By no means a universally high-quality year, it still yielded some excitingly intense whites, with Coche-Dury a prime example.

2010   A thrilling year for Burgundy full stop, but this producer and vineyard rose above the competition with rich, racy precision.

2009   Showing more delicacy than the mighty 2010, this seduced critics with its ethereal fragrance and nuanced flavors.

2006   A strong year for white Burgundy, with Coche-Dury's move to pick before the rain resulting in plenty of finesse and acidity.

2005   Dry conditions led to whites of great substance, with this star example showing Perrières to be a Grand Cru in all but name.

2002   Ideal weather gave healthy fruit and wines of great balance. For this example add to that richness, immortality, depth, and length.

2001   If it's purity you prize then look no further. This star shines bright with a dazzling array of harmoniously interwoven flavors.

1999   A generous year where the best wines such as this have taken time to show the full appeal hinted at so temptingly in their youth.

1997   A challenging year whose low yields led top estates to create intense wines made more accessible by slightly lower acidity.

1996   "Out of this world," declared Parker of a "masterpiece" effort from Coche-Dury. He was by no means alone in such loud praise.

Dream vintage: 1995   Yes, you could find pleasure in older vintages, but if you want to catch a wine close to its peak then look no further. Around nine hundred bottles were made, with critics full of unanimous praise for its harmonious composition and intensity.

DOMAINE DES COMTES LAFON
(MEURSAULT CHARMES)

The village of Meursault is packed with top-quality producers, but in the hands of its current custodian Comtes Lafon has cemented a reputation at the top of this pyramid.

In a region as fragmented as Burgundy it is quite an achievement to own a stake in the best vineyards of your village. Comtes Lafon takes this a step further by occupying top sites within those top vineyards. Such prime positioning is mostly due to the shrewd acquisitions of Comte Jules Lafon, who formed the estate as it appears today after his 1894 marriage to Marie Boch, who was from a family of Meursault vineyard owners and wine merchants. This union brought vineyard holdings in the adjacent villages of Monthélie, Volnay, and Meursault, from which base Jules then expanded into a number of mostly Premier Cru sites in the latter two areas. His only move farther afield was to buy a 0.32-hectare slice of Grand Cru Le Montrachet in 1918.

At a Glance

ADDRESS
5, rue Pierre Joigneaux
21190 Meursault, France
Tel: +33 (0)3 80 21 22 17

PEOPLE
Dominique Lafon (managing director)
Stéphane Thibodaux (estate manager)

SIZE
16.3 hectares spread across four villages and fifteen appellations, including the 2.1-hectare Meursault monopole Clos de la Barre.

KEY WINES
Grand Cru: Le Montrachet in Chassagne-Montrachet
Premier Cru: Meursault Charmes, Gouttes d'Or, Porusot, Bouchères, Genevrières, Perrières; Volnay Santenots du Milieu, En Champans, Clos des Chênes; Monthélie les Duresses

GRAPE VARIETIES
Chardonnay
Pinot Noir

That same auspicious year saw the title of *comte* awarded to Jules by the pope after he refused to use his position as inspector at the public registry office to force churches to declare their wealth. Following his appointment as mayor of Meursault, Jules established the Paulée de Meursault in 1923 to celebrate the end of the grape harvest. Today that event has evolved into a banquet for six hundred people and is one of the most high-profile occasions on the Burgundian calendar.

With Jules's death in 1940, his sons Pierre and Henri took over, but Pierre's early death in 1944 saw Henri rent out most of the estate, which looked set to be sold. That fate was averted thanks to the intervention of Henri's son René, who took the reins in 1956 and embarked on a major vineyard restoration drive and a move to bottling under the domaine's own label. Since 1984, Dominique Lafon has built on his father's work, steadily bringing the entire property back under direct control. As of 1998, Comtes Lafon has been certified biodynamic. Then in 1999 the family expanded south, making Mâconnais wines that are sold under the label of Les Héritiers du Comte Lafon. For all its acclaimed reds and whites from other parts of Burgundy, this estate's fame is rooted in its reputation as the top producer in Meursault.

MEURSAULT

For a village with no Grand Crus, Meursault certainly has more than

its fair share of top producers. Their profile, combined with the relatively large scale of this appellation and its seventeen-strong clutch of Premier Crus—most notably Les Perrières, Les Charmes, and Les Genevrières—has helped to make this one of the best-known and most highly regarded areas for white Burgundy.

While this fame is well deserved for the best wines, which offer full-bodied, savory, ageworthy pleasure, Meursault's reputation often commands a higher price than wines of equal quality from less celebrated villages.

Apart from Comtes Lafon, other prestigious names to look out for in this appellation include Coche-Dury, Patrick Javillier, Arnaud Ente, Guy Roulot, Jean-Philippe Fichet, Michel Bouzereau, and François Jobard.

TOP VINTAGES

Of the many Premier Crus in Meursault, Les Charmes together with its neighbors Les Perrières and Les Genevrières are widely agreed to be the stars. Comtes Lafon holds a 1.9-hectare slice of the thirty-hectare Charmes *climat*, which borders Puligny-Montrachet at the southern end of Meursault.

Until Dominique Lafon took the helm in the mid-1980s, the domaine was known for some outstanding if not entirely consistent wines. Today quality is far more reliably outstanding.

The following vintages of Comtes Lafon Meursault Charmes are particularly noteworthy:

2012   An expressive style and no little concentration are neatly harnessed by a cool, mineral framework, indicating a bright future.

2010   Less open than many vintages of Lafon Charmes, this wine nevertheless suggests that it has plenty to unfurl over time.

2007   Some great white Burgundy emerged from this vintage, with this example consistently impressing as it evolves.

2006   Attracting comparisons with the acclaimed 1992 vintage, this year produced a tense, structured Charmes built for the long term.

2005   So ripe and Grand Cru–worthy was the fruit in this year that it was easy to overlook the structure driving this wine forward.

Dream vintage: 1995   By this stage Comtes Lafon was already organic and on its way to biodynamic certification. It is impossible to tell how much of an impact this new green regime was having on the vines at this early stage, but certainly this acclaimed vintage was a resounding success across the board for Lafon. Its Charmes expression shows all the openness typical of this *climat*, with its natural generosity tempered by lively minerality and zippy acidity.

DOMAINE COMTE GEORGES DE VOGÜÉ (MUSIGNY, BONNES MARES, LES AMOREUSES)

Over 550 years after it was founded and still in the same family, this estate enjoyed a revival in the late 1980s and is now producing wines as consistently aristocratic as its name.

Of all the illustrious vineyards in the Côte d'Or, few make a Burgundy lover's heart beat faster than Le Musigny. Although split between several producers, the lion's share of this Chambolle-Musigny Grand Cru—7.2 out of 10 hectares—is owned by Domaine Comte Georges de Vogüé. Such prime positioning is partly explained by the fact that the estate has been around for longer than most, with an even more remarkable continuity of ownership. Founded in 1450 by Jean Moisson, twenty family generations later de Vogüé is currently in the hands of Marie de Ladoucette and Claire de Causans, who took over in 1987 after the death of their grandfather Comte Georges de

Vogüé. It was he who changed the estate's title, which had previously been Comte Arthur de Vogüé, after his father. For all the benefits of this stable ownership, quality dipped between the 1970s and late 1980s. According to Robert Parker, de Vogüé's former manager Alain Roumier blamed this decline on "Americans' obsession with brilliant, clear wines," which led the domaine to filter. Whatever the cause, quality rose rapidly after Comte Georges's death and the arrival of technical director François Millet, swiftly followed by Jean-

Luc Pépin as commercial director. By the late 1980s de Vogüé was firmly back on track, and the 1996 advent of aptly named vineyard manager Eric Bourgogne completed a strong team that remains in place today. However welcome this revival, even de Vogüé's relatively large share of Musigny yields no more than about nine hundred cases a year of Grand Cru wine, with prices to reflect such scarcity.

MUSIGNY

Located at the opposite end of the village from its fellow Chambolle Grand Cru Les Bonnes Mares, this ten-hectare Musigny plot also offers a very different personality: fragrant delicacy rather than velvety vigor. Although almost entirely planted with Pinot Noir, Musigny stands out as the only Côte de Nuits Grand Cru to produce white wine as well as red. That 0.66-hectare Chardonnay parcel was planted by de Vogüé, which owns over 70 percent of the entire vineyard, including all of *sub-climat* Les Petits-Musigny. Other producers with a significant presence here include Frédéric Mugnier, Jacques Prieur, and Joseph Drouhin, while the likes of Georges Roumier and Leroy also hold a small share.

TOP VINTAGES

As indicated by the "vieilles vignes" on its label, de Vogüé's Musigny comes from vines with an average age of about forty years (fruit from younger vines goes into its Chambolle-Musigny Premier Cru). Given the dip in quality during the 1970s and much of the 1980s, there is little to recommend in this age bracket, although devoted lovers of very mature Burgundy may find rewarding signs of life from the domaine's greatest wines of the preceding three decades.

The following vintages of de Vogüé Musigny are particularly noteworthy:

2012   Impossible to penetrate in its extreme youth, nonetheless this wine hides immense character and structure for the very long term.

2011   All the hallmark violet perfume of Musigny with great fruit purity and intensity that was relatively approachable even in youth.

2010 Dense, fragrant, and precise, this wine will take some time to reveal the many layers of complexity buried beneath its surface.

2009 Managing to avoid the over-balancing richness of some wines in 2009, this wine is all about finesse and gently persistent fruit.

2008 For all its florality, this is a very serious wine with great intensity yet restraint, keeping its powder dry for the future.

2005 A very complete, highly complex, and seductive wine even in its youth, this is set to intrigue and delight drinkers for some time.

2002 Enormously expressive on the nose with elegantly textured palate and a wealth of flavor from this exciting Burgundy vintage.

2000 Lots of charm and delicate sweetness for Burgundy fans to enjoy over the coming years.

1999 "Perfect!" declared Burgundy specialist Clive Coates MW upon tasting this "profound" wine in its youth.

1993 Far from an easy vintage, but one that produced some great wines such as this; highly structured but now softening with age.

Dream vintage: 1949 Nudging toward the end of its optimum drinking window perhaps, this wine came from a great vintage and was still full of energy and richness well into its second half century. Ethereal and with great length, it would nevertheless benefit from a few hours in the decanter to show at its most expressive.

DOMAINE DE LA ROMANÉE-CONTI (ROMANÉE-CONTI, LA TÂCHE)

Its fame can prove a double-edged sword, but this producer shows time and again the magic that patient perfectionists can conjure from such incomparably fine vineyards.

Are these the most highly prized wines in the world? Certainly the thieves and fraudsters seem to think so, with co-owner Aubert de Villaine increasingly drawn away from the more pleasurable aspects of his role to do battle with counterfeiters. So what is it that makes the estate known as DRC—or in Burgundy simply "La Domaine"—so special? Quite simply, unrivaled vineyards, whose twenty-five hectares comprise entirely major shares in Grand Cru vineyards, including the bright monopole jewel in its crown, Romanée-Conti.

The "Conti" suffix is a legacy left by Louis François de Bourbon, Prince de Conti, just one of this site's many own-

At a Glance

ADDRESS
1, place de l'Eglise
21700 Vosne-Romanée, France
Tel: +33 (0)3 80 62 48 80

PEOPLE
Aubert de Villaine and Henri-Frédéric Roch (co-managers)
Bernard Noblet (winemaker)

SIZE
Twenty-five hectares, including the 1.8-hectare monopole Romanée-Conti, which has an annual average production of around five thousand bottles.

KEY WINES
Grand Cru: Romanée-Conti, La Tâche, Richebourg, Romanée-Saint-Vivant, Grands Echézeaux, Echézeaux, Montrachet, Corton Clos du Roi

GRAPE VARIETIES
Pinot Noir
Chardonnay

ers since it was first planted in the twelfth century. The "Romanée" origin is less clear, but it appears in the seventeenth century; prior to this, the site had been known as Cros des Cloux. Romanée-Conti last changed hands in 1869, when it was sold to Jacques-Marie Duvault Blochet, a prominent owner in the nearby Richebourg, Echézeaux, and Grands Echézeaux Grand Crus, and ancestor of Aubert de Villaine, who has jointly held the reins since 1977.

La Tâche, also a monopole and second in prestige after Romanée-Conti, was added in 1933, while Romanée-Saint-Vivant was bought off a long lease in 1988. Another big step came in 1940 with the arrival of André Noblet as winemaker; his son Bernard holds this role today. DRC's only white wine debuted in 1963 in the suitably aristocratic form of Montrachet. Meanwhile in 2008 it took a lease on Corton Clos du Roi. Today the suffocating expectation on this estate is matched only by the perfectionist approach of its team.

PINPOINTING GREATNESS

No self-respecting Burgundian would ever refer to Romanée-Conti as the greatest Pinot Noir on the planet. That is not to diminish its standing, just a reflection of the prism through which Burgundy producers in particular view their wines. Here, Pinot Noir is not the star of the show, but simply, albeit crucially, the best vehicle that has been found to express the one truly prized factor: terroir. This nebulous, fragmentary concept may cause headaches for the world's marketing teams but certainly when you taste a wine from Romanée-Conti, or indeed the other great sites of Burgundy, its flavor, energy, and substance go well beyond what could be expected of grapes alone.

TOP VINTAGES

The high-profile 2014 court case of fraudster Rudy Kurniawan showed the peril of buying a celebrated wine such as DRC at auction, although buying directly from approved merchants, as the estate itself urges, means a long wait for even a sniff of an allocation. For all the temptation to seize upon a bottle of Romanée-Conti from the 1945, 1947, or 1949 vintages, resist: despite just six hundred bottles being produced in 1945, thousands have appeared on the market. With phylloxera rendering these vines unproductive, they were pulled up after the 1945 harvest, with production not resuming until 1952. Caveat emptor, as they say. On the plus side, the quality of this vineyard and its expert, consistent management by essentially the same team since 1977 means that "off" vintages tend to be very much a relative term; however, the following more recent vintages of DRC Romanée-Conti are particularly noteworthy:

2012   Great presence and an ever-shifting array of dancing flavors, from red currants to herbs and game, all wrapped in a velvety texture.

2011   Wild but delicate, packing in great complexity with no sense of obvious force at all, just a lingering, multilayered finish.

2010   A monumental wine, combining poise and density with grace and vibrancy. Endlessly layered and with majestic length.

2009   A wine of great richness yet purity, described by de Villaine as "seductive" as he noted the quality and quantity was excellent this year.

2006   A hot, dry July gave way to a cold, wet August, creating problems for the team but a fine, fragrant wine of impressive depth.

2005   Top marks from several corners for this vintage, accompanied by effervescent descriptors trying to do justice to this jewel.

1999   Even the cool heads behind DRC were moved by the quality of fruit, with de Villaine calling this "our legacy to the Domaine."

1996   The estate's late harvesting ethos paid off with a late burst of welcome dry weather to create a majestic wine of quiet intensity.

1990   While some vintages are immediately approachable, this has required considerable patience, but its beautiful shape won through.

1985   A perfect score from Parker and praise all around for a wine with such a rich spectrum of lingering flavor and sparkling vitality.

Dream vintage: 1966   Without wishing to overlook the equally exciting 1978 vintage, the focused intensity of this wine even after fifty years has astonished several critics. All the flavor complexity seen in a young expression appears here but in a more developed phase of dried flowers and herbs, which linger so tantalizingly after the final sip.

DOMAINE DUJAC (CLOS DE LA ROCHE, CLOS SAINT-DENIS)

From a standing start in 1967, Domaine Dujac has amassed a treasure trove of great Burgundy vineyard sites, all the while attracting a loyal following for its wines.

It would be impossible in today's market for a newcomer to build such an impressive vineyard portfolio as Jacques Seysses did upon arrival in Burgundy in 1967. At a time when many estates were struggling to survive, he founded Domaine Dujac ("Domaine du Jacques") by buying the 4.5-hectare Domaine Marcel Graillet in Morey-Saint-Denis. Once the new estate had weathered its first harvest, the disastrous 1968 vintage, Seysses expanded his holdings with small parcels in the prestigious areas of Echézeaux and Bonnes Mares, all the while working to build a client base from scratch. Fortunately 1969 offered far more favorable weather and Dujac's wines quickly attracted attention from the market.

At a Glance

ADDRESS
7, rue de Bussière
21220 Morey-Saint-Denis, France
Tel: +33 (0)3 80 34 01 00

PEOPLE
Jeremy Seysses (managing director)

SIZE
Owns around 11.5 hectares of vineyard but manages 15.5 hectares in total.

KEY WINES
Grand Cru: Romanée-Saint-Vivant, Echézeaux, Clos de Vougeot, Clos Saint-Denis, Clos de la Roche, Bonnes Mares, Chambertin, Charmes-Chambertin
Premier Cru: Morey-Saint-Denis, Les Monts Luisants, Chambolle-Musigny Les Gruenchers, Gevrey-Chambertin Les Combottes, Vosne-Romanée Les Beaux Monts, Aux Malconsorts

GRAPE VARIETIES
Chardonnay
Pinot Noir

Since the early 1990s the domaine has shunned herbicides, farming organically since 2001 and biodynamically since 2009. Much of this shift was led by Jacques's son Jeremy, who now manages Dujac, aided by his Californian enologist wife, Diana, and his brother Alec. Jeremy also set up a *négociant* with his father called Dujac Fils & Père.

In 2005 the family acquired a very considerable assortment of prime vineyard land via a joint purchase with the de Montille family of eighteen hectares formerly owned by the Société Civile du Clos de Thorey. For the most part, the Seysses family kept the parcels lying in the Côte de Nuits, which included gems such as Clos de Vougeot, Vosne-Romanée Aux Malconsorts, and Romanée-Saint-Vivant. Indeed, with no fewer than eight Grand Crus and a complementary host of Premier Crus, Dujac now boasts some of the most enviable holdings in the whole of Burgundy.

CLOS DE LA ROCHE

This 13.41-hectare Grand Cru lies on Morey-Saint-Denis's northern border with Gevrey-Chambertin. Unsurprisingly therefore, Clos de la Roche wines tend to show a similarly firm texture to those from their neighboring appellation. By contrast, fellow Morey-Saint-Denis Grand Cru Clos de Tart lies on the commune's southern border with Chambolle-Musigny, with its wines sharing that village's lighter, strawberry-scented charms. Although it would be a considerable overstatement to describe Morey-Saint-Denis as undiscovered, its wines have historically struggled to enjoy the prices of either neighbor. That said, the rising reputation of top sites such as Clos de la Roche looks set to remove this discrepancy of good value in the Côte de Nuits. Certainly the caliber of producers in Clos de la Roche is impeccable. Alongside the 1.95-hectare collection of parcels owned by Dujac—making this grand cru one of the domaine's largest vineyard holdings—other top names here include Ponsot, Rousseau, Leroy, Drouhin, and the recently emerged Burgundy superstar Olivier Bernstein.

TOP VINTAGES

Firm, deep, and highly structured, Clos de la Roche makes Pinot Noir that is very much in the traditional Côte de Nuits style. This is balanced by the Dujac wariness of overextraction and preference for charm over too much tannic grip.

The following vintages of Dujac Clos de la Roche are particularly noteworthy:

2012   Structured and powerful but with a very attractive sweet Pinot character that gives this wine a welcoming generosity too.

2010   Bright and precise, floral but still muscular, this wine won praise for its perfectly judged balance, length, and intensity.

2009   Plenty of rich, sweet fruit, but also some welcome tension here, this was attractive in youth but with plenty of mileage left.

2005   Elegant and energetic to counterbalance its richness of body, creating a very harmonious wine of enormous class.

1999   Beautifully balanced with great charm and freshness, this wine shuns concentration in favor of complexity and length.

1995   More complete than the also highly rated 1996, this brings characteristic energy to a rich wine with plenty of backbone.

1989   Developed now but still singing with a perfumed, gamy nose and complexity that will delight fans of mature Burgundy.

Dream vintage: 1978   A high-quality year, the best wines offer a very classic style and have aged beautifully. This particular example appears to be enjoying a long plateau of maturity, retaining its finesse, vigor, and complexity with plenty to intrigue the drinker.

DOMAINE LEFLAIVE
(MONTRACHET,
BÂTARD-MONTRACHET)

*It may sit among the greatest producers of white Burgundy,
but Domaine Leflaive is certainly not afraid to rock the boat,
implementing bold changes to improve its wine still further.*

It's difficult to believe that the very same workhorse grape that provides the world with millions of liters of cheap refreshment can become so transformed by the top sites of Burgundy into an unrecognizably thrilling, aristocratic beauty. For many people who have been seduced by great white Burgundy, the name Leflaive represents the apogee of this costly passion. Based in the white Burgundy heartland of Puligny-Montrachet, Leflaive first began making wine under its own label thanks to the efforts of Joseph Leflaive. During the 1920s he gradually replanted and extended his family vineyards with better-adapted rootstock. Upon his death in 1953, Joseph's four children divided

the running of their estate among themselves until 1990, when control passed on to the next generation in the form of Anne Claude Leflaive and her cousin Olivier. From 1994 Anne Claude took on sole management of the estate, implementing its conversion to biodynamic viticulture. In 2013 Domaine Leflaive moved its barrels into the result of another notable departure from mainstream practice: an egg-shaped cellar. Holding up to 180 barrels, "La Cave de l'Oeuf" was built according to the proportions laid out by the

Golden Ratio using a mixture of wood, clay, straw, and earth bricks, which create a natural humidity of 80 percent and a constant temperature of 54 degrees Fahrenheit. Anne Claude countered skeptics by insisting that wines matured in this facility were more elegant. Her sudden death in 2015 aged just fifty-nine robbed Burgundy of one of its most determined, free-thinking personalities.

MONTRACHET

The suffix used since 1879 by both the villages of Puligny and Chassagne highlights their proud link to the most famous vineyard in this southerly corner of the Côte de Beaune: Montrachet.

Often called Le Montrachet (pronounced "Mon-rachay") to dispel any doubt of its preeminence over the handful of neighboring sites that incorporate its name into their own titles, this 7.99-hectare vineyard produces around forty-seven thousand bottles annually between the various domaines that own or lease a stake in this hallowed site. Alongside Leflaive, which owns less than 0.1 of a hectare here, other Montrachet producers include Domaine de la Romanée-Conti, Joseph Drouhin, Louis Jadot, and Château de Puligny-Montrachet. The latter is believed to have paid over half a million euros for its 0.04-hectare share in 1993.

TOP VINTAGES

At their best, the wines of Montrachet show an extraordinary structured intensity with spicy, honeyed flavors not obviously derived from grapes. In contrast to most white wines, it can take a decade for Grand Cru white Burgundy such as this to fully unleash its full appeal and complexity.

The following vintages of Leflaive Montrachet are particularly noteworthy:

2010   A great year for both red and white Burgundy, this rich but vibrant expression has all the fruit and structure to last many years.

2009   Big and bold with exciting tension, this has the weight and energy to carry it powerfully into the future.

2006   An excellent year for white Burgundy so no surprise to see one of its greatest producers and vineyards create a thrilling wine.

2005   Good luck getting hold of anything from the one and a half barrels of majestic Leflaive Montrachet made this year.

2002   Bad for Bordeaux but excellent for Champagne and white Burgundy, this year produced wines with great aging potential.

1999   Golden and ripe yet savory and structured, is it too much to attribute this wine's great liveliness to its newly biodynamic roots?

Dream vintage: 1992   For fans of white Burgundy, this was an exceptional vintage whose wines are now at their peak. In theory, of course, there are older great vintages such as 1990, 1989, and 1985, but these Montrachet wines are so rare that tracking them down at auction—and then paying for them—is the preserve of only the most dedicated collector.

DOMAINE LEROY
(ROMANÉE-SAINT-VIVANT)

The fact that this domaine was set up as recently as the late 1980s hasn't stopped it from leaping almost immediately into the very top tier of Burgundy producers.

If Domaine Leroy is one of very few estates to be mentioned in the same breath as the mighty DRC, it is worth noting the link between these Burgundian powerhouses. Until she was ousted in 1992, the formidable Lalou Bize-Leroy was joint manager of Domaine de la Romanée-Conti as well as running her eponymous estate, which she founded in 1988. Three generations previously, Burgundian winemaker François Leroy had extended his ambitions to found a *négociant*, Maison Leroy. Having subsequently expanded under his son Joseph and grandson Henri, the business flourished still further with the arrival in 1955 of his great-granddaughter Lalou. Among the most notable of her activities was a regular tasting in her home of the house's wines, an event that was famously and enthusiastically attended by top writers, critics, sommeliers, and chefs.

The creation of Domaine Leroy arose from the struggle to find growers capable of meeting the standards demanded by Maison Leroy. The core of the new property came from the purchase of estates from Charles Noellat in Vosne-Romanée and, a year later, Philippe Rémy in Gevrey-Cham-

At a Glance

ADDRESS
15, rue de la Fontaine
21700 Vosne-Romanée, France
Tel: +33 (0)3 80 21 21 10

PEOPLE
Marcelle (Lalou) Bize-Leroy (owner)

SIZE
Twenty-three hectares, including parcels in nine Grand Cru and eight Premier Cru vineyards. Total annual production: thirty-five to forty-five thousand cases.

KEY WINES
Grand Cru: Corton-Charlemagne, Corton-Renardes, Richebourg, Romanée-Saint-Vivant, Clos de Vougeot, Musigny, Clos de la Roche, Latricières-Chambertin, Chambertin
Premier Cru: Volnay Santenots du Milieu, Savigny-lès-Beaune Les Narbantons, Nuits-Saint-Georges Aux Vignerondes and Aux Boudots, Vosne-Romanée Aux Brulées and Les Beaux Monts, Chambolle-Musigny Les Charmes, Gevrey-Chambertin Les Combottes

GRAPE VARIETIES
Pinot Noir
Chardonnay
Aligoté

bertin. Much of this top-class vineyard acquisition was funded by Maison Leroy's Japanese importer and shareholder, Takashimaya.

Biodynamic from the very start, Domaine Leroy is also known for its extreme crop thinning, with a yield of just four bunches per vine. Rather than large-scale replanting, vines are replaced on an individual basis with cuttings from the same vineyard. It's a perfectionist approach that shines through in the end product.

VOSNE-ROMANÉE

No commune in Burgundy boasts such a concentration of top-quality vineyards as this small section of the Côte de Nuits. Sandwiched between Nuits-Saint-Georges and Chambolle-Musigny, Vosne-Romanée packs in an impressive eight Grand Crus: Romanée-Conti, La Romanée, Romanée-Saint-Vivant, La Tâche, La Grande Rue, Richebourg, Grands Echézeaux, and Echézeaux. Together these account for seventy-five hectares, with a further fifty-six hectares of Premier Cru vineyards.

Hardly surprisingly, Vosne-Romanée is also home to a starry collection of producers. Alongside Domaine de la Romanée-Conti and Leroy, other names to look out for include Grivot, Cathiard, Engel, Rouget, and Liger-Belair.

TOP VINTAGES

At just under one hectare, Domaine Leroy's share of Romanée-Saint-Vivant represents one of its largest Grand Cru parcels. Although generally known more for a silky finesse than the voluptuousness of its neighbors Romanée-Conti and Richebourg, Romanée-Saint-Vivant from Leroy tends to demonstrate a particular concentration and depth in keeping with other wines from this domaine.

The following vintages of Leroy Romanée-Saint-Vivant are particularly noteworthy:

2012   All the elegant finesse you expect from this vineyard, but with a striking density too, thanks no doubt to the super-low yields.

2011   Leroy was one of several producers whose wines outshone the overall reputation of this vintage, and did so in impressive style.

2009   A very serious, savory expression with plenty of energy and great length; a bright future lies ahead of it.

2008   A small vintage even by Leroy's extreme standards, the result was an enormously charming, multilayered wine.

2005   Considerable restraint will be required to allow this bright, vivacious, finely constructed wine to reach full maturity.

2002   Despite its restraint in youth, this wine packs in an excitingly complex combination of flavors, perfume, and waves of intensity.

1997   As with many wines from this vintage, freshness and delicacy are the defining characteristics here: Pinot at its prettiest.

Dream vintage: 1990   Just a couple of years after its creation, Leroy laid down a marker with this highly impressive wine. Showing what would rapidly become recognized as the estate's hallmark concentration, this wine remains rather firm and masculine in character: a very serious wine.

DOMAINE MARQUIS D'ANGERVILLE (CLOS DES DUCS)

Run by the third generation of the d'Angerville family, this aristocratic estate's top vineyard demonstrates an even longer history and the delicate qualities of Volnay.

Guillaume d'Angerville is hardly the first person to make the transition from finance into winemaking, but his background and motivation, not to mention the caliber of the estate itself, make for a unique scenario. Once owned by the Dukes of Burgundy—whose name endures in its most famous vineyard—the estate lies at the heart of Volnay and occupies some of the commune's top parcels. The property passed into its current family via the Baron of Mesnil, who acquired Clos des Ducs in 1804. When his son Eugène died in 1888 without an heir, the property passed to his fifteen-year-old nephew Sem, Marquis d'Angerville. Having fallen out with merchants during the 1930s over their fraudulent practices, the marquis was forced to become one of the first producers to manage his own bottling and sales. This quality focus saw the marquis, along with Henri Gouges of Nuits-Saint-Georges, given a key role in setting the appellation rules for Burgundy. Legend has it that the pair declined to request Grand Crus for their communes to avoid claims of bias. From 1952, Jacques d'Angerville continued his father's focus

At a Glance

ADDRESS
Clos des Ducs
21190 Volnay, France
Tel: +33 (0)3 80 21 61 75

PEOPLE
Guillaume d'Angerville
(managing director)
François Duvivier (estate manager)

SIZE
Around fifteen hectares, most of which—just over eleven hectares—lie in Volnay's Premier Cru sites, but with other small parcels in Meursault and Pommard.

KEY WINES
The domaine has no Grand Cru sites but the following Premier Crus: Volnay Clos des Ducs (monopole), Caillerets, Champans, Clos des Angles, Fremiet, Mitans, Pitures, Taillepieds; Meursault Santenots; Pommard Combes-Dessus.

GRAPE VARIETIES
Chardonnay
Pinot Noir
Aligoté

on quality and integrity, heading the Comité Interprofessionnel des Vins de Bourgogne and helping to set up the Institut Universitaire de la Vigne et du Vin in Dijon. His sudden death in 2003 fast-tracked son Guillaume d'Angerville's move from heading up the French investment arm of JP Morgan to taking over the family estate. Despite his banking career, Guillaume had also worked almost every harvest, is a qualified winemaker, and has now converted the domaine to biodynamics.

VOLNAY

Sandwiched on the Côte de Beaune between the famously powerful reds of Pommard and rich whites of Meursault lie the surprisingly feminine wines of Volnay. Such delicacy may well come from the lighter, chalky soils that characterize this appellation, which perches on the slopes of the hill of Chaignot. At 206 hectares of vineyard in total, it may be relatively small, but this Pinot Noir–focused appellation packs in twenty-nine Premier Cru *climats*, covering more than half the total production area. Most of these top vineyards lie on the lower slopes by the main road where the limestone soil is deeper and more gravelly. Among the most highly regarded Premier Crus are Clos des Chênes, Taillepieds, and Les Caillerets. Alongside Marquis d'Angerville, other top Volnay producers to look out for include Lafarge, Comtes Lafon, and de Montille.

TOP VINTAGES

Of Marquis d'Angerville's eight Premier Cru sites in Volnay, its 2.15-hectare walled Clos des Ducs monopole is not only the most historic vineyard but can arguably present the appellation's strongest case for Grand Cru promotion. The fact that this vineyard is not only owned in its entirety by one estate, but that the estate itself has enjoyed three generations of family-run stability makes it even more rewarding to follow from year to year.

The following vintages of Marquis d'Angerville Clos des Ducs are particularly noteworthy:

2010 Proof, if any were needed, that pale color does not mean weak wine; nose and palate are full of complex yet delicate intrigue.

2009 Even an appellation known for delicacy could not avoid the richness of this year, but channels it in a gorgeously feminine style.

2007 Not generally regarded as a stellar vintage but it certainly seemed to suit this site, whose wines offer great forward charm.

2005 Intense, ripe, energetic, this showed well in its youth but is clearly built for the long term.

2002 A very charming expression that shows Volnay at its most delicately feminine and vibrant.

1997 Similar to 2007, this was a year for fans of more delicate styles and appears to have made a particularly charming wine here.

1993 A year when the best sites and producers achieved lovely purity of Pinot Noir fruit that has lingered enticingly with age.

Dream vintage: 1990 Offering a longer drinking window than many Volnay wines, the caliber of this vineyard meant that the richness of this year did not override the wine's attractive

femininity. The end result was an expression offering great depth, coolness, and fine-boned structure.

DOMAINE MÉO-CAMUZET
(CLOS DE VOUGEOT)

Nurtured for many decades by the renowned Henri Jayer, this domaine has seen its reputation soar since the Méo family stepped up their involvement during the 1980s.

It seems astonishing now to think that an estate with a reputation as stellar as Méo-Camuzet was selling off its grapes in bulk until the late 1980s. In this respect, the Vosne-Romanée property reflects a wider revival of Burgundy's fortunes to the lofty prestige—and prices—that its wines command today.

The domaine's story begins in the early twentieth century when Etienne Camuzet began to buy up parcels within his favorite vineyards. It is thanks to him that Méo-Camuzet can boast such a strong collection of sites, in particular its large single plot within the Clos de Vougeot.

When Camuzet's daughter Maria Noirot died childless in 1959, she left the estate to her cousin Jean Méo, whose government career in Paris saw him sell off the produce of this inheritance through local merchants until 1985, when Méo-Camuzet began bottling under its own name. From 1988 onward the domaine also took back greater control of the land, bringing vineyards under its own management as leases expired. This more hands-on involvement saw Jean's son Jean-Nicolas settle full-time in Burgundy to direct

At a Glance

ADDRESS
11, rue des Grands Crus
21700 Vosne-Romanée, France
Tel: +33 (3)80 61 55 55

PEOPLE
Jean-Nicolas Méo (technical director)
Christian Faurois (vineyard manager)

SIZE
About six hectares of vineyard, of which three hectares lie in Clos de Vougeot. Another five hectares are managed under contract.

KEY WINES
Grand Cru: Richebourg, Clos de Vougeot, Corton Clos Rognet, Corton Les Perrières, Corton La Vigne au Saint, Echézeaux
Premier Cru: Vosne-Romanée Aux Brûlées, Au Cros Parantoux, Les Chaumes; Nuits-Saint-Georges Aux Boudots, Aux Murgers, Aux Argillas, Les Perrières; Chambolle-Musigny Les Cras, Les Feusselottes; Fixin Clos du Chapitre

GRAPE VARIETIES
Pinot Noir (Chardonnay also appears in Hautes Côtes de Nuits expression), Saint-Philibert

operations with guidance from the legendary Henri Jayer, who had worked on the estate's top vineyards since 1945. While Jayer's pursuit of lush, fruit-forward wines, achieved through destemming and a cold soak to slow fermentation, continues to divide opinion in Burgundy, Méo-Camuzet remains loyal to his legacy. The greatest tribute to Jayer lies in Méo-Camuzet's Cros Parantoux, a challenging, formerly maligned site whose image was transformed by the dedication of this one individual.

CLOS DE VOUGEOT

Of the many walled vineyards (*clos*) that make up Burgundy's landscape, at just over fifty hectares in size Clos de Vougeot is the largest with Grand Cru status. Unsurprisingly for such a large plot, the soils vary from one end to another with the result that, for all its single classification, not all Clos de Vougeot is equal. On top of this geological variation, its division among over eighty growers creates even further quality distinctions.

The bottom section along the road is composed of poor-draining, heavier clay soils. It is no coincidence that so few Côte de Nuits top vineyards sit at this lower level. Moving uphill, the middle section has a higher limestone and gravel content, with a resulting step up in drainage and quality—neighbors here include several Premier Crus. However, the most highly regarded expressions from Clos de Vougeot—among them Méo-Camuzet—tend to come from its upper part around the château that shares its name. Here, on the border of fellow Grand Crus Musigny and Grands Echézeaux, the soils become light and chalky with free-draining gravel.

Other domaines to look out for here include Leroy, Mugner-et-Gibourg, Anne Gros, and Grivot. The latter's vines lie at the bottom of the clos, proving that there's an exception to every rule.

TOP VINTAGES

In keeping with other top expressions from Clos de Vougeot, this is a wine that tends to be dense, muscular, and often backward, even unfriendly in its youth. With a decade or so in bottle, however, it can blossom into a very complete, rewarding expression of Burgundy.

The following vintages of Méo-Camuzet Clos de Vougeot are particularly noteworthy:

2013   Not a wine to be approached young, this is a structured, full expression with firm tannins keeping some refined fruit in check.

2008   Roasted meat, blackberries, and dark, savory notes brood over this wine, whose tannins surround a dense core of fruit.

2005   A ripe burst of black cherry fruit, pepper, and herbs pops out of this particularly expressive vintage.

2003   Packed with plum and cassis fruit, this ripeness is lifted by great mineral freshness with tannins pushed to the background.

1999   Supple and appealing even in youth, this has blossomed into a harmonious, elegant, finely structured expression of Vougeot.

1996   A bold, intense style with velvety texture and a showy mix of black cherry fruit, spice, and earthy undertones.

Dream vintage: 1985   A pivotal year for Méo-Camuzet as it began bottling wine under its own label for the first time. And what a vintage to choose: arguably the top example from this decade, whose wines have matured with great flair. "Gets better with every sip," raved the *Wine Spectator* of this flying start for the domaine.

DOMAINE GEORGES ROUMIER (LES BONNES MARES)

Now securely in the hands of its third family generation, Domaine Georges Roumier produces wines that offer the drinker a crystal-clear reflection of their vineyard origin.

In 1924 Georges Roumier moved from the cattle country of Charolais to the winelands of Chambolle-Musigny. Here he settled with new wife Geneviève Quanquin to farm her vineyard dowry that became Domaine Georges Roumier. Despite containing some high-quality sites, its small scale led Georges to take on a second job as vineyard manager for Comte Georges de Vogüé, a role that was later inherited by his son Alain. Together with the likes of d'Angerville and Gouges, the domaine was one of the first to begin bottling and selling its own wine, although some of the bottling was still outsourced as recently as 1984. During the 1950s, Georges slowly ceded control to one of his seven children, Jean-Marie. This decade was also a period of expansion for the domaine, which added parcels from Les Bonnes Mares and Clos de Vougeot Grand Crus, as well as Premier Cru monopole Clos de la Bussière. After the full retirement of Georges in 1961, Jean-Marie's leadership brought the addition of land in Corton-Charlemagne and the famed Musigny vineyard, while shared agreements gave the domaine access to sites in Ruchottes-Chambertin and Charmes-Chambertin. As

At a Glance

ADDRESS
4, rue de Vergy
21220 Chambolle-Musigny, France
Tel: +33 (0)3 80 62 86 37

PEOPLE
Christophe Roumier
(managing director)

SIZE
Twelve hectares, centered on Chambolle-Musigny, including a 1.39-hectare parcel of Les Bonnes Mares, which produces around five hundred cases annually.

KEY WINES
Grand Cru: Bonnes Mares, Musigny, Corton-Charlemagne, Charmes-Chambertin, Ruchottes-Chambertin
Premier Cru: Morey-Saint-Denis Clos de la Bussière, Chambolle-Musigny Les Cras and Les Amoureuses

GRAPE VARIETIES
Pinot Noir
Chardonnay
Pinot Beurot (the Burgundian name for Pinot Gris, used as part of the Chambolle-Musigny village blend)

with many wine estates, French inheritance law led the Roumier siblings to create a limited company, which rents land to the domaine. Although this has largely succeeded in keeping it unified, 1996 saw Georges Roumier's Clos de Vougeot holdings break off to form part of a cousin's new domaine.

Emulating the gradual transition of the previous generation, in 1981 Jean-Marie's son Christophe started working with his father, who finally retired in 1990. Christophe has continued his forebears' approach, making wines with minimal intervention or use of new oak in order to show off the personality of each site. Under Christophe, this pursuit of precision has stepped up a gear to make the Roumier wines stand out as benchmark expressions from some of the most prestigious vineyards in the Côte de Nuits.

LES BONNES MARES

Located on the border of Morey-Saint-Denis, Les Bonnes Mares shares an element of its neighbor's more full-bodied, structured style than is usually associated with Chambolle-Musigny. At 16.24 hectares, Bonnes Mares is relatively large by the modest standards of Burgundy, but in terms of soil structure it splits into two distinct personalities. Much of the northern section at the Morey end is composed of *terres rouges*, a heavier soil with higher clay content, which tends to produce wines with a more masculine, powerful style. To the south, this gives way to white marl, or *terres blanches*, made from fossilized oyster shells. Producers whose land spans both parts of the vineyard tend to vinify the latter's daintier output separately and then blend it back in as a civilizing influence on the final wine.

Along with De Vogüé and Drouhin Laroze, Roumier holds one of the largest stakes in this Grand Cru. Other names to look out for include Bruno Clair, Groffier, Vougeraie, Dujac, and Mugnier.

TOP VINTAGES

The Roumier wines are known for showing particularly vibrant fruit in their youth, but also the capacity to age well over many decades.

The following vintages of Roumier Les Bonnes Mares are particularly noteworthy:

2012   A serious, rich, textured wine showing plenty of meaty flavor that is clearly destined to develop well over many years.

2011   Although the lighter *terres blanches* soil accounted for over half the final blend, in youth this wine showed great density.

2010   "Breathtakingly good," according to Burgundy specialist Allen Meadows, who highlights the mineral lift to this muscly style.

2009   If anything, this vintage attracted even higher scores than the 2010; a gamy, spiced, solid vintage shot through with huge energy.

2008   Rich but precise too, with characteristic spice and animal character alongside vibrant fruit to create a very complete wine.

2007   A stunning interpretation of an unshowy vintage, this is packed with savory cherry fruit and silky tannins but great length.

1999   Mixed recent reviews suggest that this wine needs to be caught on the right day as it matures, but patience should pay off.

1995   Fine and full with a seductive sweetness that is balanced by plenty of structure. This wine set new auction records in 2013.

Dream vintage: 1983   "The best 1983 red Burgundy I can remember tasting," declared Jancis Robinson MW. Evolved and showing off its pedigree in some style, this would offer an exciting encounter for anyone lucky enough to have a bottle stashed away.

DOMAINE ARMAND ROUSSEAU (CHAMBERTIN, CLOS DE BÈZE, MAZY-CHAMBERTIN)

The biggest name in Gevrey-Chambertin, Domaine Armand Rousseau possesses an enviable clutch of vineyards, with even a Premier Cru that commands Grand Cru prices.

A producer with just one of this domaine's Grand Cru holdings might consider himself lucky. As it is, Rousseau's prestige is particularly linked to no fewer than three sites: Chambertin, Clos de Bèze, and Clos Saint Jacques, the latter considered a Grand Cru in all but name. Such a clutch of great vineyards can mean that some other top holdings such as its Clos des Ruchottes monopole and Mazy-Chambertin can be overshadowed when in other hands they would be stars of the show. Nevertheless, third-generation custodian Eric Rousseau appears to have leveled out the balance of quality between this family of gems. Established by Armand Rousseau

At a Glance

ADDRESS
1, rue Aumonerie
21220 Gevrey-Chambertin, France
Tel: +33 (0)3 80 34 30 55

PEOPLE
Eric Rousseau (managing director and winemaker)

SIZE
A little over fifteen hectares, all in Morey-Saint-Denis and Gevrey-Chambertin and of which more than half are Grand Cru level. Average annual production is 5,400 cases.

KEY WINES
Grand Cru: Clos de la Roche, Charmes-Chambertin, Chambertin, Clos de Bèze, Mazy-Chambertin, Clos des Ruchottes
Premier Cru: Clos Saint Jacques, Lavaux Saint-Jacques, Les Cazetiers

GRAPE VARIETIES
Pinot Noir

at the start of the twentieth century, the domaine took further shape when his initial vineyard inheritance was bolstered through marriage. Further expansion came as Armand bought land in Charmes-Chambertin, Clos de la Roche, Chambertin, Mazy-Chambertin, and Clos Saint Jacques. By the time Armand died in a car accident in 1959 on his way home from hunting, his son Charles had already been working at the estate for fourteen years. As well as continuing to add vineyard land, Charles carried out a major export push.

In 1982, Charles was joined by his son Eric, who today manages the domaine with the assistance of his own daughter, Cyrielle. Although little has changed in the cellar under Eric's leadership, vineyard work is now far more precise, especially in terms of yield management. Despite the surging price of top vineyards in Burgundy, in 2009 the Rousseaus managed to expand their share of the prized Chambertin Grand Cru.

GEVREY-CHAMBERTIN

For Burgundy specialist Clive Coates MW, the "rich and masculine" wines from Gevrey-Chambertin are "more flamboyant than Vosne and more substantial than Chambolle." It manages to combine being the largest wine-producing village area in the Côte d'Or with providing some of the region's fullest, finest, longest-lived expressions. Among the nine Grand Crus here, spreading over a total of fifty-five hectares, the most prestigious are the 13.22-hectare Chambertin and the 14.67-hectare Chambertin Clos de Bèze, with the latter swapping power for more feminine charm.

The name Chambertin is thought to come from a man by the name of Bertin, who originally planted vines here. Such was their high quality that the vineyard was dubbed "Champs de Bertin."

Alongside Rousseau, other Gevrey producers to look out for include Serafin, Bachelet, Mortet, Rossignol-Trapet, and Bernstein.

TOP VINTAGES

The distinction between Chambertin and Clos de Bèze is one of personal stylistic preference rather than quality. However, since Rousseau has a larger holding of Chambertin vineyard, there is a marginally greater chance of being able to track down these wines.

The following vintages of Armand Rousseau Chambertin are particularly noteworthy:

2012   Despite the standard use of 100 percent new oak for this wine, such is the richness of fruit that its influence is barely perceptible.

2011   After rigorous sorting, this year proved a remarkable success here. Tight and bright in youth, it may take a while to unwind.

2010   A year that will demand enormous patience from the drinker, but looks set to repay that long wait with immense rewards.

2008   A year that showed off the character of individual sites, with this vineyard depicted with great precision and purity.

2005   Masculine, rich, and spicy, this is a wine of great complexity that will benefit from considerable aging.

2001   A wine that has fulfilled its initial introvert hint of greatness ahead with panache; not so much power here, but much grace.

1999   Rich, full-bodied, and with an exciting array of flavors, this is a very fine expression of Chambertin.

1995   Flagged by Rousseau for long aging, this dense, vibrant wine does indeed appear to be taking its time to open fully.

1993 Showing plenty of sweet fruit, but no little class with it, this offers plenty of charm for the drinker.

1990 An energetic and rich wine with lots of depth, both in terms of flavor and overall profundity of character.

Dream vintage: 1988 A beautifully straightforward vintage in Burgundy, while some lesser wines are not unreasonably showing their age, the pedigree of Rousseau's Chambertin shines through with great vigor and class.

LOUIS ROEDERER (CRISTAL)

It may mix in glamorous circles, but Louis Roederer Cristal is also highly regarded as a serious, ageworthy wine produced from some of the top vineyards in Champagne.

Sitting at the pinnacle of Louis Roederer's Champagne portfolio is its historic prestige cuvée, Cristal. First created back in 1876 for Tsar Alexander II, the cuvée's name links to its distinctive flat-bottomed, clear bottle made of lead crystal. Fearful of assassination (justifiably so, as it turned out), the tsar is said to have requested this packaging to make it more difficult for would-be killers to conceal a bomb in the bottle.

It was not until 1945 that Cristal was sold to the public. A rosé expression was added from the 1974 vintage, with much of its 55 percent Pinot Noir quota based on old-vine Grand Cru sites in Aÿ. As with its white sibling, the rosé is kept on its lees for about six years in the house's cellars prior to release.

Unusually for Champagne, Roederer is in the strong position of owning

At a Glance

ADDRESS
21, boulevard Lundy
51722 Reims, France
Tel: +33 (0)3 26 40 42 11

PEOPLE
Frédéric Rouzaud (president)
Jean-Baptiste Lécaillon (cellarmaster)

SIZE
Over 240 hectares of Grand Cru and Premier Cru vineyard, supplying about two-thirds of the house's fruit. Annual production of Cristal is estimated at around fifty to sixty-five thousand six-bottle cases.

KEY WINES
Cristal Brut, Cristal Rosé (there are plans for a late-disgorged, late-release expression of Cristal), Louis Roederer Brut Premier NV, Vintage, Vintage Rosé, Blanc de Blancs, "Carte Blanche" Demi-Sec, "Brut Nature" (zero dosage)

GRAPE VARIETIES
Pinot Noir (about 60 percent of the final blend for both Cristal and Brut Premier)
Chardonnay (40 percent)

around two-thirds of the vineyard area required to meet production needs and it is from these sites, nearly all Grand Cru with a few Premier Cru additions, that most of the fruit used to make Cristal comes. Such control has enabled *chef de cave* Jean-Baptiste Lécaillon to impose rigorous quality measures, with a large proportion of the top sites now cultivated biodynamically.

Long celebrated for its ability to age, Cristal is now showing off this attribute more formally via a limited release of its 1995 vintage, matured on lees for ten years with a further ten years of aging post-disgorgement. Roederer also stands out as one of the few big Champagne names still in family hands: Frédéric Rouzaud is the seventh generation to hold the reins since ancestor Louis Roederer founded the house in 1833.

THE RIGHT DOSE

You may rarely detect its presence in the glass, but added sugar is a long-established and important element of the Champagne-making process. Indeed, many houses will take great care over the "recipe" for their *liqueur d'expédition* used for this dosage stage, whereby a sugar solution is added after disgorgement to balance its naturally high acidity.

In recent years the combination of warmer weather and improved winemaking know-how, not to mention changing consumer tastes,

has led many producers to lower this dosage, or in the case of extra brut styles, to leave it out entirely. At Roederer, the warm 2006 vintage saw just such a move with the launch of "Brut Nature," a zero-dosage style that represented its first new expression since the creation of Cristal Rosé in 1974. Likewise, the added richness of the house's new late-disgorged, late-release version of Cristal meant that Jean-Baptiste

Lécaillon was able to drop the dosage from the standard nine grams per liter—a level similar or lower than that of many brut Champagnes—to just seven grams per liter.

Just as cheaper Champagnes can use sugar to mask poor-quality fruit, a low-dosage expression leaves the wine—and its producer—with nowhere to hide.

TOP VINTAGES

Champagne may be most commonly associated with sipping on its own as an aperitif, a scenario where youthful freshness is key; Cristal, however, is a very different animal. With so much structure and intensity, young vintages can often prove too tightly wound if sipped solo. Food matching is one option to explore, but otherwise treat this like the serious fine wine that it is and wait for it to mature.

The following vintages of Cristal are particularly noteworthy:

2006   A warm year that shows through in the richness of this expression. Needs time for that mix of power and acidity to mellow.

2005   Not a universally declared vintage in Champagne, this offers a nuanced delicacy, finesse, and precision.

2004   A glorious, vibrant, and expressive wine from a great year in Champagne. Looks set to become even more majestic with age.

2002   Razor sharp, yet with plenty of delicate, mineral complexity simmering below the surface, this shows great poise.

1999   A really exciting expression of Cristal, perfectly balanced with depth, delicacy, and a luxurious dash of *crème pâtissière*.

1996   Those who had the patience to wait for this highly structured, tight expression to evolve can hope to find great depths emerging.

1995   A far bigger, more structured style than many of the excellent Champagnes produced this year. As ever, consider it with food.

1989   This appears to have retained greater vibrancy and acidity than Cristal's effort in the acclaimed 1990 vintage. Fully mature.

Dream vintage: 1985   For lovers of very mature Champagne, this should prove a fascinating, pleasurable experience. Not the most powerful of vintages, its well-balanced structure seen in youth should have carried this wine through to an elegant old age.

DOM PÉRIGNON

*One of the world's most recognized luxury brands, this cuvée
nevertheless retains strong credibility among wine lovers
for its consistently high quality, flair, and longevity.*

Named in honor of the seventeenth-century monk who spent his life working to improve the quality of wine from Champagne, Dom Pérignon is the prestige cuvée of this region's most famous brand, Moët & Chandon.

Despite such a historic link, Dom Pérignon did not actually appear on the market until 1936, when Moët decided to launch an extra-mature version of its 1921 vintage under this new label. By the 1947 vintage, Dom Pérignon's production was entirely separate from Moët, while 1952 saw the introduction of its first rosé. Despite these developments, the original ethos of focusing solely on vintage styles and its program of extended aging remain very much at the heart of the brand's identity.

At a Glance

ADDRESS
18, avenue de Champagne
51200 Epernay, France
Tel: +33 (0)1 48 13 00 00

PEOPLE
LVMH (owner)
Richard Geoffroy (cellarmaster)

SIZE
No official figures are ever released,
but industry insiders suggest that
production for each vintage is at least
two million bottles.

KEY WINES
Dom Périgon Brut
Dom Pérignon Brut Rosé

GRAPE VARIETIES
Pinot Noir
Chardonnay
Proportions can vary but tend
to be a maximum of 60 percent
of either variety.

Led by its charismatic if enigmatic cellarmaster Richard Geoffroy since 1990, Dom Pérignon has stepped up its promotion of the concept of late-disgorged, mature Champagne. First came its "Oenothèque" series from 2000 until 2014, when Geoffroy renamed and expanded this concept into a trio of "Plenitudes," a title referring to Champagne's three main stages of development. The scheme effectively allows the house to launch each vintage three times at intervals of more than a decade.

If all this sounds like too much focus on the cellars at the expense of the vineyard, that has much to do with the nature of Champagne, where the grower-producer is a rarity. Talk of specific vineyards would also be impractical at this scale: although Dom Pérignon is famously silent on volumes, production is said to reach well into seven figures. That makes its quality all the more impressive.

DISGORGEMENT DECISIONS

Disgorgement—the moment when the lees are separated from the Champagne—has been a particularly hot topic in the region of late. For top houses such as Dom Pérignon, Bollinger with its "RD" (i.e., "Recently Disgorged") label, and now Cristal with its plan to release an extra-mature expression, the term "late disgorgement" is closely tied to Champagnes with added weight and texture.

More widely, the separate question of whether houses should feature the disgorgement date on bottles or cases of their nonvintage style has provoked animated discussion. Some argue that, with numerous disgorgements during the year, such a scheme is complex to implement and in addition risks confusing the consumer, some of whom may mistakenly view the numbers as a "best before" date. However, a growing number of houses, including Pol Roger, Veuve Clicquot, Lanson, and Philipponnat have now adopted this practice in order to provide more engaged consumers with as much detail as possible. If nothing else, it should help less-organized wine lovers to establish roughly how long that forgotten bottle of nonvintage Champagne has been languishing in the corner of their cellar.

TOP VINTAGES

In theory, every vintage Champagne should be of top quality, as the style is only made in the best years. At Dom Pérignon, the ever-expanding "Plenitude" system means it is vital to know which level of maturity you are drinking, although for the purposes of this list it makes sense to focus on the initial "P1" brut release.

The following vintages are particularly noteworthy from this estate:

2004   An excellent vintage year for Champagne, with Dom Pérignon making a notably fine, precise wine, rounded off with toasted notes.

2003   An idiosyncratic, opulent, rich, but somehow still controlled style from a hot year when few producers made a vintage.

2002   Another great year for Champagne, which produced this very structured, powerful, lively expression that is clearly built to last.

1998   Characterized by what Geoffroy refers to as a "creamy chew," this was a ripe year enlivened by Dom Pérignon's citrus edge.

1996   A high-acid year, which this wine balances with impressive concentration to create a serious expression crying out for food.

1995   Plenty of brioche and honey flavors gave this early appeal, although it clearly has the building blocks to mature well too.

1990   Brimming with character, this wine from a warm vintage is evolving with exuberant, richly padded style.

1988   For fans of mature Champagne, this vintage should now be fulfilling the maturation promise of its youth.

Dream vintage: 1961   Famously served at the 1981 wedding of Prince Charles and Princess Diana, even decades later this expression was astonishing critics with its youthful citrus vibrancy.

KRUG (CLOS DU MESNIL)

From a house built on a commitment to working with only the best grapes and sites, Clos du Mesnil shows what Krug can achieve when channeling its focus to a single vineyard.

Certainly one of the grandest names in the luxury world of Champagne, Krug prides itself on producing not one prestige cuvée but five. From the Grande Cuvée nonvintage to its famed single-vineyard expressions—a rarity in Champagne—these are rich, nutty, long-lived wines.

The distinctive Krug style is proudly based on principles set down in 1848 by founder Joseph Krug for his young son. Stressing the importance of working only with the best-quality sites, Krug's message is applied today across the range. Although most obviously expressed through single-vineyard Champagnes Clos du Mesnil and Clos d'Ambonnay, this selective ethos is also evident in the flagship Grande Cuvée, which comprises a blend of around 120

At a Glance

ADDRESS
5, rue Coquebert
51100 Reims, France
Tel: +33 (0)3 26 84 44 20

PEOPLE
LVMH (owner)
Maggie Henriquez (CEO)
Olivier Krug (director)
Eric Lebel (cellarmaster)

SIZE
Owns around twenty hectares of vineyard—about 30 percent of total requirements. Production from the 1.84-hectare Clos du Mesnil is around two thousand six-bottle cases per vintage.

KEY WINES
Krug Grande Cuvée, Rosé, Vintage, Clos d'Ambonnay (100 percent Pinot Noir), Clos du Mesnil (100 percent Chardonnay)

GRAPE VARIETIES
Pinot Noir
Chardonnay
Pinot Meunier

wines made from separately vinified plots and ten or more vintages. Another factor that distinguishes Krug is the house's loyalty to oak fermentation, even when most houses transferred their allegiance to stainless steel during the 1960s. While there has since been a slight shift back from some quarters, Krug has always stood by its use of old 205-liter barrels across the range, which further helps to explain the house style. For all their freshness, these are not light aperitif wines, but call for food, contemplation, and perhaps even a cigar.

Absorbed by luxury giant LVMH in 1999, Krug retains its family link in the form of sixth-generation member Olivier Krug. With this new backing, the house stepped up investment in its already impressive reserve wines. Since 2011, bottle ID codes have allowed customers to trace the exact makeup of the wine in their glass.

CLOS DU MESNIL

This historic 1.84-hectare vineyard lies in the middle of the Grand Cru Chardonnay village of Mesnil-sur-Oger in the Côte des Blancs. Enclosed by a wall since 1698, Clos du Mesnil was bought by Krug in 1971 and completely replanted so its first vintage under

new ownership did not come until 1979, released by the house in 1986. With production standing at around twelve thousand bottles, this is widely acknowledged as one of the world's great *blanc de blancs* styles and a particular star within the glittering Krug portfolio. Nevertheless, the challenge of meeting such high expectations became clear in 2012 when the house confirmed that it would not release a Clos du Mesnil from the acclaimed 1999 vintage. Despite having gotten as far as labeling the wine, cellarmaster Eric Lebel found himself making the difficult call that after twelve years of maturation it had somehow failed to develop the character and flair associated with Clos du Mesnil. Breaking the news to his bosses at LVMH can't have been easy, but at least this luxury powerhouse had sufficiently deep pockets to place long-term reputation ahead of immediate cash flow concerns.

TOP VINTAGES

As is common practice in a region that has built its business model on nonvintage expressions, the vintage Clos du Mesnil style is only produced in the best years. Built to age, today it is usually matured by Krug for at least ten years before release.

The following vintages of Krug Clos de Mesnil are particularly noteworthy:

2003 A tricky year, especially for those who prize acidity, but this microclimate produced a charming, expressive style.

2000 After the disappointment of the 1999 vintage, this seductive, rich, textured wine showed why Mesnil is so highly prized.

1998 Described by Olivier Krug as "like a sparkling Montrachet," this has evolved quickly and will reward relatively early drinking.

1996 In keeping with many other Champagnes from 1996, this showed huge intensity and cried out for long-term aging.

1995 Suited to earlier drinking, this has developed plenty of rich, nutty notes and even more mature mushroomy characteristics.

1992   Sliding gently into a mellow old age, this is full of forest floor and mushroomy notes, but retains that crucial spark of vitality.

1990   For dedicated lovers of mature Champagne, this wine has been showing off its pedigree since release with no shortage of flair.

1989   In the middle of a trio of strong vintages, this is perhaps the most delicate, but with no shortage of candied fruit and spice.

Dream vintage: 1988   Top marks from Parker here and a host of glowing reviews from other corners, even with considerable maturity this has retained its solid, savory core and should perhaps be treated more like a mature white Burgundy than Champagne.

POL ROGER
(SIR WINSTON CHURCHILL)

With its top cuvée Sir Winston Churchill, this famously anglophile Champagne house pays tribute to one of its greatest supporters and a historic style of Champagne.

It is hardly surprising that Pol Roger has allied its top cuvée with a British statesman: From the very start this Champagne house has forged strong links with the English market.

Founded by a man called Pol Roger in the mid-nineteenth century, by 1855 the house was already leaning toward a brut style in order to cater to the drier tastes of his English clientele. By the time its founder died in 1899, his business was well established. Sons Maurice and Georges forged ahead, changing the family name to Pol-Roger in their father's honor. However it was Odette Pol-Roger, wife of Maurice's son Jacques, who would play such a major role in the house's fortunes. Her friendship with British prime minister Winston Churchill saw him become one of the house's best customers and even name his racehorse Pol Roger.

When Churchill died, the house placed a black border on its UK labels of brut nonvintage. Then, a decade on in 1975, it created Cuvée Sir Winston Churchill, launched in 1984 to mark the fortieth anniversary of D-Day. Modeled on vintages such as 1928 and 1934 that Churchill himself used to enjoy, the expression uses exclusively Grand Cru grapes with a high level

At a Glance

ADDRESS
1, rue Winston Churchill
51200 Épernay, France
Tel: +33 (0)3 26 59 58 00

PEOPLE
Hubert de Billy (director)
Laurent d'Harcourt
(managing director)
Dominique Petit (cellarmaster)

SIZE
Around ninety hectares of its own vineyard, with additional grapes sourced from growers. The cellars hold a total of 1.8 million bottles with the house's core brut nonvintage maturing for three years prior to release.

KEY WINES
Pol Roger Sir Winston Churchill, Brut Reserve Nonvintage, Vintage, Blanc de Blancs, Rosé, "Pure" Extra Brut, "Rich" Demi-Sec

GRAPE VARIETIES
Pinot Noir (33 percent of NV blend, and a dominant proportion of Sir Winston Churchill)
Chardonnay (34 percent of NV blend, minority part of Churchill)
Pinot Meunier (33 percent of NV blend)

of Pinot Noir and spends a decade on lees prior to release. Today, the family link continues via Hubert de Billy, great-grandson of Maurice, and momentum remains strong. The last two decades have brought a new winemaker, a revamped winery, and the addition of both demi-sec and extra brut styles. Pol Roger received the royal seal of approval in 2011 when it was served at the wedding of the Duke and Duchess of Cambridge.

WHY SO SPECIAL?

With so many sparkling wines out there, many of them of very high quality, the Champenois are under increased pressure to explain just what makes their product so special. First of all comes the region, which comprises around thirty-four thousand hectares divided into four main areas: the Montagne de Reims, where Pinot Noir dominates; the Marne Valley, which is Pinot Meunier country; the Côte des Blancs, where Chardonnay rules; and the Côte des Bar, whose southern location provides a more friendly spot to ripen Pinot Noir. Within these areas, top villages are marked out as either Premier Cru or Grand Cru. No other region may call its product Champagne, a rule that the region polices vigorously. With annual production at well over three hundred million bottles, Champagne treads a tricky balance in setting a maximum yield that will satisfy demand without sacrificing quality. It's a political decision that must strike a balance of interests between the region's fifteen thousand growers, who own 90 percent of the vineyards, and the houses, which dominate production.

While many sparkling wine regions have copied Champagne's mix of Chardonnay, Pinot Noir, and Pinot Meunier, as well as its *méthode Champenoise* of secondary fermentation in bottle, few have such strict rules on aging. Bottles must be stored a minimum of fifteen months before release, although the top houses tend to mature even their nonvintage for double that. Another big asset for Champagne is its large reserve stocks of older wine, which are vital to achieving consistency for the big-volume nonvintage styles. Despite such controls, quality varies greatly. Although the best houses do indeed produce extraordinary wines, rising competition means that Champagne as a whole must do more to justify its luxury price tag.

TOP VINTAGES

"Robustness, structure, and maturity" is how Champagne Pol Roger chooses to sum up the characteristics of its prestige cuvée. Although the blend itself remains a closely guarded secret, the inspiration of great vintage expressions from the time of Churchill points to a high proportion of Pinot Noir—Chardonnay only became widespread in Champagne during the second half of the twentieth century.

The following vintages of Sir Winston Churchill are particularly noteworthy:

2002 Only released in 2014, and it was easy to understand the wait upon tasting the richness and depth here, shot through with citrus.

2000 Plenty of rich, creamy, brioche-tinged pleasure here, but all that breadth is balanced with a streak of citrus fruit freshness.

1999 Very serious, combining purity with power and dense layers of spice: a grand, impressive first vintage for the new winemaker.

1998   Real purity and finesse were on show when this was released in 2009, still retaining the cuvée's characteristic breadth.

1996   A hugely structured expression, packing in tightly wound layers of flavor, from biscuits to lemon meringue.

1993   This vintage may lack the reputation of others from the 1990s, but Churchill surprised many with its intriguing style and poise.

1990   Bold and rich in keeping with the style of the vintage as a whole, this is likely to have peaked now but impressed in its day.

1988   Even if it was more delicate than the 1990, this seems to have kept its freshness rather better.

Dream vintage: 1985   Although considerably older than the recommended drinking date for most Champagne—made just a decade after the inaugural vintage—this comes from a particularly good Pinot Noir year for the region; if it's as harmoniously put together as tasting notes suggest, it should be lingering on into a delicate, dignified old age.

CHÂTEAU DE BEAUCASTEL
(HOMMAGE À JACQUES PERRIN)

In the hands of the Perrin family, this southern Rhône estate makes full use of the region's palette of grape varieties while celebrating Mourvèdre in particular with its special cuvée.

While Châteauneuf-du-Pape draws its name from the region's role as wine supplier to the popes during their fourteenth-century sojourn in nearby Avignon, its arguably most famous estate today does not enter the history books until 1549. This was the year when Pierre de Beaucastel bought land in Coudoulet, which lies a few kilometers beyond the modern borders of Châteauneuf-du-Pape. Despite the majority of its vineyards today lying inside this appellation, Beaucastel continues to make a wine from its Coudoulet vines that is widely regarded as a cut above the standard of its generic Côtes du Rhône classification.

The modern history of Beaucastel really dates to 1909, by which time the estate was in the hands of Pierre Tramier. He passed it on to his son-in-law Pierre Perrin, whose scientific background did much to advance quality at Beaucastel. Pierre's son Jacques Perrin continued

At a Glance

ADDRESS
Chemin de Beaucastel
84350 Courthezon, France
Tel: +33 (0)4 90 70 41 00

PEOPLE
Jean-Pierre and François Perrin (estate directors)

SIZE
A 130-hectare estate, of which one hundred hectares are planted with vineyards and seventy hectares lie within the Châteauneuf-du-Pape appellation. Annual production of Château de Beaucastel red is about eight thousand cases. In years when Hommage à Jacques Perrin is made, quantities are about 350 cases.

KEY WINES
Hommage à Jacques Perrin
Château de Beaucastel (red)
Château de Beaucastel (white)
Château de Beaucastel Roussanne Vieilles Vignes
Coudoulet de Beaucastel (red)
Coudoulet de Beaucastel (white)

GRAPE VARIETIES
Mourvèdre, Grenache, Syrah, Cinsault, Vaccarèse, Counoise, Terret Noir, Muscardin, Clairette, Picpoul Noir, Picardin, Bourboulenc, Roussanne

this work until his death in 1978. It was in his honor that the next generation of Perrins created a special cuvée in 1989, to be made only in the best years: Hommage à Jacques Perrin. Today that family link endures with Jean-Pierre and François Perrin at the helm, aided

by several members of the fifth generation.

While Beaucastel remains very much the jewel in their crown, Perrin winemaking interests now extend to ventures across the Rhône, while Brad Pitt and Angelina Jolie hired the family's expertise for their Provençal rosé, Miraval. The Perrins also hold a stake in Tablas Creek, which re-creates Beaucastel's varietal mix and wider winemaking ethos in the Californian hills of Paso Robles.

THE ART OF BLENDING

If northern Rhône reds are all about Syrah, winemaking in the southern Rhône is about finding the right balance each year between the veritable tapestry of grape varieties that exist here. Beaucastel is a particular master of this art, proudly offering a home to all thirteen

varieties permitted in Châteauneuf-du-Pape. Each of these will be picked and vinified separately to show off their individual attributes before the final blend is put together, spending a further year aging in barrel then another year in bottle before release. As a result, Château de Beaucastel red represents a union of the warm, rounded Cinsault and Grenache, along with Mourvèdre's structure, the ageworthiness of Syrah, the dark color of Muscardin, and the aromas of Vaccarèse. Finally there come Counoise and Picpoul Noir, bringing freshness and an extra layer of aromatic interest.

In years deemed good enough for Beaucastel to produce its top wine, Hommage à Jacques Perrin, the majority of this long-lived cuvée—around 60 percent—comes from very old, low-yielding Mourvèdre vines, with the remainder accounted for by Grenache, Syrah, and Counoise.

TOP VINTAGES

With such a high proportion of this cuvée derived from old-vine Mourvèdre, Hommage à Jacques Perrin is a very different wine from the broader blend of Beaucastel's flagship red. Made only in the years when the dark, tannic, heat-loving Mourvèdre can shine, this is a wine that needs considerable aging to reveal its full animal, leathery, tar-flecked flavor.

The following vintages of Hommage à Jacques Perrin are particularly noteworthy:

2011 Widely viewed as a lighter, relatively early drinking year for the Rhône, this dense, gamy tour de force is a notable exception.

2010 "I don't know what more a wine could offer," enthused Parker, describing it as "ageless in potential"—a retirement wine.

2009 All the richness, smoke, forest fruits, and gaminess that you associate with this wine, but in a softer, more approachable shell.

2007 One merchant's description of "quietly sensational" seems to sum up this wine rather elegantly. Voluptuous but in proportion.

2005   Like several of these vintages, this has been comfortably given a fifty-year-plus window to unfurl its considerable character.

2004   A wine that manages to pull off an unlikely balance of huge intensity with a lightness of touch in the way its many layers align.

1998   Typically voluptuous and packed full of black fruit, licorice, and incense, this retains its vigor after a relatively forward youth.

1990   Hedonistic yet intellectual according to Parker, who described the second-ever vintage of this wine as "perfection."

Dream vintage: 1989   The maiden vintage for this *grande cuvée* from Beaucastel set the tone for future expressions in no uncertain style. Big but well balanced, the sweet fruit does not prevent this from being an enormously sophisticated fine wine with a structure that is set to carry it forward for many years to come.

DOMAINE JEAN-LOUIS CHAVE (HERMITAGE)

With sixteen generations' experience in the vineyards of the northern Rhône, Chave's restrained winemaking approach is geared toward accentuating that regional signature.

Few winemaking families can boast the sort of history in evidence at this star of the northern Rhône. The domaine's name, Jean-Louis Chave, refers to the current generation in a very long line indeed, as noted by the proud neck label declaration: "Vignerons de Père en Fils depuis 1481." Although today this producer is best known for its Hermitage, Chave's origins actually lie in Saint-Joseph on the opposite, Ardèche side of the river. It was the arrival of phylloxera in the nineteenth century that forced the family to broaden their focus, first by moving south to the village of Mauves, where they diversified into fruit farming and continue to base themselves today. The second step was to look across the Rhône to Hermitage, where Chave now owns 14.5 hectares. A considerable portion of this land was added during the 1970s by Gérard Chave, who did so much to establish the international reputation of the estate's Hermitage. It is his son, Jean-Louis Chave, who now runs the family business. An enology graduate of UC Davis with an MBA from the University of Hartford, Jean-Louis has built on his father's work by creating *négociant* business J-L Chave Sélection and restoring the steep terraces of Saint-Joseph, many of which were top-quality sites left fallow in the wake of phylloxera and two world wars. With such deep Rhône roots, it is little surprise that Chave has a reputation as a traditionalist. In practice, that means minimal use of new oak, as little intervention as possible, and blending separately vinified plots across the Hermitage hill in a bid to capture the ultimate expression of this appellation.

NAVIGATING THE NORTH

Running south from Lyon along the river that gives this region its name, the northern Rhône joins the Douro and Mosel as home to some of the world's most dramatically steep vineyards. This is Syrah country, although white grapes also have a strong track record here, primarily in the form of Marsanne and Roussanne, but also with Viognier, which shines in Condrieu. The most northerly of this region's eight wine appellations is Côte-Rôtie, whose fragrant reds offer a stylistic contrast with the full-bodied expressions in the other great name of Hermitage. In part this delicacy comes from the Côte-Rôtie tradition of adding a dose of peach-scented Viognier to its Syrah. Downstream of Condrieu lies the anomaly of Château-Grillet, a 3.5-hectare appellation owned in its entirety since 2011 by businessman François Pinault. Stretching along much of the right bank (as the river flows) is Saint-Joseph, whose best wines come from the steep terraced area near Tournon. Opposite lies Crozes-Hermitage, a flat area that accounts for about half this region's production. Rising up from this plain is the famous hill of Hermitage, home to the Rhône's most prestigious, long-lived wines—both red and white. Back on the right bank lies Cornas, another source of serious wine, which typically requires long aging to show at its best. Finally comes Saint-Péray, a white-focused region whose output extends to sparkling wine.

TOP VINTAGES

With vineyards spread across Hermitage's most acclaimed plots, Chave's expression represents a triumph of blending to capture the right amount of the attributes offered by each. Of these, it is the granite soils of Les Bessards whose structured style is widely seen as providing much of the backbone of Chave Hermitage.

The following vintages of Chave Hermitage are particularly note-worthy:

2012 A year that showed off the character of this wine's different components with a collective display of muscular purity.

2011 Not a year associated with highly structured wines, but this wine showed off its pedigree with great density and minerality.

2010 The various component sites delivered a majestic mix of freshness, tension, silkiness, and backbone.

2009 As with the 2010, this expression received top marks from Parker, combining flamboyance with precision.

2005 A challenging wine in its youth, those tannins are softening gradually to reveal a fine-toned mix of fruit, minerals, and tar.

2003 The extremes of this hot year are reflected in the wine, which is full of cedar-tinged spice and ripe fruit but retains a vital energy.

2000 Like 1997, this was a slightly lighter year, but nevertheless very complete, nuanced, and with a relatively early drinking appeal.

1995 Supple, suave, and enormously appealing, this has flourished with age to show blackberry fruit with spice, herbs, and game notes.

1991 Seamless and long with real charm from the sweet fruit, smoky nose, and underlying acidity that propels this wine forward.

1990　A great expression of Hermitage, this offers a heady richness layered with roasted fruit, black tea, and spice—flourishing now.

1989　Rich and concentrated even well into its third decade, this is full of wild fruit, spice, freshness, and great length.

1988　Another year that took a while to soften and reveal its charms, but is now full of smoke, spice, black pepper, and lush fruit.

Dream vintage: 1983　This was a stellar year for the northern Rhône, for some the finest vintage of the decade. Chave's effort appears to be right at its peak, offering an enticingly aromatic nose that gives way to equally appealing complexity in the mouth. This is what mature Rhône wine is all about.

PAUL JABOULET AINÉ (HERMITAGE LA CHAPELLE)

For all the challenges facing this estate in recent years, the halo of its glory days continues to burn brightly as fans hope fervently for a return to form under recent new ownership.

Other estates may perhaps lay claim to greater overall appeal, but for wine lovers there is one name in the Rhône that has acquired iconic status: Hermitage La Chapelle.

For nearly two hundred years, its producer was a family-run affair. Founded by Antoine Jaboulet in 1834, the firm took its name from his elder son, Paul Jaboulet. Although Hermitage had long been admired—until AOC law kicked in, Bordeaux estates often looked here to pad out their own wines—it was Paul's heir Louis who caught the world's attention with the 1961 Hermitage La Chapelle. This legendary wine formed part of a wider effort to raise quality and with it the international reputation of Jaboulet. Although he lived until the age of one hundred, only dying in 2012, Louis handed the reins to his highly capable and charismatic son Gérard in 1977. The 1978 vintage set the tone for an exciting era until the 1990s, when this house appeared to have lost its way slightly. Before the issue could be fully felt or analyzed, disaster struck with the sudden death of Gérard in 1997, aged just fifty-five. The next generation struggled to keep their wines on the right path,

At a Glance

ADDRESS
BP 46, La Roche de Glun
26600 Tain l'Hermitage, France
Tel: +33 (0)4 75 84 68 93

PEOPLE
Frey family (owners)
Caroline Frey (winemaker)

SIZE
Although Jaboulet has sizable vineyard holdings across the northern and southern Rhône, its heart lies in twenty-two hectares of Hermitage.

KEY WINES
Hermitage La Chapelle red
Hermitage La Chapelle white
(revived in 2006)
Hermitage La Petite Chapelle
(since 2001)
Le Chevalier de Sterimberg
(white Hermitage)
Domaine de Thalabert
(red Crozes-Hermitage)
Domaine de Saint Pierre (Cornas)

GRAPE VARIETIES
Syrah (100 percent La Chapelle red)
Marsanne (80 percent La Chapelle white) Roussanne (20 percent La Chapelle white)
Also: Viognier (Condrieu) and Grenache, Cinsault, Mourvèdre (Châteauneuf-du-Pape)

with critics raising concerns about a dramatic increase in production and wines that seemed very light and rapidly evolving in comparison

with their illustrious forebears. Jaboulet's purchase in 2006 by the Frey family, owners of La Lagune in Bordeaux and with a long involvement in Champagne, was met with cautious optimism. Eyebrows were raised when they pulled up the old vines of Le Méal, historically a big part of La Chapelle, but recent vintages suggest this wine is back on track.

HERMITAGE

The wines produced on this granitic, sun-drenched hill of Hermitage have long been revered, with the region receiving mentions in the work of Roman authors. Two thousand years later, Hermitage's 136 hectares tend to produce the most imposing, ageworthy wines of the northern Rhône. This grandeur and longevity also applies to the

peach-scented white wines from this appellation. Nevertheless, this is a region most famous for Syrah, to the extent that until the late 1990s Australian Shiraz often went by the name Hermitage. Unlike many of the world's great wines, Hermitage La Chapelle is simply a brand name rather than denoting a specific vineyard. Indeed, this wine has historically been very much a blended effort, drawing on grapes from different aspects of the Hermitage hill (and, if you believe the rumors, from even farther afield in Cornas in the case of the fabled 1961 vintage). Nevertheless, it seems eminently suitable that such a distinctive wine should bear the name of one of the Rhône's most evocative landmarks, the thirteenth-century chapel that sits on top of the hill of Hermitage.

Alongside Jaboulet, other names to look out for in Hermitage are Chave, Chapoutier, and Delas.

TOP VINTAGES

Given the various changes in management at Jaboulet, the performance of its wines has been notably less consistent since the early 1990s. While the producer's fortunes appear to be on the rise once more, the conditions in which its legendary 1961 vintage was made could possibly be once in a lifetime.

The following vintages of Jaboulet Hermitage La Chapelle are particularly noteworthy:

2010 A weighty, dense wine packed with fruit and smoky game flavors, but retaining an invigorating dose of acidity.

2009 Great concentration here from a wine packed full of flavor and fruit more than capable of withstanding the considerable oak.

2007 An exciting year for the Rhône, with La Chapelle giving black fruit, meat, and a roasted, sweet character that is utterly seductive.

2005   The last vintage before the estate was sold, this excellent year gave a dense expression full of velvety black cherry fruit and spice.

1990   "The modern-day equivalent of 1961," according to Parker, as others lavished praise on a wine of great profundity and purity.

1989   Something of a blockbuster, the fierce tannins sparked debate about this wine's future, but patience appears to be paying off.

1978   Top marks all around and hailed as "exceptional" by Rhône expert John Livingstone-Learmonth, this is enjoying a glorious peak.

1972   Hail hit hard this year and the yield was tiny but left a very complete, violet-edged wine of enormous charm and length.

1964   For those unable to secure a precious bottle of the 1961, this may not reach quite the same heights but offers mature delights.

Dream vintage: 1961   Holding an undisputed place as one of the world's great wines, this star continues to burn brightly, thrilling those drinkers lucky enough to find a bottle as its drinking window extends ever further.

FE TRIMBACH
(CLOS SAINTE HUNE)

With varying sugar levels making Alsatian wines tricky to understand, Trimbach presents a welcome model of high-level consistency across its broad range of very classic wines.

Alsace may have seen its nationality chop and change over the years, but the Trimbach family and its prized Clos Sainte Hune vineyard have remained a constant through the centuries. The name Trimbach has been associated with wine since 1626, when Jean Trimbach settled in the town of Riquewihr. Among the most notable figureheads over the next twelve generations was Frédéric Emile Trimbach, who did much to raise the producer's international prestige during the late nineteenth century and gave his name to one of its top wines, Cuvée Frédéric Emile. Today the firm is headed by Hubert, supported by his two nephews Pierre and Jean Trimbach, as well as daughter Anne.

While modern Alsace wines range confusingly across a full spectrum from bone dry to sweet expressions, Trimbach has—with the exception of a handful of late-harvest labels—stuck firmly to the traditional dry styles. With Clos Sainte Hune this house demonstrates the impressive heights that such dedicated focus on ageworthy, mineral Riesling can achieve. Owned by the Trimbach family for over two hundred years, this small parcel within the Rosacker vineyard does not officially share the site's Grand Cru

At a Glance

ADDRESS
15, route de Bergheim
68150 Ribeauvillé, France
Tel: +33 (3)89 73 60 30

PEOPLE
Hubert, Pierre, Jean, and
Anne Trimbach (owners)

SIZE
Clos Sainte Hune is a 1.67-hectare parcel within the Rosacker vineyard, producing about 650 cases per year.

KEY WINES
Clos Sainte Hune, Cuvée Frédéric Emile, Pinot Gris Réserve Personnelle, Gewürztraminer Cuvée des Seigneurs de Ribeaupierre
Reserve range: Muscat, Pinot Gris, Riesling, Pinot Noir, Gewürztraminer
Classic range: Sylvaner, Pinot Blanc, Gewürztraminer, Riesling
A selection of late-harvest and *Séléction de Grains Nobles* sweet wines

GRAPE VARIETIES
Riesling (100 percent
Clos Sainte Hune)
Pinot Blanc, Sylvaner, Muscat, Gewürztraminer, Pinot Gris, Pinot Noir

status, awarded in 1983, on the grounds that the Trimbachs chose to keep using the more famous Clos Sainte Hune name. Trimbach is one of the world's few producers to successfully combine significant scale with sublime peaks. The company's entry-level "Classic" Riesling offers an ideal introduction to both the Alsace and Trimbach style, while top wines like Clos Sainte Hune fly the flag for this all-too-often overlooked region.

ALSACE

It may currently be part of France, but Alsace's German history is clearly seen in its place names, cuisine, and an architectural style that is straight out of a Brothers Grimm fairytale.

Despite Alsace's northerly latitude, thanks to the rain shadow created by the Vosges Mountains, this is one of the driest wine regions in France, a factor that lends itself well to biodynamic and organic viticulture.

Traditionally the Alsatian style has been dry, full-bodied, inherently food-friendly wines, although sugar levels today may vary from pro-

ducer to producer. Riesling is generally the star of the show, but Gewürztraminer, Muscat, Pinot Gris, Pinot Blanc, and Sylvaner all make distinctive wines here. With global warming Pinot Noir is also performing well and the region produces good quality Crémant d'Alsace, made using the same method as Champagne.

Other producers to look out for include Zind Humbrecht, Hugel, Domaines Schlumberger, Josmeyer, Ostertag, Kreydenweiss, Blanck, Marcel Deiss, Domaine Weinbach, and Rolly Gassman.

TOP VINTAGES

The combination of Clos Sainte Hune's southern exposure, limestone soil, and Riesling vines with an average age of fifty years all contribute to this wine's striking concentration, mineral character, and ability to age. Generally viewed as being less austere in style than Trimbach's other star, Cuvée Frédéric Emile, the family cellars bottles of both these wines for at least five years before release.

The following vintages of Trimbach's Clos Sainte Hune are particularly noteworthy:

2007   A kaleidoscope of flavor emerges from this wine, showing off a stony, saline quality and grapefruit character with real energy.

2005   Tightly wound in its youth, this wine is bursting with all the ageworthy promise you would expect of Riesling in a great site.

2001   A wine of huge concentration, precision, and intensity, this shows a rich lime character balanced with a steely mineral edge.

1998   An impressive balance of fruity breadth and mineral focus, this harmonious wine should be approaching its peak about now.

1996   Dense, focused, and showing layers of lime-tinged mineral character, a vibrant texture, and no shortage of length on the finish.

1995   A great expression of this wine, which shows thrilling vibrancy, richness, and complexity that ensures a captivating future.

1990   Few Clos Sainte Hune vintages set critics' pulses racing like this one, packed with richness and maturing slowly with real flair.

1985   Showing some age now with kerosene and nutty notes, but in a very delicate, restrained way that reflects this cool vintage.

Dream vintage: 1976   A hot, ripe vintage whose top wines have nevertheless proved lively and long-lived. Showing its age now, there is nevertheless plenty to delight the drinker with peaty notes sitting alongside some lingering fruit and tingling energy.

CHATEAU MONTELENA
(MONTELENA ESTATE
CABERNET SAUVIGNON)

Resurrected in the 1970s, just in time for the event that made the world wake up to Californian wine, Chateau Montelena remains a leading player in the same family hands.

Not only does Chateau Montelena have one of the longest histories in Californian winemaking, it also played a starring role in the most pivotal event in this region's wine annals to date.

Back in 1882, one Alfred L. Tubbs, a San Francisco entrepreneur, acted on received wisdom that Napa Valley was the best place in California to grow grapes by buying a wild patch of land north of Calistoga at the foot of Mount Saint Helena. The next few years saw him build a "chateau" called Montelena—a contraction of Mount Saint Helena—and hire a French winemaker. By 1896 Chateau Montelena was one of the largest producers in Napa Valley, although the advent of Prohibition brought an end to that. In 1958 the Tubbs family sold their estate to a couple looking for a quiet place to retire. By the time Jim Barrett bought the property with a view to turning his winemaking dream into reality, the vineyards and disused winery were in need of a major overhaul. Hav-

At a Glance

ADDRESS
1429 Tubbs Lane
Calistoga, CA 94515, USA
Tel: +1 (707) 942-5105

PEOPLE
James "Bo" Barrett (CEO)
Matt Crafton (winemaker)
Dave Vella (vineyard manager)

SIZE
About forty-nine hectares of vineyard with a total annual production of around thirty-five thousand cases. About 7,500 cases of the Montelena Estate Cabernet Sauvignon are made each year.

KEY WINES
Montelena Estate Cabernet Sauvignon
Napa Valley Chardonnay
Napa Valley Cabernet Sauvignon
Montelena Estate Zinfandel
Napa Valley Sauvignon Blanc
Potter Valley Riesling

GRAPE VARIETIES
Cabernet Sauvignon (around 98 percent of the Montelena Estate Cabernet Sauvignon blend)
Cabernet Franc (2 percent)
Chardonnay
Merlot
Zinfandel
Sauvignon Blanc
Riesling

ing made his first wine in 1972, Barrett's 1973 Chardonnay—made by Mike Grgich, who has since founded his own winery—trounced some of the biggest names in Burgundy to take first place in the  blind-tasting event known as the Judgment of Paris. It may have been a Chardonnay that put Montelena on the map, but in 1978 this flagship style was joined by an estate Cabernet Sauvignon. Although Barrett's son Bo took on winemaking duties in 1982, in 2008 Montelena came close to being sold to Cos d'Estournel owner Michel Reybier. That deal collapsed and Barrett died in 2013, but Bo remains at the helm of this family affair.

THE JUDGMENT OF PARIS

Back in 1976, few fine-wine lovers would have cast their gaze beyond France, or at least Europe. However, English wine writer Steven Spurrier, at that time running a wine shop and school in Paris, was intrigued by the Californian wines brought to him by his many American students based at the nearby IBM offices. Spurrier therefore brought together a selection of Californian Cabernet Sauvignon and Chardonnay with some of the most admired names in Bordeaux and Burgundy from the same vintage, pouring them blind for a group of top French critics. The results saw the 1973 Stag's Leap SLV Cabernet Sauvignon triumph in the red class, outscoring the likes of Mouton Rothschild and Haut-Brion. Meanwhile, the Chardonnay contest was won by Chateau Montelena, which fought off competition from wines including Roulot's Meursault Charmes and Joseph Drouhin's Clos des Mouches. That might have been the end of it had not a French-speaking journalist from *Time* magazine brought this result—together with disparaging comments made about wines the judges believed to be Californian, and their outrage when the scores were revealed—to a wider audience. Today a bottle of each winning wine sits in the Smithsonian National Museum of American History. Thirty years later, Montelena enjoyed another publicity boost when it starred in the film *Bottle Shock*, a Hollywood remake of the tasting that catapulted California so firmly onto the world wine map.

TOP VINTAGES

Montelena's gently sloping vineyards feature alluvial outshoots from the Napa River. These, combined with the warm Calistoga climate—but moderated by cooling afternoon breezes—act as key factors behind this estate's rich, aromatic Cabernet Sauvignon style.

The following vintages of Montelena Estate Cabernet Sauvignon are particularly noteworthy:

2010 A highly expressive style with great ripeness but in need of some years' cellaring for its various elements to knit together fully.

2009 Plenty of depth and intensity to complement this wine's up-front array of spicy aromas and immediate appeal even in youth.

2007 This strong vintage for Napa resulted in a fragrant mix of sweet black currant fruit, rocky notes, and powerful drive.

2004 Dense and structured, this brings sweet fruit, licorice, and spice in a forward style that nevertheless looks built to age well.

2002 A flamboyant vintage for California, this is no exception, but retains a structured Cabernet character to control that richness.

1997   One of the most highly acclaimed vintages in Montelena's history, this full-bodied style incorporates exciting complexity too.

1995   Plenty of power here, featuring cassis, wild undergrowth, and spice that explodes on the midpalate and lingers on the finish.

1991   The brooding intensity of its youth has translated into a thrilling experience after two decades of evolution.

1987   A top performance from this estate, bringing a rich, highly extracted display of black currant, violets, and licorice.

Dream vintage: 1986   Still showing enormously youthful character a decade after it was harvested, this forms part of a particularly strong run of vintages for Chateau Montelena and features the estate's characteristic sweet black currant fruit in a harmonious, seductive package that was accessible in youth but built for the long term.

HANZELL VINEYARDS (HANZELL VINEYARDS CHARDONNAY)

*One of Sonoma's oldest wine estates, Hanzell has always forged
a distinct path that sees its wines, especially the Chardonnay,
age with all the panache of top-end Burgundy.*

Among the less well-documented effects of the Marshall Plan, a US scheme to rebuild Europe's economy after World War II, is its indirect role in creating some of California's most admired wines. Tasked by President Truman with implementing this billion-dollar initiative, businessman-turned-diplomat James Zellerbach spent time in Burgundy, where he became determined to replicate the quality of wines there at his own estate in the Mayacamas Mountains of Sonoma. He renamed this place Hanzell, a contraction of his wife Hana's name and his own surname, with the first vintage produced in 1957. As a mark of the historic place Hanzell holds in the annals of US winemaking, its Ambassador's 1953 Vineyard is said to contain the oldest productive Pinot Noir and Chardonnay vines in North America.

In order to satisfy Zellerbach's bold vision, Hanzell boasts a proud track record of innovation, from the world's first temperature-controlled stainless steel fermenters to modern-day trials of different clones and rootstock. This inventive outlook combines with an ethos of minimal intervention that sees oak used only

At a Glance

ADDRESS
18596 Lomita Avenue
Sonoma, CA 95476, USA
Tel: +1 (707) 996-3860

PEOPLE
Alexander de Brye (owner)
Michael McNeill (winemaking director)
José Ramos Esquivel (vineyard director)

SIZE
18.6 hectares of vineyard, with annual production of around six thousand cases, of which about three quarters is Chardonnay.

KEY WINES
Chardonnay: Three single-vineyard expressions—Ramos Vineyard, Ambassador's 1953 Vineyard, and de Brye Vineyard—and the flagship Hanzell Vineyards Chardonnay, a blend of the property's five vineyards. The Sebella label is used for fruit from younger vines.
Pinot Noir: Three single-vineyard expressions from Sessions Vineyard, de Brye Vineyard, and Ambassador's 1953 Vineyard, as well as the flagship Hanzell Vineyards Pinot Noir, a barrel selection of these three vineyards.

GRAPE VARIETIES
Chardonnay
Pinot Noir
Cabernet Sauvignon

modestly, along with meticulous care for the old vineyards here, to create wines that are defined above all by their impressive ability to age.

Indeed, Hanzell has shown a notable consistency of style across its seven decades, a fact undoubtedly aided by the incumbency of just four winemakers during that time and the same vineyard manager since 1975. Having taken the winemaking reins in 2008, Michael McNeill is quietly nudging up quality without altering the essence of Hanzell.

NOT SO COOL

When James Zellerbach embarked on his ambitious mission to replicate Burgundian quality in California, his estate in the Mayacamas Mountains was perhaps not the most obvious place to start. Despite its altitude and the influence of fog on certain vineyards,

this remains a relatively warm corner of Sonoma—a position at odds with the "cool-climate" buzzword that is cited by so many winemakers pursuing elegance in Pinot Noir and Chardonnay. Nevertheless, the Hanzell team defied the naysayers by showing that it is perfectly possible to achieve restrained, balanced, and above all ageworthy expressions of these varieties here, thanks to thoughtful management of its now venerable vineyards. The producer has even developed its own "Hanzell Clone," subsequently adopted by many other wineries. In addition to this well-suited raw material, Hanzell pays close attention to the positioning and canopy management of its various vineyards, while adopting a rigorous approach to harvest dates and fruit sorting. Meanwhile, French oak barrels are coopered to fit this estate's precise needs and employed sparingly to enhance rather than smother the fruit character.

TOP VINTAGES

One reason why Hanzell wines, although widely admired, have never enjoyed quite the same profile as other Californian producers is surely down to the fact that its wines can often be quite reticent when first released and therefore tend not to attract headline-grabbing scores. That doesn't deter an army of loyal followers, who prize this winery's ability to turn out consistently high-quality Pinot Noir and especially Chardonnay that reward considerable aging. These wines also reward decanting at least an hour in advance.

The following most recent vintages of Hanzell Vineyards Chardonnay are particularly noteworthy:

2011   Enticing aromas of everything from lime zest to cloves and honeysuckle, which give way to intense apple flavors and tight acid.

2010   A combination of limey nectarine and jasmine scents merges with rich white fruit on the palate and a lively lemony finish.

2009   Noted for its Chablis-style flintiness, but also recalling Côte de Beaune–levels of rich intensity that bodes well for future aging.

2008 A few years of bottle age have unveiled bright, tropical fruit character sitting alongside a cool, mineral, structured framework.

2007 A lively mix of citrus fruit and mineral undertones, showing off great richness in the mouth and finishing with bright acidity.

2006 There's no shortage of rich body here, but it's kept in check by a mineral edge and citrusy acidity to leave a complex, elegant result.

2005 "Addictively brilliant," raved the *Wine Enthusiast*, noting its mix of pear, lemon drops, and anise with a honeyed but crisp finish.

2004 Showing the estate's signature opulent fruit coupled with intensity of flavor and acid framework, this looks set to age in style.

2003 In keeping with the warmth of the vintage, this is a notably rich style but keeps its characteristic precision and purity.

2002 Defined by its mineral core and elegant texture, this marks quite a contrast with the fatter Chardonnays prevailing at this time.

2001 At over a decade old, this wine was still on an energetically upward curve, showing peaches, lemon curd, and herbs.

1996 Rated an "exceptional" year by the estate itself, this wine has matured to show a structured mix of dried fruit, fresh hay, and nuts.

Dream vintage: 1995 While there's plenty of evidence that Hanzell Chardonnays can age much further, this example has now unfurled to show its full complexity, from the petrol character seen in mature Riesling to baked pear and the energy to run still further.

HARLAN ESTATE

In a region full of cult wines, Harlan was one of the earliest trailblazers, whose founder's ambitious vision inspired many other Napa producers to aspire to a higher level.

The wild, wooded mountains of Oakville may be a far cry from the flat, aristocratically landscaped Médoc peninsula, but that didn't deter Bill Harlan from his vision to create a Californian "first growth."

This conviction saw Harlan Estate emerge as one of the first cult wineries to emerge from Napa and set a benchmark that remains today. It was by no means an easy journey. Having bought the property in 1984, Harlan set about clearing the steep, forested hillside to plant vines. Despite making a wine in 1987, 1988, and 1989, it was not until 1990, after hiring Bordeaux consultant Michel Rolland, that the quality was deemed worthy of commercial release. Even then, the first bottles did not

At a Glance

ADDRESS
PO Box 352
Oakville, CA 94562, USA
Tel: +1 (707) 944-1441

PEOPLE
Bill Harlan (owner)
Don Weaver (estate director)
Bob Levy (director of winemaking)

SIZE
Seventeen hectares of vineyard with an average annual production of the top wine of 1,800 cases.

KEY WINES
Harlan Estate
The Maiden—second wine, introduced in the 1995 vintage
The Mascot—made from young vines and bought-in grapes—introduced in the 2008 vintage

GRAPE VARIETIES
Cabernet Sauvignon (70 percent of vineyard plantings)
Merlot (20 percent)
Cabernet Franc (8 percent)
Petit Verdot (2 percent)

reach the market until 1996, more than a decade after the project got under way.

Unsurprisingly, given the striking contrasts in terroir, the Harlan style is very different from a Médoc first growth. For those raised on the cool, savory, gravelly Left Bank wines, Harlan's unashamedly voluptuous expression of the same grape varieties might come as a shock, but often an exhilaratingly seductive one. Not that this strong Californian character undermines its owner's original aim, which was primarily inspired by the Bordelais dedication to crafting a wine that is as much a high art form as a drink. Another aspect of Bill Harlan's Bordeaux trip during the 1980s with the late Robert Mondavi that left a deep impression was the idea of an estate being passed down the generations. With son Will Harlan joining the winery team in 2008, that long-term perspective looks assured.

MAIDENS AND MASCOTS

Such is the demand for Harlan's limited quantities that the estate's top wine is strictly allocated and attracts ever more inflated prices after release. As a result, fans looking for a taste of this Napa legend may wish to consider its younger siblings.

Introduced from the 1995 vintage onward, The Maiden emulates the Bordelais approach of creating a second wine from fruit that didn't make the cut for the *grand vin*, but shares the same vineyard pedigree. The arrival of second-generation representative Will Harlan saw him keen to make his own mark on the family business. The result was The Mascot, a blend of grapes from younger vines on the property, as well as the family's Bond and Promontory ventures, which apply the Harlan philosophy to other top sites in Napa.

TOP VINTAGES

Harlan undoubtedly owes much of its commercial success to the consistently glowing recognition it has received over the years from Robert Parker. Not content with giving five vintages a perfect score, the critic has gone so far as to suggest, "Harlan Estate might be the single most profound red wine made not just in California, but the world." Not all will share such a superlative judgment, but the impact of Harlan both among wine lovers and the Napa style is less open to debate.

The following vintages from Harlan Estate are particularly note-worthy:

2012   A great vintage for much of California manifested itself here in a rich, velvety display of chocolate, dark fruit, and great length.

2010   A cooler year is reflected in a wine show-ing plenty of fresh acidity alongside nuanced notes of cedar, tobacco, and black tea.

2007   Top marks from Parker, who described it as a "splendidly opulent, pure wine with a skyscraper-like texture" and built to last.

2004   Particularly accessible in its youth, even by the precocious standards of Harlan, this is a lush, fleshy style with thrilling length.

2003   Densely textured, with over a decade's maturity, this has evolved to show an explosive array of graphite, smoke, and forest floor.

2002   Another top score from Parker; other critics also praised its flattering richness that does not use power at the expense of finesse.

2001   Full marks again from Parker, this reveals more and more layers in the glass, achieving richness without being too heavy.

1997   "One of the greatest Cabernet Sau-vignon–based wines I have ever tasted," said Parker, noting in particular its lingering finish.

1996   This blockbuster shows great intensity of black currant, spice, and tobacco, tipping over into rich fruitcake flavors.

1995   Another vintage to assure early fans that Harlan estate was no one-trick pony; this has evolved to show a wild, smoky character.

1994 "Comes close to immortality in a glass," said Parker, giving this vintage top marks after following Harlan since its inception.

1991 Just the second commercial vintage, this was eagerly awaited and reassured critics that there was a new star in the making.

Dream vintage: 1990 While reviews of this wine were glowing rather than effervescent, this has to be the Harlan for fans of the estate to track down. Just three hundred cases were made of the maiden commercial vintage from an estate whose subsequent track record has only added to the appeal of such an historic artifact from its early anonymous days.

HUNDRED ACRE
(KAYLI MORGAN
CABERNET SAUVIGNON)

One of the most provocative, blockbuster cult Cabernets to come out of Napa, Hundred Acre launched with a bang as the new millennium dawned and hasn't looked back.

It's difficult to think of another wine estate that can tell such an overnight success story as Hundred Acre. Even Le Pin in Pomerol took a decade to really catch the collector's eye. For both of these cult producers, but especially Hundred Acre, a major factor propelling them to such an enviable supply and demand balance is undoubtedly the influence of US critic Robert Parker. Having won its first hundred-point score in 2002, only the estate's third vintage, this Napa producer has consistently racked up a shelfload of perfect or near-perfect accolades.

All this critical acclaim should not overshadow the driving force behind Hundred Acre's astonishing rise: charismatic founder Jayson Woodbridge. Having found an initial channel for his energy in the Canadian army, then the means to support his winemaking dream via a career in investment banking, by 2000 Woodbridge was able to buy his own prime slice of Napa Valley real estate at the foot of Howell Mountain. The name Hundred Acre came not from the property's size, but its resemblance in Woodbridge's eyes to the

At a Glance

ADDRESS
PO Box 380
Rutherford, CA 94573, USA
Tel: +1 (707) 967-9398

PEOPLE
Jayson Woodbridge (owner)
Philippe Melka (consultant winemaker)
Jim Barbour (vineyard manager)

SIZE
Average annual production from the four-hectare Kayli Morgan Cabernet Sauvignon is one thousand cases.

KEY WINES
Cabernet Sauvignon wines: Kayli Morgan Vineyard, Ark Vineyard, Few & Far Between, Deep Time, Precious
Also: Dark Matter Zinfandel Fortification, The Duke Brandy, and, from a sister venture set up in Australia's Barossa Valley, Hundred Acre Shiraz Ancient Way

GRAPE VARIETIES
Cabernet Sauvignon
(100 percent of Kayli Morgan)
Zinfandel
Shiraz (Australian venture)

Hundred Acre Wood of Winnie-the-Pooh fame. Here he wasted no time or expense in hiring the expertise of consultant Philippe Melka for the winemaking and Jim Barbour in the vineyard, fostering an approach of meticulous attention to detail for each of his single-vineyard, single-variety wines. First came the Kayli Morgan Vineyard, then, as Woodbridge acquired more land, other Cabernet Sauvignon labels, a Zinfandel, and a port-style fortified wine. All share a powerful intensity and prices as high as their praise.

NAPA AND BEYOND

For those unable to secure the very limited allocation, top-dollar wines from the Hundred Acre collection, Woodbridge has extended his considerable energies in several more accessible directions. These include Cherry Pie, a Pinot Noir from Carneros, and Layer Cake, a range that pitches itself as offering "affordable luxury." This latter brand moves well beyond the confines of Napa, featuring a broad sweep of single-varietal wines from as far afield as Italy, Argentina, Spain, and Australia.

Australia is also the home of another Hundred Acre wine, Ancient Way. Having produced its first vintage in 2004, this aims to express the same plush intensity with Barossa Shiraz as the original property does with Cabernet Sauvignon in Napa.

TOP VINTAGES

The clay rich soils of Kayli Morgan Vineyard, together with the rich style of wine produced here, have led some commentators to draw a stylistic parallel with Le Pin, whose quantities are similarly minute. Certainly Right Bank Bordeaux was a major inspiration for Hundred Acre, but the character of these wines also shows an unmistakable Californian ripeness, combined with a creaminess derived from an extreme oak regime that can see these wines spend up to thirty months in new French barriques.

The following vintages of Kayli Morgan Vineyard are particularly noteworthy:

2010   An already tiny production was 75 percent down this year, but what remained impressed critics with its voluptuous, black currant style.

2009   Rain during harvest saw helicopters deployed to dry off the fruit, a move repaid with this rich, sensual, toasty flavor explosion.

2008   More noticeable acidity and marked tannins have seen this dubbed a comparatively European style, with plenty of personality.

2007   One hundred points for what Parker describes as a "bigger than life" Cabernet Sauvignon of "extraordinary intensity, purity, and depth."

2006   "Built like a skyscraper, with terrific intensity, but no heaviness," enthuses Parker, who urged patience before opening.

2005   Showing all the opulence you would expect from this wine, it has taken time to move beyond exuberant youth and really unfold.

2004   Another vintage of this wine that, despite its Cabernet rather than Merlot makeup, drew stylistic comparisons with Le Pin.

2003   A vintage that shows all the rich plum, cassis fruit, and smoky, caramel oak influence that is so characteristic of this wine.

2002   "A terrific example of great Napa Cabernet Sauvignon," raved Parker as he awarded it top marks after just three vintages.

2001   This second vintage confirmed Hundred Acre's impressive debut and reinforced its bold stylistic signature with conviction.

Dream vintage: 2000   Good luck getting hold of a rare bottle from this maiden vintage, which immediately grabbed critics' attention, especially Parker's, who praised the "brash newcomer" for its "incredibly sexy, opulent, 'pedal to the metal' Cabernet." Far from taking time to find its feet, Hundred Acre came straight out of the blocks with an energy and panache that would set a firm tone for the future.

KISTLER VINEYARDS (KISTLER VINEYARD CUVÉE CATHLEEN)

A prime example of vineyard-led expression and bellwether for California's wider stylistic evolution, Kistler Vineyards has proved a source of inspiration for many.

Anyone keen to get under the skin of an individual vineyard's influence on wine should spend some time getting to know the Kistler portfolio. From sites dotted across Sonoma, Kistler produces ten single-vineyard Chardonnays and four Pinot Noirs. Each plot is planted with the same clone and its grapes vinified in the same way, leaving the wines to act as a liquid interpretation of their origin. While this Burgundian ethos has formed a continuous thread since Steve Kistler established the venture back in 1978, that's not to suggest the style of these wines has stayed the same. As Americans developed a serious thirst for Chardonnay in the 1980s and 1990s, Kistler fueled this demand with its collection of full-bodied, buttery, opulent expressions of the variety that met with great critical acclaim. Indeed, Kistler's success with this style inspired others to create still richer versions. However, as the new millennium dawned, Kistler gradually embraced a "less is more" outlook, applied both to the flagship Chardonnays and also its highly regarded Pinot Noirs. This shift saw the producer move toward picking earlier—and even reorienting some sections of its vineyards to facilitate this—as well as using fewer new oak barrels and adopting wild yeasts in place

At a Glance

ADDRESS
7095 Trenton-Healdsburg Road
Forestville, CA 95436, USA
Tel: +1 (707) 657-7665

PEOPLE
Steve Kistler (CEO)
Jason Kesner (winemaker)

SIZE
Total annual production is around twenty-five thousand cases, of which about one fifth is Pinot Noir and the rest Chardonnay. About five hundred cases of Cuvée Cathleen are produced a year.

KEY WINES
Chardonnay: Dutton Vineyard, Vine Hill Vineyard, Trenton Roadhouse, McCrea Vineyard, Kistler Vineyard, Kistler Vineyard Cuvée Cathleen, Hyde Vineyards, Hudson Vineyards, Durell Vineyards, and Stone Flat Pinot Noir: Kistler Vineyard Cuvée Natalie, Cuvée Catherine, and Cuvée Elizabeth

GRAPE VARIETIES
Chardonnay
Pinot Noir

of commercial ones. These decisions not only made sense in the context of Kistler's drive to show the character of individual vineyards; they also placed this estate at the head of a wider sea change, as winemakers moved to balance the benefits of Californian sun with techniques geared toward a more vibrant, toned, food-friendly style.

SONOMA

Stretching sixty miles along California's northern coastline, Sonoma County is home to some twenty-four thousand hectares of vineyard and over five hundred wineries. Although Chardonnay dominates, Sonoma is home to more Pinot Noir than any other county in the state. Meanwhile subregions such as Dry Creek produce top Zinfandel and Sonoma Mountain shows that Napa doesn't have a monopoly on high-class Cabernet. Indeed, in order to reflect the various climatic

and geological influences within its boundaries, Sonoma is divided into seventeen AVAs. At the coolest end of this spectrum is Sonoma Coast, where the fog rolls in like clockwork each morning before giving way to more characteristic Californian sunshine. Thanks to the Petaluma Wind Gap, this fog also penetrates through to another major AVA, Russian River Valley. Another high-profile subregion is Carneros, where Sonoma overlaps with its Napa neighbor. Fog plays a key cooling role here too, leading this area to cultivate a strong reputation not just for its still Chardonnay and Pinot, but also sparkling wines.

Alongside Kistler, among the many other high-quality Sonoma names to look out for are Littorai, Williams Selyem, Ridge, Dry Creek Vineyard, Flowers, Matanzas Creek, Hanzell, Marcassin, Sonoma-Cutrer, Schug, Saintsbury, and Seghesio.

TOP VINTAGES

Made from a single block of the Kistler Vineyard planted in 1989, Cuvée Cathleen is a reflection of the distinctive geology here, where the soil changes to a mixture of shale and volcanic ash. The Kistler team clearly thinks highly of the resulting character, referring to this wine as "one of our most complete and complex Chardonnays, and nears perfection on an annual basis."

The following vintages of Kistler Vineyard Cuvée Cathleen are particularly noteworthy:

2012   An expression that shows off the typically more structured, highly mineral style of this wine, balanced by great breadth of fruit.

2011   There's gener-
ous body and opulent tangerine-tinged fruit here, but the wine is given shape by its texture and gravelly edge.

2009   Richer   than the main Kistler Vineyard wine, this cuvée is full of honeyed tangerines,   showing depth, intensity, and a lifted finish.

2006   A year when bad weather forced earlier picking with winning results, this wine shows no lack of body but some lively acidity too.

2005   Backward in youth, this wine's tropical vibrancy, mineral edge, richness, and depth saw it hailed as a world-class Chardonnay.

2003   "Undeniably sexy, full-throttle stuff," said Parker, hailing this as representing the best of California and Burgundy combined.

2001   Maturing with style, this is full of brioche, hazelnuts, and honeyed citrus in an impressive display of full-bodied Chardonnay.

Dream vintage: 1992   An important year for Kistler, which saw the first vintage of this cuvée coincide with the completion of a new, state-of-the-art winery, allowing the team to ensure quality achieved in the vineyard was not undermined by practices in the cellar. The warm reception of this wine by critics served to strengthen even further Kistler's reputation as a confirmed star of Sonoma.

KONGSGAARD
(THE JUDGE CHARDONNAY)

*Displaying the kind of resolutely "hands-off" winemaking
approach rarely seen outside Burgundy, John Kongsgaard
has shown Napa producers an alternative philosophy.*

John Kongsgaard is not so much a winemaker as a school of thought. In a region where producers present technical sheets packed with detail of their minutely controlled, state-of-the-art process, this fifth-generation Napa native preaches a contrary philosophy of benign neglect. Classically trained in winemaking at UC Davis, Kongsgaard spent a formative period working at Stag's Leap under the pioneering Warren Winiarski before taking another pivotal post at Newton Vineyard. Here he was packed off to discover how the Burgundians crafted their famous Chardonnays, witnessing the minimal intervention—and very persuasive results—deployed by Coche-Dury and Comtes Lafon. This experience gave Kongsgaard courage to put his own fruit through the same unnerving vinification process, one in which fermentation with wild yeasts takes a year and the oxidized juice turns brown before resurrecting in dramatic, intensely flavored and textured style.

Since the 1996 vintage, Kongsgaard and his wife, Maggy, have deployed this aggressively natural approach under their own label.

At a Glance

ADDRESS
4375 Atlas Peak Road
Napa, CA 94558, USA
Tel: +1 (707) 226-2190

PEOPLE
John, Maggy, and son Alex Kongsgaard
(owners and winemakers)

SIZE
Just three hundred cases of top wine
The Judge are made each year from a
total production of about 2,500 cases.
Grapes come from the family's own
land as well as managed long-term
leases.

KEY WINES
The Judge
Chardonnay
Cabernet Sauvignon
The Fimasaurus
Merlot
Syrah
Viorous
Also, The Kings Farm, a range
of "little brothers and sisters"
offered only via mailing list

GRAPE VARIETIES
Chardonnay (100 percent of The Judge)
Cabernet Sauvignon
Merlot
Syrah
Viognier
Roussanne

Heading this portfolio is The Judge, from a parcel named after his father, Thomas, a Napa Superior Court judge. It was none other than Napa guru André Tchelistcheff who had advised his young neighbor to plant this family plot with Chardonnay back in 1970. Over four decades, Kongsgaard has mentored a host of disciples, from Blair Walter, now of New Zealand star Felton Road, to Abe Schoener, whose Scholium Project is one of the most proudly provocative producers in a notoriously conformist Napa.

ANYTHING BUT CHARDONNAY?

A long-term hit with wine drinkers around the world, but particularly in the US, Chardonnay has proved a victim of its own success. California was by no means the only place to ramp up the buttery, tropical, oak-driven character of this variety during the 1980s and 1990s, but thanks to a solid US consumer support base, it has been slower than many other wine regions (such as Australia, New Zealand, and South Africa) to embrace a collective shift toward more restrained, acid-driven styles. Nevertheless, while the ubiquitous Kendall Jackson Vintner's Reserve may remain the style template for California's most widely planted variety, those in search of a more refined experience can dip into an expanding array of options. Some such as Hanzell have quietly been treading this path for decades; others have sensed the zeitgeist that was given form by the "In Pursuit of Balance" movement.

Among the steadily growing band of elegant Californian Chardonnays are Sandhi, Littorai, Jordan Vineyard, Hanzell, Stag's Leap, Patz & Hall, Arnot-Roberts, Hirsch, Lioco, Au Bon Climat, Mathiasson, Red Car, Mount Eden, Domaine de la Côte, and Hyde de Villaine, the latter a joint project with the co-owner of Domaine de la Romanée-Conti.

TOP VINTAGES

The Judge Chardonnay was inaugurated in 2002 as a memorial to John Kongsgaard's late father. Yields from this single vineyard are low so the tiny quantities of wine that result are quickly snapped up by the winery's mailing list. For those unable to secure a bottle, Kongsgaard makes another Chardonnay, whose 2001 vintage was likened by Jancis Robinson MW to DRC 1978 Montrachet no less, at slightly more accessible production levels.

The following vintages of The Judge are particularly noteworthy:

2012 Described by Parker as a "sexy beast of a Chardonnay," this shows huge concentration, rich fruit, and "undeniable minerality."

2010 Like a good Burgundy, there's much more here than just fruit. This is packed with minerals and spice in a richly nuanced package.

2009 Rich but full of dancing energy, this wine carries substantial weight with the lightest, most elegant of mineral-laced steps.

2008 A multilayered array of ripe stone fruit, honeysuckle, and cool minerality, this gently unfurls with a lingering finish.

2007 Energetic and in youth show-ing a tannic element reminiscent of red wine, this shows off a dense array of stones, smoke, and citrus.

2005 "Flirts with perfection," teases Parker; this packs in an intense mix of honey, tropical fruit, and floral notes with a buoyant vitality.

2004 The mind-blowing concentration of this wine is saved from tipping over the edge by an invigorating mineral streak.

2003 Not for the fainthearted, this came out as California's priciest Chardonnay and hit nearly 15 percent ABV but still won over wary critics.

Dream vintage: 2002　This wine made quite an impact with its maiden vintage, demonstrating a clear common thread with the original Kongsgaard Chardonnay but ratcheting everything up a gear. In youth, this thick texture and extreme concentration gave its sibling the edge in terms of vitality, but critics nevertheless viewed The Judge as a wine requiring maturity to show off its true class.

RIDGE VINEYARDS (MONTE BELLO)

Another Californian star from the 1976 Judgment of Paris,
Ridge's caliber and idiosyncratic ethos is validated by an
impressive track record of elegant, ageworthy wines.

It may seem paradoxical for such greatness to be achieved by doing as little as possible, but that's what happens when your winemaker trained in philosophy rather than enology. Since being asked to join Ridge Vineyards back in 1969 by a group of Stanford scientists who had bought the Monte Bello property to indulge their low-tech winemaking hobby, Paul Draper has spent five decades demonstrating the validity of this minimalist mind-set.

His theory behind some of the most unashamedly claret-style wines outside the Médoc is that fruit from well-tended vineyards should be interfered with as little as possible. At Ridge, this means harvesting by hand and using natural yeasts and the bare minimum of additives such as sulfur dioxide. Indeed, so transparent is Ridge in this respect that since 2011 the estate has listed all ingredients on its back label.

One other element that sets Ridge apart, both from Bordeaux châteaux and most of the many producers around the world who seek to emulate their style, is its loyalty to American oak over French. Draper maintains that, when air-dried

At a Glance

ADDRESS
17100 Monte Bello Road
Cupertino, CA 95014, USA
Tel: (408) 867-3233

PEOPLE
Paul Draper (CEO and head winemaker)
Eric Baugher (winemaker, Monte Bello)
David Gates (vineyard manager)

SIZE
Eleven estates spread across
Sonoma, Paso Robles, and Santa Cruz
Mountains. Annual production of Monte
Bello is about three thousand cases.

KEY WINES
Monte Bello, Monte Bello Chardonnay,
Estate Cabernet Sauvignon,
Torre Merlot, Torre Petit Verdot,
Merlot Estate, Lytton Springs,
Lytton Estate Late Harvest Viognier,
Pagani Ranch Zinfandel,
Three Valleys Sonoma County
A wider range is available exclusively
to Ridge members.

GRAPE VARIETIES
Cabernet Sauvignon (about
75 percent of Monte Bello blend),
Merlot, Cabernet Franc, Petit Verdot.
Also: Chardonnay, Petite Sirah,
Zinfandel, Syrah, Carignan, Grenache,
Mourvèdre, Viognier, Alicante Bouschet

and coopered correctly, US oak barrels are as good, if not better than, their revered French counterparts.

This patriotism is not limited to oak: Ridge can also claim a

major role in showing the exciting quality of which California's native but often derided grape Zinfandel is capable, thanks to old-vine expressions from its Lytton Springs and Geyserville estates. However, it is the Cabernet Sauvignon–based Monte Bello that flies the flag for a contrary but thoroughly convincing philosophy.

PAUL DRAPER

The idea of a winemaker's signature would no doubt appall Paul Draper, but his five decades at the helm here mean that the Ridge character is inextricably linked to this man and the experiences that have shaped his highly individual approach. Farming may be in his blood, but growing up in Illinois meant that it was not until he spent weekends with the family of a Swiss roommate while studying philosophy at Stanford that Draper really caught the wine bug. After spending time in Italy and France, he ended up in Chile offering wineries advice on how to develop their export sales. While there he rented a vineyard and taught himself winemaking with the help of nineteenth-century French and Californian textbooks, whose tenets inform his approach today. Having been invited to speak at his alma mater Stanford about Chilean wines, he met one of the Ridge owners who felt that his approach offered a perfect match for their own noninterventionist ethos. Draper took on the job if winemaker in 1969 and the rest, as they say, is history.

TOP VINTAGES

High up in the Santa Cruz Mountains and fifteen miles from the Pacific Ocean, the Monte Bello vineyard lies in California's coolest site for Cabernet Sauvignon and features a limestone component not found in Napa or Sonoma. The blend each year will vary considerably, based on extensive tasting and preparation of different assemblages, but it's always Cabernet Sauvignon–led with supporting roles from any or all of the other classic Bordeaux varietal components: Merlot, Cabernet Franc, and Petit Verdot.

Almost every vintage of the ever-consistent Ridge Monte Bello wins critical acclaim, but the following are particularly noteworthy:

2012 In its youth this wine displays great purity with intense wild, peppery fruit and fine tannins to set it up for a long life ahead.

2010 Very savory, showing herbal notes, dark fruit, and a graphite character enrobed in firm but fine tannins.

2009 A majestically layered mix of dark red fruit, spice, and mineral edge brought together with a silky yet firmly structured framework.

2008 A muscular but strikingly harmonious and complex wine, even in its youth this hinted loudly at even greater things to come.

2005 Explosive black currant and cherry fruit is tempered by floral notes and spice to create a dense, highly textured but polished wine.

2001 Exuberant yet nuanced rather than brutish, a higher than usual Merlot component gives this wine particular voluptuousness.

1991   Showing an austerity reminiscent of claret in its youth, this wine has blossomed to show a richer, more opulent, spicy side.

1988   Even more than two decades on, this was showing huge vigor and concentration, with a mineral finish and plenty still to come.

1984   Happily outlasting most Bordeaux from the same vintage, this beautifully balanced wine retains an attractive richness and warmth.

1981   Three decades on this wine was still vibrating with mineral character, purity, and superb balance.

1978   Showing a touch of fragility and sweetness now, this wine nevertheless retains a plushness and charm in its maturity.

1971   The vintage that saw Ridge shine in the 1976 "Judgment of Paris" showed its caliber when the same wines lined up thirty years on.

Dream vintage: 1970   Draper's first solo vintage and a testament to Monte Bello's considerable aging potential. This wine retains a more youthful spring in its step than some junior expressions and its 100 percent Cabernet Sauvignon composition lends a firm structure even after all these years.

SCARECROW

Boasting links to the golden age of the silver screen and
a past grape supplier to famous Napa wines, Scarecrow
represents a very modern generation of Californian icons.

A scruffy name for a smart wine, Scarecrow represents a tribute to the achievements of founder Bret Lopez's grandfather Joseph Judson Cohn. Born into poverty in New York to Russian emigrant parents, he moved west in time to catch the wave of Hollywood's Golden Age, ending up as chief of production at MGM with responsibility for many classic films such as *Ben-Hur* and *The Wizard of Oz*. It is the latter's scarecrow character, evoking in Lopez's view "a distinctly American agricultural icon and American optimism," that lends its name to this cult Napa Cabernet.

However, JJ Cohn's link to this wine runs deeper than simply giving his name to the estate he bought in 1943.

At a Glance

ADDRESS
PO Box 144
Rutherford, CA 94573, USA
Tel: +1 (707) 963-3361

PEOPLE
Bret Lopez (owner)
Celia Welch (winemaker)
Michael J. Wolf (vineyard manager)

SIZE
Ten hectares of vineyard, including
0.8 hectare of Cabernet vines
planted in 1945. Annual production
of Scarecrow ranges between four
hundred and eight hundred cases.

KEY WINES
Scarecrow
M. Etain

GRAPE VARIETIES
Cabernet Sauvignon
(100 percent of Scarecrow blend)
Petit Verdot

Encouraged to plant vines by John Daniel Jr., who at the time headed up neighboring property Inglenook, Cohn supplied grapes over time not just to this famous winery but to other big names such as Opus One. His fruit had strong appeal since JJ Cohn Estate boasts a small plot of Cabernet Sauvignon planted in 1945 (he had avoided a widespread switch to "better" rootstock, which turned out to be very susceptible to phylloxera). When Cohn died aged one hundred, Lopez bought his sisters out with the help of current Inglenook owner Francis Ford Coppola, who took most of the land. But Lopez's small parcel contained the old vines, a treasure that helped him to attract the winemaker Celia Welch. The first Scarecrow vintage came in 2003, followed in 2008 by a second wine, M. Etain—French for "Mr. Tin" or "Tin Man."

For those able to gain an allocation, this wine is in many ways a tidy metaphor for the American Dream.

NAVIGATING NAPA

Just thirty miles long, Napa Valley's eighteen thousand hectares of vineyard make this region about an eighth the size of Bordeaux in terms of plantings and account for around 4 percent of California's total wine production. This relatively modest scale hasn't stopped the region from cultivating a reputation as home to some of the world's top-quality wines, an image kickstarted by Napa's triumph in the 1976 "Judgment of Paris." As investment and winemakers subsequently flocked to this corner of northern California, in 1981 it became the state's first American Viticultural Area, today divided into sixteen official subregions.

Although Napa sees less of the cooling Pacific fog that is such a defining feature of Sonoma next door, there remains a diverse sweep of climatic influence between and even within different AVAs. One of the cooler regions is Los Carneros, where temperatures are kept in check by marine winds blowing through the Petaluma Gap. This makes it one of the few Napa AVAs where Pinot Noir can achieve truly elegant results. At the opposite end of the region in Calistoga AVA it is a much warmer story, with summer temperatures about 10 degrees Fahrenheit higher than in Los Carneros. Here you can find not only warmer-climate expressions of Cabernet Sauvignon but heat-loving grapes such as Petite Sirah. Somewhere in the middle, both geographically and climatically, is Rutherford AVA. Its western edge is milder with a higher proportion of gravelly/sandy soil that retains water well. In addition to Scarecrow, other top Rutherford producers include Inglenook, Joseph Phelps, Beaulieu Vineyard, Frog's Leap, and Caymus Vineyard.

TOP VINTAGES

With a decade of harvests in the bag, little has changed in the Scarecrow formula. Its top wine still comes from the oldest plots, which are separately vinified and matured in French barrels for a year before the final blend is created and undergoes a further ten months' barrel aging.

The following vintages of Scarecrow are particularly noteworthy:

2012 A long, even growing season resulted in a healthy crop that produced a wine full of spiced plum fruit and caramel oak notes.

2010 Its explosive fruit character does not mar this wine's wet stone minerality, enchanting perfume, structure, and long finish.

2007 A perfect score from Parker was echoed by other critics for this panoply of flavor, cooling mineral edge, and striking intensity.

2005 Rich and full-bodied, this wine was quick to show secondary elements, but critics remained confident in its ability to mature well.

2004 In only its second vintage Parker hailed this "staggeringly great wine" for its striking personality and balance.

Dream vintage: 2003 This debut vintage was warmly welcomed by critics, especially Parker, who noted its "sensational richness" and a distinctive character, qualities found in the wine's later vintages as well. At the time he suggested that the wine would thrive for "15–20 or more years," a prediction that those in possession of a bottle will soon be able to test.

SINE QUA NON

Anyone finding Napa and Sonoma a bit too straitlaced and predictable should cast their gaze down south to Sine Qua Non's Rhône-inspired shifting smorgasbord of blends.

For anyone laboring under the delusion that California's fine-wine scene is all about the Cabernets and Pinots of Napa and Sonoma, Sine Qua Non will come as something of a shock. In fact, this maverick outfit seems to delight in keeping its long waiting list of disciples on their toes, changing grape varieties, vineyards, names, and label design each year as owners Manfred and Elaine Krankl work with sites across the southern end of the Central Coast AVA.

If there is any unifying theme to this resolutely quixotic approach, then it would be a Rhône-inspired style, with Syrah a particular sweet spot. Indeed, it was four and a half barrels of a Syrah called Queen of Spades that kickstarted the Sine Qua Non story back in 1994, with the critical reception transforming this hobby into a full-time obsession.

Rather than allow success to pigeonhole their style, the duo have chosen to blend freely across the Rhône varietal spectrum. As in this French region, Syrah and Grenache tend to take the lead, but anything from Mourvèdre to Roussanne and Viognier could be brought in to play a supporting role. On top of these come other grapes such as Touriga Nacional, Petit Manseng, Graciano, and Petite Sirah, which, while falling outside the Rhône sphere, are seen as complementary partners.

At a Glance

ADDRESS
PO Box 1048
Oak View, CA 93022, USA
Tel: +1 (805) 649-8901

PEOPLE
Manfred and Elaine Krankl
(owners and winemakers)

SIZE
Grapes come from Sine Qua Non's own four vineyards located across the southern end of the Central Coast AVA, as well as two plots under contract. Total annual production is around 3,500 cases.

KEY WINES
The range varies across red, white, and rosé with each vintage, although Syrah and Grenache tend to play lead roles in the red blends. A sweet wine, "Mr. K," was produced in partnership with Austrian winemaker Alois Kracher until his death in 2007.

GRAPE VARIETIES
Syrah, Grenache, Mourvèdre, Roussanne, Marsanne, Viognier, Petit Manseng, Graciano, Petite Sirah, Touriga Nacional, Chardonnay

Far from alienating customers, this iconoclastic disregard for the "rules" of building a fine-wine brand has given each vintage the irresistible allure of a limited edition artwork. As Manfred Krankl once told the *Los Angeles Times*, "People buy Sine Qua Non. They don't seem to give a toot where it's from."

CENTRAL COAST

Stretching from San Francisco for three hundred miles right down toward Los Angeles, California's sprawling Central Coast AVA encapsulates a patchwork of subregions, each with its own character and strengths. To the north lie the fog-influenced AVAs of San Francisco Bay and Livermore Valley, the cool elevation of Santa Cruz Mountain, and then, moving inland, the Mediterranean climate of Santa Clara Valley. Stretching down the midsection of the California coast is Monterey County, home to forty-two different grape varieties but perhaps best known for the Pinot Noir and Chardonnay from its northern end, especially the Santa Lucia Highlands.

Drive on south down the old missionary route Highway 101 and you come to Paso Robles, home of the "Rhône Rangers" movement. Finally, at the southern edge of the Central Coast AVA lies Santa Barbara County. At this latitude you might expect a continuation of the Mediterranean grapes found in Paso Robles, as indeed is exemplified by Sine Qua Non's vineyard holdings around this region. However, the cooling combination of coastal fog and hills means that in certain places, most notably within the Santa Ynez Valley and Santa Rita Hills, Pinot Noir and Chardonnay can both thrive too—as highlighted so effectively in the film *Sideways*.

TOP VINTAGES

If the offbeat Sine Qua Non does have anything at all in common with the more conventional cult Cabernets of Napa, it must surely lie in the discernible influence of critic Robert Parker, whose early high scores heralded almost overnight demand for these wines. Indeed, the idiosyncratic blends produced each year by Sine Qua

Non have not stopped this winery from racking up more perfect Parker scores than all except Rhône giants Guigal and Chapoutier. It will be interesting to track the ongoing popularity of these favored producers as Parker nudges toward inevitable retirement. That said, his Californian successor Antonio Galloni also appears to be a Sine Qua Non fan, reporting, "The sheer drive for perfection and attention to detail at Sine Qua Non is something I have rarely witnessed anywhere else in the world."

The following expressions from Sine Qua Non are particularly noteworthy, all attracting 100 points from Parker:

2006 "A Shot In The Dark" Syrah; "In The Cross Hairs" Grenache

2005 "Atlantis Fe_2O_3-1A" Syrah/Grenache; "Mr. K The Straw Man" Marsanne; "The 17th Nail in My Cranium" Syrah

2004 "Ode to E" Grenache/Syrah; "Mr. K The Straw Man" Sémillon

2003 "The Inaugural" Syrah/Grenache

2002 "Just for the Love of It" Syrah

2000 "Suey" Roussanne Trockenbeerenauslese; "Incognito" Grenache

SPOTTSWOODE (SPOTTSWOODE ESTATE CABERNET SAUVIGNON)

Staying true to classically structured, elegant wines doesn't seem to have done Spottswoode any harm, with this Napa estate's style famously compared to Château Margaux.

Subtlety is not the first word that springs to mind when you think of Napa Cabernet. As many of its neighbors embraced a critic-backed trend for extended hang-time and expensive oak regimes from the 1990s onward, Spottswoode stayed loyal to old-fashioned values of elegance and restraint.

Is it too simplistic to attribute this attitude to the female team in charge at this St. Helena estate? The Novak family transformed Spottswoode from pre-Prohibition grape grower to full-fledged wine business when they bought the property in 1972 as a rural retreat in which to raise their children. After the sudden death of Jack Novak in 1977, his widow, Mary, took charge, selling fruit to nearby wineries until 1982 when, exactly one hundred years after the estate's creation, Spottswoode produced its first wine.

Since 1987, daughter Beth Novak has steered the family business, which was one of the first to adopt organic viticul-

At a Glance

ADDRESS
1902 Madrona Avenue
St. Helena, CA 94574, USA
Tel: +1 (707) 963-0134

PEOPLE
Novak family (owners)
Beth Novak Milliken (CEO)
Aron Weinkauf (winemaker and
vineyard manager)

SIZE
Just over forty acres of vineyard, planted
primarily with Cabernet Sauvignon.
Around four thousand cases of the
estate Cabernet Sauvignon blend are
produced each year.

KEY WINES
Spottswoode Estate Cabernet
Sauvignon
Spottswoode Sauvignon Blanc
Lyndenhurst Cabernet Sauvignon
Field Book Syrah (available to club
members only, made from fruit
grown in Paso Robles)

GRAPE VARIETIES
Cabernet Sauvignon (about 85 percent
of the estate flagship red)
Cabernet Franc (10 percent)
Petit Verdot (5 percent)
Sauvignon Blanc
Also, Syrah and Grenache,
both grown in Paso Robles

ture in California. Both the original winemaker Tony Soter and his

1997 successor, Rosemary Cakebread, focused firmly on ensuring the fruit expressed its origins, spending as much time in the vineyard as cellar. In 2002 the Lyndenhurst Cabernet Sauvignon arrived, an expression using fruit from the estate's younger vines. Since 2011 the winemaking baton has passed, apparently seamlessly, to Aron Weinkauf.

As a new generation of Californian producers swings the pendulum back toward wines that celebrate refreshment and site above power and winemaker signature, it is important to recognize operations such as Spottswoode that never deviated from this path.

ST. HELENA

While some producers in Napa prefer to promote themselves via their own brand or vineyard joined with the starry but vague association of this wider region, Spottswoode celebrates the individuality of St. Helena. Indeed, the Novak family played an important role in defining this AVA back in 1995.

Located toward the northern end of Napa territory, where the valley narrows between the Mayacamas and Vaca mountain ranges, this 3,600-hectare AVA is where the region's oldest winery was founded by Charles Krug back in 1861. While technically one of the warmer parts of Napa thanks to its sheltered position, certain areas of St. Helena (such as where Spottswoode is located) do enjoy a winning combination of cooling breezes and the gravelly alluvial soil that is so key to the Médoc's success. Alongside Spottswoode, other St. Helena producers to look out for include Corison Winery, Duckhorn Vineyards, and Beringer Vineyards.

TOP VINTAGES

In addition to sensitive winemaking and vineyard management, Spottswoode is able to achieve such finesse with its flagship Cabernet Sauvignon thanks to the cool air that regularly pours into the gap between the Mayacamas Range and Spring Mountain, where this vineyard is located. As other winemakers fight to keep alcohol levels in check, Spottswoode has maintained the steady 13 percent ABV that used to be so commonplace during Napa's early days.

The following vintages of Spottswoode Estate Cabernet Sauvignon are particularly noteworthy:

2012 "Close to a dream come true" is how the estate describes this vintage, whose silky tannins meld with bright, lingering cassis fruit.

2010 Parker gave this wine a perfect score, drawing a parallel with Château Margaux for its elegantly integrated flavor and structure.

2009 Firm tannins envelop a wine of great depth and muscularity, showing flavors of black currant, tar, and pencil shavings.

2007 A stellar year for Spottswoode, this sets power aside in favor of a floral, black-fruited character put together with real delicacy.

2005 One of this wine's bolder expressions, it explodes with cedar and dark fruit, but the presence of Cabernet Franc adds charm too.

2004 A decade on, this was showing beautiful balance that, for all its ready accessibility, looked set to propel the wine for another two.

2003 This warm vintage brought an enticing array of blueberries, spice, and floral character, backed by substantial texture and length.

2002 Another year that sparked Parker parallels with Margaux, this mixes a charmingly soft texture with pure fruit and great poise.

1994   Enchanting notes of cassis, pencil shavings, and spice show no shortage of flavor, all housed in a polished, elegant framework.

1989   Surprisingly good after rain hit a big crop, this impressed with its saline edge, ripe fruit, and subtle, savory finish.

Dream vintage: 1985   This third vintage from the estate put Spottswoode on the wine map when it was included in the *Wine Spectator*'s Top 100 wines. Critics were quick to draw favorable comparisons with serious claret and, like good Bordeaux, this wine has continued to reward drinkers with an ever more expressive, sophisticated personality as it has matured along a beautifully balanced keel.

STAG'S LEAP (CASK 23)

Having played a legendary role in not just Californian but American history, this estate is now carving out a new chapter in the hands of one of the world's great wine names.

It's difficult to imagine now, but back in 1970 when Warren Winiarski founded Stag's Leap Wine Cellars, Napa Valley still bore the scars of Prohibition. The wine industry here had been decimated, but from the mid-1960s it began to revive, although few would have guessed this region could reach the international heights of today. Many played a role in this renaissance, but Stag's Leap created a major boost when its SLV Cabernet Sauvignon 1973, the estate's second vintage and made from vines just three years old, took first place over established greats such as Mouton Rothschild and Haut-Brion in the famous 1976 "Judgment of Paris." The result resonated far beyond the wine trade, with a bottle of the giant-slaying wine selected for inclusion in the Smithsonian's National Museum of American History. Having won further critical acclaim for its Cask 23 Cabernet Sauvignon, in 1986 Stag's Leap took another big step when Nathan Fay, who had sold Winiarski the original SLV plot, offered him the adjacent vineyard too. Planted in 1961, this oldest Cabernet vineyard in the district was renamed Fay in his honor.

Another watershed year for Stag's Leap was 2007, when Winiarski decided to step back from the running of the estate. His search for

At a Glance

ADDRESS
5766 Silverado Trail
Napa, CA 94558, USA
Tel: +1 (707) 944-2020

PEOPLE
Piero Antinori and Ted Baseler
(co-owners)
Marcus Notaro (winemaker)

SIZE
Forty hectares, split between the SLV and Fay vineyards. The fifty-two-hectare Arcadia vineyard in Coombsville is still owned by the Winiarski family but supplies grapes on contract. Production of Cask 23 is around 1,500 cases.

KEY WINES
Cask 23, SLV, and Fay Cabernet Sauvignons are this estate's top wines, along with its Arcadia Vineyard Chardonnay. Stag's Leap also produces the following using fruit from across Napa Valley: Artemis Cabernet Sauvignon, Merlot, Karia Chardonnay, Aveta Sauvignon Blanc, and Rancho Chimiles Sauvignon Blanc.

GRAPE VARIETIES
Cabernet Sauvignon
(100 percent of Cask 23)
Also: Petit Verdot, Chardonnay,
Merlot, and Sauvignon Blanc

a suitable custodian led him to approach none other than Marchese

Piero Antinori, the man behind Tignanello. He took on the challenge in partnership with Ted Baseler of Washington State's Chateau Ste. Michelle. Followers of this legendary estate will be eyeing the impact of winemaker Marcus Notaro, appointed in 2013, on the Stag's Leap success story.

A TOP TRIO

Stag's Leap SLV may have been this estate's first wine and the one that catapulted it onto the world map, but that same vineyard soon gave rise to a second expression: Cask 23. In 1974, consulting winemaker André Tchelistcheff identified one barrel, number 23, whose wine showed a particularly distinct and exciting character, so he suggested that it should be bottled separately. Following the 1986 acquisition of Fay vineyard, selected blocks were incorporated into the Cask 23 blend. The result is a collector's favorite that combines the signature perfume seen in Fay's own single-vineyard Cabernet Sauvignon with the more structured, mineral elements of SLV.

TOP VINTAGES

Bordeaux lovers have often found Stag's Leap to provide an ideal bridge between Napa and the Médoc. Ripe but steering well clear of the port-like tendency that can characterize some blockbuster Californian Cabernets, this wine is not afraid to show some tannin and rewards those with the patience to hide it away in the cellar.

The following vintages of Cask 23 are particularly noteworthy:

2009 Despite the relatively mild growing season, this wine is full of richness, but with plenty of controlling structure and texture.

2008 A vintage that suggested the Antinori touch marked a revival for this estate, this elegantly textured wine is strong but refined.

2007 Showing plenty of this estate's characteristic restraint, there's nevertheless plenty of black currant, plum, and spicy pleasure here.

1997 Ripe, but savory rather than sweet in style, there's a subtlety and restraint here to give this wine a serious, ageworthy edge.

1994 A cool harvest period brought bright acidity to match this wine's

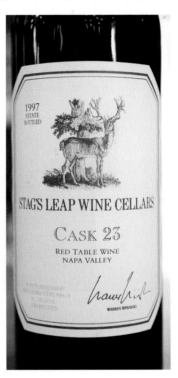

hallmark firm tannins, with supple fruit to balance.

1992 Succulent and graceful, this has been maturing with great style to reveal an array of earthy, tobacco, and roasted herb flavor.

1991 One of the top-rated expressions of this wine to date, this was flattering in youth but has matured gracefully.

Dream vintage: 1985 Made a year before Fay vineyard joined its blend, this was hailed as a star performer from Napa in this vintage. A firm tannin structure made this wine relatively slow to show off its full charm, which gradually emerged to show off a compelling spectrum of exotic perfume and spicy fruit flavors. Although some other top Cask 23 expressions such as 1979 or even the inaugural 1974 may well still have pleasure to offer, this vintage looked particularly well poised to age with flair.

EGON MÜLLER
(SCHARZHOFBERGER AUSLESE)

Tucked away up the Mosel's Saar tributary, Egon Müller and his Scharzhofberg vineyard produce some of the region's most famous and consistently stellar wines.

Just across the border from both France and Luxembourg, the Saar region has formed part of various kingdoms and provinces before being absorbed as part of a newly created German Empire in the late nineteenth century. Indeed, it was from the French Republic that the Scharzhof estate was originally acquired in 1797 by Jean-Jacques Koch, although there are believed to have been vines on the famous Scharzhofberg since Roman times.

Following Koch's death, the property was split among his seven children. One of these, Elisabeth, married a man named Felix Müller, and the couple steadily managed to double the size of

At a Glance

ADDRESS
Scharzhof
D-54459 Wiltingen, Germany
Tel: +49 (0)6501 17232

PEOPLE
Egon Müller IV (owner)

SIZE
Around sixteen hectares in the Saar, including the 8.5-hectare Scharzhofberg vineyard.

KEY WINES
A range of styles, all Riesling, come from the following vineyards: Scharzhofberg, Wiltinger Braune Kupp, Saarburger Antoniusbrunnen, Wawerner Jesuitengarten, Oberemmeler Rosenberg, Wiltinger Braunfels, Wiltinger Kupp

GRAPE VARIETIES
Riesling

their holdings. It was their son Egon Müller who really began to build the reputation that is today preserved by his direct descendant, the fourth consecutive Egon Müller to hold the reins at this widely admired German producer. The intervening period saw the estate survive difficult war years, followed by the 1954 acquisition of a nearby estate called Le Gallais. However, it is the range of styles, from Kabinett right through to the rare Trockenbeerenauslese made on the gray shale of the family's Scharzhofberg vineyard, that is its most famous. Many of these Riesling vines date from the nineteenth century and yields across the board are low, while winemaking shows minimal intervention. Lest there be any doubt about where his focus lies, Müller explains: "One hundred percent of the quality of a wine is generated in the vineyard. It is impossible to reach even 101 percent in the cellars but it is a great achievement to pack the full potential of the vines into a bottle."

MOSEL-SAAR-RUWER

A famous tributary of the mighty Rhine River, the Mosel and its even smaller offshoots the Saar and Ruwer help to produce some of the most inimitable white wines in the world. Few places in the world offer such an obvious demonstration of the impact of terroir—from the vines perching goatlike on steep slopes to the different exposures created by the meandering river, the strikingly mineral flavor given to the wines by these slate soils, and the challenge of ripening grapes in such a marginal northern European climate.

This is not a cheap place to produce wine, and as elsewhere in Germany the Mosel suffered from a quality slide during the 1960s and 1970s. While varieties such as Müller-Thurgau and Elbling are now common, the key to exciting quality is Riesling. Although the sweetest styles often command prices to match their rarity, there is often exceptional value to be found in the Kabinett and Spätlese categories.

Today most of the valley's top producers and famous sites—as in Burgundy, vineyard ownership may be divided among many estates—lie in the Mittelmosel region between Bernkastel and Enkirch, although upstream areas such as Mühlheim and Brauneberg also offer plenty to excite.

Smaller, higher, and cooler are the Saar and Ruwer valleys, which flow into the Mosel near the historic Roman town of Trier.

Among the many names to look out for across these three valleys are Van Volxem, Karthäuserhof, Fritz Haag, JJ Prüm, Zilliken, von Hövel, Willi Schäfer, Max Ferd. Richter, and St. Urbans-Hof.

TOP VINTAGES

While Egon Müller's Scharzhofberger Trockenbeerenauslese is a true jewel of the wine world, it would be a shame to overlook the same vineyard's other superlative—not to mention significantly cheaper and more widely available—styles. Offering exciting appeal both in its accessible youth and impressive old age, the Auslese is perhaps especially worthy of attention.

The following vintages of Egon Müller Scharzhofberger Riesling Auslese are particularly noteworthy:

2010 A year of intense concentration and small quantities, this is a soaring masterpiece of candied peach, spice, and subtle minerality.

2005 Golden and smoky with candied fruit, spice, and lemon zest, this very complete wine is built for the long term.

2003 A thrilling combination of opulence with huge tension, this warm year brought ripe charm but the site added finesse.

1999 A superb vintage for Müller, his wines this year combine ripeness with exciting complexity and vibrant mineral tones.

1994 A difficult vintage with very variable quality across the region, but the best sites and producers achieved superb results.

1993 Another tricky year but Müller was clearly more than satisfied with the end result, picking this out as a great year for his Auslese.

1990 A bumper year for botrytis, this vintage produced some great sweet wines with searing acidity setting this up for the long term.

1989 Some fabulously profound wines came out of the Mosel this year, and Müller's Auslese proved a real standout.

1983   Not a big botrytis year, but with maturity this is showing enticing flavors of tarte Tatin, roses, and a vibratingly alive finish.

1976   This has evolved well beyond familiar mature Riesling flavors into the exotic territory of mint and toffee with a deep color.

1959   Egon Müller's birth year proved exciting on the wine front too. This is almost dry now with huge depth and freshness.

Dream vintage: 1949   Dark in color now, this wine still shows an astonishing burst of fruit and acidity. Although there are telltale signs of gentle decay that one might expect after so many decades, this wine retains an energetic thread and lingering flavor that are a real testament to the quality of this producer.

WEINGUT JOHANN JOSEF PRÜM (WEHLENER SONNENUHR TROCKENBEERENAUSLESE)

This star of the Mosel has an enviable and consistent track record of excellence, delighting Riesling fans with its notably long-lived wines, including some especially rare treasures.

Among the many top-quality estates that line the winding Mosel River, JJ Prüm is often one of the first names to fall from a Riesling lover's lips. Although the Prüm family can trace its wine-making links with this scenic corner of Germany back to the twelfth century, the JJ Prüm estate was created relatively recently in 1911 when Johann Josef took his share of the family inheritance. His brother Sebastian Alois took another slice of the large estate to create neighboring producer Weingut SA Prüm.

The JJ arm saw its reputation flourish during the 1930s and 1940s under the management of Johann Josef's son, also named Sebastian. Today Sebastian's son Dr. Manfred Prüm creates thrilling expressions of Mosel Riesling in partnership with his daughter Dr. Katharina Prüm. The family's twenty-two hectares of vineyard span the Mittelmosel's top sites, reaching across the famous villages of Wehlen, Graach, Zeltingen, and the estate's Bernkastel base.

Although high-quality dry styles do exist here, the Mosel is celebrated for its vertiginous vineyards' sweet expressions of Riesling.

At a Glance

ADDRESS
Uferallee 19
D-54470 Bernkastel-Wehlen, Germany
Tel: +49 (0)6531 3091

PEOPLE
Dr. Manfred Prüm and Dr. Katharina Prüm (owners)

SIZE
Twenty-two hectares spread across the Mittelmosel, with a total annual production of ten to thirteen thousand cases.

KEY WINES
A range of styles ranging across Kabinett, Spätlese, Auslese, Beerenauslese, Eiswein, and Trockenbeerenauslese from several vineyards, most notably: Wehlener Sonnenuhr, Zeltinger Sonnenuhr, Graacher Himmelreich, Graacher Domprobst, Bernkasteler Lay, Bernkasteler Badstube, and Bernkasteler Bratenhöfchen

GRAPE VARIETIES
Riesling (95 percent of production)
Optima (a Riesling/Silvaner/Müller-Thurgau cross)

Here sugar and acidity collide with pure fruit and a cool mineral edge from the local slate to create highly original wines of thrilling energy, tension, and age-worthiness. A century ago, top Mosel wines commanded prices on a par with, or even exceeding, Médoc first growths, but Germany's disastrous slide downmarket in the 1960s and 1970s alienated a generation of consumers. Even today, these wines' sweet profile can perturb the uninitiated, but houses such as JJ Prüm consistently show off the Mosel at its most sublime.

SWEET SENSATION

Even within the Mosel's sweet wine specialism there remains a broad spectrum of styles to explore. Although technically based on ripeness level rather than sweetness, Germany's stylistic spectrum, which runs from Kabinett at the lightest end through to Spätlese, Auslese, Beerenauslese, Eiswein, and Trockenbeerenauslese, offers a useful guide of what to expect.

Both Kabinett and Spätlese can offer an attractive aperitif alternative to Champagne, while also providing a useful match for spicy dishes or even game, where their sweet fruit is complementary in a similar way to apple sauce or red currant jelly.

From Auslese upward it may be best to consider a dessert pairing such as a fruit tart. However, once these wines reach several decades of maturity, then it's often best to savor their complexity without food—or maybe try the German tradition of serving old Auslese with wild boar or venison ragù and mushrooms.

TOP VINTAGES

Translated as "dried berry selection," Trockenbeerenauslese (or TBA) is a style only possible in the best years, when fog and sun mix in the perfect combination to create ripe grapes affected by botrytis. As in Sauternes, the shriveled grapes soar in concentration and will be harvested berry by berry in the middle of winter from the Mosel's vineyards of staggering steepness. The rarity, longevity, and sheer mouthwatering intensity of these wines mean that they often attract high prices at auction. Indeed, JJ Prüm's Wehlener Sonnenuhr TBA recently appeared alongside the likes of Leflaive Montrachet and Henri Jayer Cros Parantoux in a list of the world's most expensive wines. It will easily outlive most of them.

Such is the scarcity of this wine that critical reviews are even rarer, although mature styles inevitably attract perfect scores. The following vintages of JJ Prüm Wehlener Sonnenuhr Riesling Trockenbeerenauslese are worth looking out for at specialized wine merchants or at auction: 2000, 1989, 1976, 1971, 1959, 1949, and 1938.

ALLEGRINI
(AMARONE CLASSICO)

Valpolicella and its specialty style Amarone are by no means of uniformly high quality, but producers such as Allegrini make these original wines well worth discovering.

The pale red wines of Valpolicella rarely arouse much excitement, but where this northern Italian region has managed to grab the world's attention is with its Amarone. In the wrong hands this style can be offputtingly alcoholic and heavy, but Allegrini offers a prime example of how to inject freshness and nuance. While the roots of Amarone as an officially recognized, protected style are relatively shallow, Allegrini has been making wine in this part of the Veneto since the sixteenth century.

It was Giovanni Allegrini who catapulted the estate into the modern company of today, improving the vineyards and winery, working to gain official recognition for Valpolicella's best sites, and building a market for his wines in Italy and farther afield. Following the untimely death of their father in 1983, Giovanni's children continued his work. Sadly, vineyard manager Walter Allegrini also died young, but his brother Franco and sister Marilisa head the winemaking and marketing divisions.

Amarone represents just one part of a broad portfolio, whose other highlights include a focus on single-vineyard wines, rare in

At a Glance

ADDRESS
Via Giare 9-11
37022 Fumane Valpolicella, Italy
Tel: +39 (0)45 6832011

PEOPLE
Franco Allegrini (winemaker)

SIZE
Ninety hectares of vineyard and a total annual production of around eighty-three thousand cases. Of this, Amarone accounts for about ten thousand cases.

KEY WINES
Recioto della Valpolicella Classico
Giovanni Allegrini
Amarone della Valpolicella Classico
La Poja
La Grola
Palazzo della Torre
Valpolicella
Soave

GRAPE VARIETIES
Corvina (80 percent of the Amarone blend)
Rondinella (15 percent)
Oseleta (5 percent)
Corvinone
Syrah
Sangiovese
Garganega
Chardonnay

this region. These include La Poja, a 2.65-hectare parcel within the cru of La Grola, where the region's star grape variety Corvina can

really shine. However, Allegrini extends its focus to foreign grapes too, most notably the Syrah that is also cultivated in a section of this prime La Grola site. Also worth looking out for is Allegrini's version of another Valpolicella specialty, the sweet Recioto, which is named in honor of Giovanni, who did so much for both the estate and its region.

THE CREATION OF AMARONE

Using dried grapes to make wine is nothing new: The Romans used it as a method to inject concentration, making this an attractive technique for those wishing to create a more serious alternative to the light reds that characterize Valpolicella. Meaning "bitter," to distinguish it from the sweet Recioto style made in a similar way, Amarone had long been made as a local curiosity but received official DOC status in 1968, upgraded to DOCG in 2010. This recognition encouraged a boom in Amarone production, but standards slipped, with too many clumsy or volatile examples being made. The best styles invariably come from the hilly regions where Amarone was originally produced. In order to distinguish their high-quality ethos, a group called "Amarone Families" was created, which includes top houses such as Allegrini, Masi, Tommasi, and Tedeschi. Within the regulations, production methods can vary, but at Allegrini the grapes are dried for between three and four months—around double the period laid down by DOC regulations. This process sees the bunches lose almost half their weight, resulting in concentrated juice, intensified flavor, and a firm tannin structure from such prolonged skin contact. After a slow fermentation, which creates a dry wine of around 16 percent ABV, the result is then matured for eighteen months in oak before the final blend is put together and aged a further seven months. A further period of bottle aging takes place before the wine is eventually released onto the market.

TOP VINTAGES

When the balance of Amarone is in tune, the famous richness of this style should be just one of several complementary elements. At their best these are wines built to last at least twenty years.

The following vintages of Allegrini Amarone are particularly noteworthy:

2010 An opulent burst of plum, vanilla, spice, and herbs encased with velvet tannins, this shows real intensity and persistence.

2004 Dark and cedary with fruitcake flavors but very much savory in style; despite its potency this retains a vital restraint and elegance.

2001 Rich, spicy, and dark, this brings notes of dried fruit but also a purity and acidity to cut through the rich, heady expression.

1998 Powerful and meaty, age is adding a leathery note to the dark cherry fruit. Smooth and rich, it opens considerably in the glass.

1990 A beautifully balanced mix of opulent, ripe fruit framed by silky tannins and increasing complexity as it evolves with age.

Dream vintage: 1988 For those looking to understand Amarone, this mature example is a thrilling place to start. Perhaps not so rich as the 1990, this allows more space for subtler notes to emerge in a package that shows a finesse and length that are absent from more overblown examples of this intriguing Italian specialty.

MARCHESI ANTINORI
(TIGNANELLO)

Many producers boast of blending tradition with innovation, but few can match Antinori's claim to over eight hundred years of history and a role in creating a radical new wine genre.

The Antinori family is no stranger to shaping history. As far back as the fourteenth century they enjoyed close ties to that great political and cultural Renaissance dynasty the Medicis. Antinori's wine roots run deep too, with Giovanni di Piero Antinori joining the Florence Winemakers Guild in 1385. By the eighteenth century the family was exporting their wine, and in 1850 they added a collection of properties in Chianti Classico, including the estate that would later produce the most famous flagship of all their domains, Tignanello.

As Europe's wine industry began to modernize during the 1960s, Piero Antinori formalized his estates' vineyard and viticultural practices, installing temperature-controlled stainless steel tanks in the winery. It all paved the way for the 1971 creation of Tignanello, a wine inspired by the creation of fellow Tuscan tear-away Sassicaia three years earlier. These wines broke the mold: First, they blended the local Sangiovese with Bordeaux varieties, using no white grapes (as the use of which was accepted practice

At a Glance

ADDRESS
Via Cassia per Siena, 133
Bargino 50026, Italy
Tel: +39 (0)55 23595

PEOPLE
Marchese Piero Antinori (president)
Albiera, Alessia, and Allegra Antinori
(vice-presidents)

SIZE
Six estates across Tuscany and Umbria: Tenuta Tignanello (of which 127 hectares are planted with vines), Pèppoli (50 hectares), Badia a Passignano (56 hectares), Castello della Sala (140 hectares), Pian delle Vigne (65 hectares), Tenuta Guado al Tasso (300 hectares)

KEY WINES
Chianti: Tignanello, Solaia, Marchese Antinori, Pèppoli, Badia a Passignano
Umbria: Cervaro della Sala
Brunello di Montalcino:
Pian delle Vigne
Bolgheri: Guado al Tasso

GRAPE VARIETIES
Sangiovese (80 percent of Tignanello), Cabernet Sauvignon (15 percent), Cabernet Franc (5 percent). Also: Syrah, Merlot, Sémillon, Pinot Nero, Sauvignon Blanc, Riesling, Chardonnay, Grechetto, Traminer, Viognier, Procanico

226

at the time); second, they were matured in new French *barriques* rather than the traditional larger Slavonian *botti*. This iconoclastic

mind-set meant that despite its quality, Tignanello was classified as a lowly *vino da tavola,* later upgraded marginally to IGT Toscana. The same applied to Solaia, a Cabernet Sauvignon–led wine that arrived in 1978, and then Cervaro, a top-end Chardonnay-led Umbrian white that was created in 1985. Today that upstart "Super Tuscan" movement kickstarted by Tignanello has gained pace and catapulted its region onto the fine-wine map.

CLASSIFYING CHIANTI

Anyone trying to get their head around the complex, strict system that governs Chianti wine production will start to see why the Super Tuscan movement looked so appealing. Both Chianti and its subregion Chianti Classico claim Italy's most prestigious label of DOCG—Denominazione di Origine Controllata e Garantita; however, Chianti Classico is widely viewed as the more consistent and higher quality. Even by European standards, the rules here are complex: Everything from yield to alcohol and acidity levels, grape varieties, time in barrel, and bottle maturation is subject to strict regulation. After the Super Tuscans decided—correctly as it turned out—that they could gain greater prestige and prices by breaking these rules, the system adapted slightly to allow other producers more leeway. Local variety Sangiovese must still play a dominant role, but Merlot, Syrah, and Cabernet Sauvignon are now also permitted. Another major development occurred in 2014 with the ratification of a new top tier for Chianti Classico: Gran Selezione. Designed to allow producers to single out particularly exciting vineyard plots, early signs suggest it has been a popular development and a further boost for the prestige of Chianti wine. That said, nothing can touch the top Super Tuscan names for glamour and international appeal.

TOP VINTAGES

Since 1982 Tignanello has settled down to a trio of varieties, typically 80 percent Sangiovese with the remainder made up of Cabernet Sauvignon and Cabernet Franc. The wine is produced from fifty-seven hectares within the Tenuta Tignanello estate, lying right next to the vineyards responsible for Solaia, where Cabernet Sauvignon plays the dominant role instead. Only produced in the best years, no Tignanello was made in 2002, 1992, 1984, 1976, and 1972–74 inclusive.

The following vintages of Tignanello are particularly noteworthy:

2010 Seductive and silky, yet still firm, the sour cherry tang of Sangiovese offers a neat balance to the velvet opulence of this wine.

2008 A standout wine from this vintage, featuring understated dark fruit softly intertwined with licorice, smoke, and tobacco.

2007 A ripe, muscular expression of Tignanello, full of warmth and richness, but clinging onto that vital dash of acidity and structure.

2004 "A modern day classic," said the *Wine Advocate*'s Antonio Galloni of this wine's vibrant cherry fruit, spice, and silky texture.

2001   A wine for those who like Bordeaux from riper vintages, the Cabernet influence shows strongly in this well-balanced wine.

1999   A warm September this year offered ideal ripening conditions that translated into an attractive, plummy, complete wine.

Dream vintage: 1985   For those curious to try older vintages of Tignanello, this looks a safe choice, although expect it to be very much into its tertiary phase. Critics praised this wine for its understated but elegantly poised style that was maturing with great cherry freshness and poise.

GAJA (BARBARESCO)

In many parts of the world there would be nothing radical in Angelo Gaja's winemaking approach, but in conservative Piedmont his ideas sparked controversy—and admiration.

Gaja and Giacosa may sit together at the pinnacle of Piedmont's wine hierarchy, but their approach could hardly be more different. In contrast to the staunchly traditionalist Bruno Giacosa, Angelo Gaja has forged a provocatively modern path, which in turn has inspired many of his neighbors and done much to shape the region we see today.

The Gaja family has been making wine in this northwestern corner of Italy since the 1850s. Even at this early stage there were signs that the producer was unafraid to break with convention: While few wineries in the region did their own bottling until the 1960s, by the end of the nineteenth century Gaja was already sending its bottled wine to Italian troops based in Abyssinia (modern-day Ethiopia). The period after World War II saw Giovanni Gaja lay the foundations for the prestige of the estate today, buying a large slice of Barbaresco and raising prices to rein-

At a Glance

ADDRESS
Via Torino, 18
12050 Barbaresco, Italy
Tel: +39 (0)1736 35158

PEOPLE
Angelo Gaja and Gaia Gaja (owners)
Guido Rivella (enologist)

SIZE
Around one hundred hectares of vineyard across Barbaresco and Barolo, producing an average annual total of thirty thousand cases.

KEY WINES
Gaia Barbaresco DOCG
Barbaresco single vineyards: Costa Russi, Sori San Lorenzo, Sorì Tildìn
Barolo single vineyard: Sperss, Conteisa, Dagromis
Langhe DOC (made from international varieties): Alteni di Brassica, Darmagi, Gaia & Rey, Sito Moresco, Rossj-Bass

GRAPE VARIETIES
Nebbiolo (100 percent of Gaja's flagship Barbaresco)
Barbera (a small proportion of the single-vineyard blends)
Cabernet Sauvignon
Cabernet Franc
Merlot
Chardonnay
Sauvignon Blanc

force the image of these wines from a region that was still relatively unknown. However, it was when son Angelo joined the business in 1961 that the biggest Gaja transformation began. Despite the reservations of Giovanni and many others, Angelo brought in a raft of new practices, ranging from green harvest and a focus on single-

vineyard expressions to the use of malolactic fermentation and smaller French *barriques*. Angelo also raised eyebrows by introducing foreign varieties such as Sauvignon Blanc, Cabernet Sauvignon, and Chardonnay as part of his mission to bring the eyes of the world to Piedmont. Whatever you think of his methods, he has certainly succeeded in considerable style.

GAJA BEYOND PIEDMONT

Given the strong influence of other regions' winemaking techniques on his Piedmont wines, it was hardly surprising that Angelo

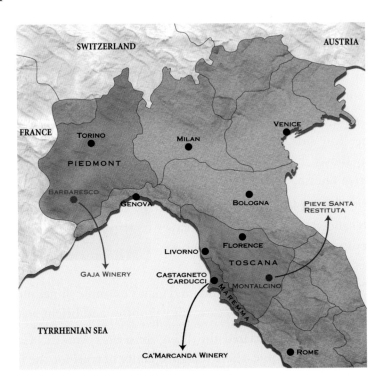

Gaja would eventually embark on his own projects farther afield. In 1994 he made his first move, acquiring the sixteen-hectare Pieve Santa Restituta in Montalcino. From these Sangiovese vineyards Gaja produces a collection of Brunello di Montalcino wines. This Tuscan presence expanded in 1996 with the purchase of a second property, Ca'Marcanda, this time in Bolgheri. Its one hundred hectares of vineyard embrace the region's Super Tuscan style, which sits so well with Gaja's use of Bordeaux varieties in Piedmont.

TOP VINTAGES

Gaja's flagship Barbaresco DOCG has been produced by the family from the very beginning, but its modern incarnation displays all the polish and richness that Angelo's once controversial—but now widely emulated—techniques aimed to achieve with Nebbiolo. Using entirely estate-grown grapes since 1961, Gaja Barbaresco draws on fourteen vineyards within this region.

The following vintages of Gaja Barbaresco are particularly noteworthy:

2011   A warm year produced accessible Nebbiolo of great perfume and elegant tannins, with Gaja adding great complexity to this mix.

2010   Wet weather left some wines on the lean side, but not this one, which shows huge personality and seductive finesse.

2006   Set for a long life, this beautifully balanced wine shows off increasing depth and intensity as it opens in the glass.

2004   A good year for Piedmont, and Gaja's example shines out with a heady perfume, dense structure, silky tannins, and bright acidity.

2001   "Gorgeous," declared the *Wine Advocate*'s Antonio Galloni. As mature notes emerge, there remains plenty of fruit for the future.

2000   From a run of good vintages for Piedmont, this wine is built for the long term and was declared a "must-have" by *Wine Spectator*.

1990   Exotic and spicy on the nose, this offers great intensity of fruit combined with the structure to ensure a long drinking window.

1989   Another great vintage for Piedmont, this wine is now showing its full, alluring spectrum of fruit, smoke, spice, and rose petals.

1978   Now autumnal in character, this is full of savory olive and balsamic notes encased in soft tannins and a fresh seam of acidity.

1974   Full of earthy tobacco and layers of mulberry fruit, this is another Gaja wine standing the test of time with considerable style.

Dream vintage: 1961   A pivotal year that saw Angelo join the family business and a change in policy to using only estate-grown grapes. Clearly a good vintage for Piedmont as it was in many other parts of Europe, this wine has retained not just its freshness but plenty of charm too. Tracking down a bottle may be difficult, however, as most of the production was sold to a local restaurant.

BRUNO GIACOSA
(LE ROCCHE DEL FALLETTO)

*Notoriously fastidious, Bruno Giacosa makes a heady array
of wines that have helped draw the world's attention to the
delights hidden within the Alpine foothills of Piedmont.*

As the wines of Piedmont have steadily amassed an ever-growing fan club, Giacosa is a name that stands out for perfectionism.

Born in 1929, Bruno Giacosa is the third generation to head his family business. Having built a network of quality-focused growers boasting vineyards in excellent sites, it was Giacosa together with Gaja who can take much of the credit for putting Barolo and Barbaresco on the world wine map during the 1960s.

This attention to detail saw Giacosa build a collection of his growers' top single-vineyard expressions. First made in 1964, his Barbaresco Santo Stefano—a vineyard in the family's home village of Neive—led the way. This reputation for being meticulous comes with a very traditional ethos. Technology is kept to a minimum and, despite a shift by many peers to *barriques*, Giacosa has remained unfaltering his in loyalty to the region's five-thousand-liter *botti*.

Despite the care lavished on these wines, Giacosa is also famous for his insistence on declassifying any that fail to meet his high standards. This has led to disappointment for many followers, even in highly regarded vintages such as 2006 and 2010. The former

At a Glance

ADDRESS
Via XX Settembre, 52
Neive, Italy
Tel: +39 (0)173 67027

PEOPLE
Bruno and Bruna Giacosa
(father and daughter, owners)
Francesco Versio (winemaker)

SIZE
About twenty hectares of vineyard
in Barbaresco and Barolo, as well
as long-term grower contracts. Total
production is around thirty-five
thousand cases per year.

KEY WINES
Barbaresco: Santo Stefano di Neive
(ceased in 2011), Asili
Barolo: Falletto, Le Rocche del Falletto

GRAPE VARIETIES
Nebbiolo (100 percent
of Santo Stefano)
Barbera
Dolcetto
Arneis
Pinot Noir (for Giacosa's
Spumante Extra Brut)

quality shortfall was partly explained by the major stroke Bruno suffered that year. Today daughter Bruna handles most of the estate's management.

Since 1996, Giacosa has split labeling into wine made from estate-grown fruit (Azienda Agricola Falletto di Bruno Giacosa) and bought-in grapes (Casa Vinicola Bruno Giacosa). With a growing focus on estate-grown fruit, 2011 was the last vintage of Giacosa Santo Stefano.

THE BURGUNDY CONNECTION

Giacosa's focus on single-vineyard wines ties in with the frequent comparisons between Piedmont and Burgundy. In few other regions do you find such a marked difference between neighboring plots of land. The most prestigious vineyards lie in Barolo and Barbaresco, located five miles apart on either side of the town of Alba. With such

variety of altitude and exposition, not to mention winemaking approach, it is difficult to generalize with any accuracy on the distinction between wines from these two regions. If anything, the smaller Barbaresco area tends to be associated with lighter expressions of the Nebbiolo grape, which may mature more quickly. That's very much a relative notion, however: Those without the patience to wait at least ten years may wish to turn their attention to the less "noble" but very appealing, gastronomic wines made from Piedmont's Barbera and Dolcetto grape varieties.

TOP VINTAGES

The fact that Giacosa's Santo Stefano (which adds a Riserva in its best years) ceased production in 2011 looks set to add to its desirability on the secondary market. It will also allow a greater share of the spotlight to shine on the domaine's Barolo flagship, Le Rocche del Falletto, which is awarded a Riserva tag in top years.

The following vintages of Le Rocche del Falletto are particularly noteworthy:

2008   This Riserva captures the mysterious essence of Piedmont Nebbiolo with its pale crimson color, yet brooding richness.

2007   Another Riserva, another exciting wine, whose dense array of leather, licorice, and rose petals builds to an impressive crescendo.

2005   A firmly structured wine of great density that blossoms in the glass to reveal dark red fruit, truffle, and spice character.

2004   "Off the charts," declared Parker of this "sensual," charismatic Riserva expression from a great, if small, vintage for Piedmont.

2001   A Riserva style that was initially imposing but then retreated into its shell. Patient Barolo lovers are promised a treat in store.

2000   "This is the Romanée Conti of Barolo," declared the *Wine Spectator* of this dazzling, velvety, endlessly unfurling Riserva.

Dream vintage: 1999   It may not have attracted the Riserva tag, but this early expression of Le Rocche del Falletto alerted critics to a bright star on the Barolo horizon. Initially less opulent than some of its neighboring vintages, this classically structured wine gradually draws the drinker in with a luxurious display of sweet-scented fruit.

TENUTA SAN GUIDO
(SASSICAIA)

Without the pioneering vision behind Sassicaia, which brought Bordeaux magic to the humble Maremma, it is hard to imagine the Super Tuscan success story ever taking off.

THE TASTING ROOM.

Sassicaia is the story of a man from Piedmont who fell in love with Bordeaux wine and discovered an ideal home for its Cabernet grapes in Tuscany. At his wife's Tenuta San Guido estate, located on the Tuscan coast, Marchese Mario Incisa della Rocchetta found the maritime climate and gravelly terrain that led him to break with local tradition in the 1940s by planting Cabernet Sauvignon—grafted from Lafite vines, no less.

This wine may have sowed the early seeds for what would become the Super Tuscan movement, but for the first two decades Sassicaia, whose name means "place of many stones," was enjoyed only by family and friends. Eventually, however, urged on by Piero Antinori,

At a Glance

ADDRESS
Loc. Le Capanne No. 27
57022 Bolgheri, Italy
Tel: +39 (0)5657 62003

PEOPLE
Nicolò Incisa della Rocchetta (owner)
Sebastiano Rosa (technical director)

SIZE
Five thousand hectare estate, of which around ninety hectares are planted with vineyards. Today Sassicaia accounts for around 60 percent of production, with an estimated annual output of fifteen thousand cases.

KEY WINES
Sassicaia
Guidalberto (since 2000)
Le Difese (since 2003)

GRAPE VARIETIES
Cabernet Sauvignon (85 percent of Sassicaia blend)
Cabernet Franc (15 percent)
Also, Merlot and Sangiovese, which are used in Guidalberto and Le Difese.

who had married into the same family, Mario was persuaded to sell his wine for the first time in 1968 at the modest price of twenty-five cents per liter. Even then, it was bottled by Antinori, who would produce his own Bordeaux-inspired Tignanello in 1971. By the 1970s, Sassicaia was being bottled in-house, appearing in export markets by the end of that decade.

Following the death of Mario in 1983, his son Nicolò continued to enhance the reputation of Sassicaia around the world. It was not until 2000 that the estate tightened up fruit selection for its flagship by adding a second wine, called Guidalberto, swiftly followed in 2003 by another, Le Difese.

Today Sassicaia remains one of the most in-demand and respected examples of the Super Tuscan wave, which owes such a debt of gratitude to the wine and visionary individual who started it all.

BOLGHERI

Thanks in no small part to the success of Sassicaia, Bolgheri is now one of the most admired subregions of Tuscany and home to some of the biggest names on the Italian fine-wine scene today. It's diffi-

THE BARREL ROOM.

cult to imagine that until the 1970s this coastal Maremma area was largely associated with fairly undistinguished white and rosé wines. However, that cooling maritime influence, which was once believed to make the production of fine wine impossible here, is now hailed as a cornerstone of what makes this region great. The acclaim generated by the Super Tuscans, which had previously been classified as simply *vino da tavola* or IGT Toscana, eventually led to the creation in 1994 of DOC Bolgheri. As a sign of how much those once controversial Bordeaux varieties have now been accepted, Sangiovese is permitted to make up no more than 50 percent of a red DOC Bolgheri wine, while Cabernet Sauvignon, Cabernet Franc, and Merlot may each account for 100 percent of the blend.

As a mark of the special respect held for Sassicaia, it became the first and only Italian single estate to be awarded its own classification: DOC Bolgheri Sassicaia.

The success of Bolgheri has attracted a huge number of ambitious, well-funded producers today, although some of these wines tend to taste expensive rather than well made.

Some producers to look out for are Antinori's Guado al Tasso estate, Gaja's Ca'Marcanda, Le Macchiole, Grattamacco, and Ornellaia, which alongside its eponymous wine is also home to the Masseto brand.

TOP VINTAGES

While Sassicaia's success has sparked a host of producers in less well-suited sites hoping to justify their prices by deploying forests of new oak barrels, the original Super Tuscan remains striking in its modesty. Prices remain relatively modest when you consider the reputation of this wine and mark-ups of its peers, nor is there a particularly flashy winery; likewise, new oak plays a minority role.

The following vintages of Sassicaia are particularly noteworthy:

2010   A tale of purity and elegance, this combines the savory cassis and structure of classic claret with dancing spice and great length.

2008   Sophisticated and restrained, in youth this was muscular but still enticing, with those buttoned-up flavors set to shine with age.

2006   Hailed as one of the top Sassicaias to date. "Lafite-like in structure," said Jancis Robinson MW; "awesome," said Galloni.

2001   Relatively light in style, this nevertheless seems to have taken some time to show off its full charm but is now full of fresh finesse.

1998   This has turned out to be a great vintage for Bolgheri, with Sassicaia offering rich fruit and tobacco, then a long savory finish.

1988   Years ending in 8 seem particularly auspicious for Sassicaia, with this dark, ripe, meaty wine balanced by racy acidity.

Dream vintage: 1985   Although Sassicaia was already building an international reputation during the late 1970s and early 1980s, this stunning vintage really caught the critics' attention and catapulted the brand into the annals of the world's great Cabernet-based wines. Compared by Parker with Mouton Rothschild of a similar age, this oozes hedonistic opulence, intensity, and, even with age, an exciting vitality that suggests there is plenty of pleasure still to come.

R. LÓPEZ DE HEREDIA (VIÑA TONDONIA GRAN RESERVA)

Amid the ever-shifting tides of fashion that buffet Rioja, one of its oldest bodegas remains resolutely traditional, creating distinctive, ageworthy wines with a real sense of history.

Rioja has done an impressive job of representing Spanish wine of every imaginable price, color, and style. Such diversity makes it all the more impressive and important that one producer remains dedicated to creating truly benchmark examples of this region's most traditional and thrillingly unique wines.

Don Rafael López de Heredia y Landeta founded the company in 1877, building a bodega in the heart of Haro that remains the producer's base today. His inspiration came from observing the many French merchants who had been driven to explore the Rioja region after their own vineyards had been wiped out by the phylloxera epidemic.

Another major step taken by Don Rafael was his 1913 planting of the hundred-hectare Viña Tondonia site on the banks of the Ebro River. In a region with a culture of blending across different regions and relying on grower contracts, this vineyard, along with three others in Rioja Alta, has created a consistent and strong identity for López de Heredia.

At a Glance

ADDRESS
Avenida de Vizcaya, 3
26200 Haro, Spain
Tel: +34 9413 10244

PEOPLE
María-José López de Heredia (managing director)
Mercedes López de Heredia (winemaker)

SIZE
The core of the estate is its one-hundred-hectare Tondonia vineyard, augmented by seventy hectares split between Viña Cubillo, Viña Bosconia, and Viña Zaconia. Total annual production is around twenty-five thousand cases, with Tondonia Gran Reserva numbering around 1,500 cases when it is made.

KEY WINES
Viña Tondonia Reserva (white and red)
Viña Tondonia Gran Reserva (white, red, and rosé)
Viña Bosconia Reserva (red)
Viña Bosconia Gran Reserva (red)
Viña Cubillo (red)
Viña Gravonia (white)

GRAPE VARIETIES
Tempranillo (75 percent of Tondonia Gran Reserva blend)
Garnacha (15 percent)
Mazuelo (10 percent)
Graciano (10 percent)
Viura
Malvasia

On top of this vineyard influence comes a strikingly long maturation period—the top Gran Reserva style will spend around eight  years in old American oak barrels and perhaps another decade in bottle before the wine is deemed ready for release. As a result, visitors to the bodega will encounter an underground cathedral of fourteen thousand barrels and even more bottles full of quietly maturing wine. While its reds are justifiably revered, López de Heredia must also be acknowledged for its vital role in preserving Rioja's vanishing art of majestically ageworthy white and even rosé styles.

RIOJA IN A NUTSHELL

The Rioja region is broadly divided into three main parts: Rioja Alta, which is home to most of the top producers, including López de Heredia; Rioja Alavesa, similarly Atlantic in influence but with  a tendency toward smaller vineyard plots sheltered by the Sierra Cantabria; and Rioja Baja, whose Mediterranean climate favors a richer, riper style.

With some notable exceptions—again López de Heredia springs to mind—Rioja houses historically tended to focus on blending and maturation rather than viticulture, with most grapes bought from growers. Although that situation is now changing, emphasis tends to remain on a classification system that is based largely on the time a wine has spent in barrel and bottle prior to release. These tiers, running from Joven to Crianza and Reserva right up to Gran Reserva, still act as a useful indicator of style, but do not tell the full story. What's more, many producers have chosen to pursue a more modern, international style of darker wines aged in French rather than traditional American oak. These often shun the official classification system entirely. Inevitably there are also bodegas that tread a middle ground between these two extremes.

Names to look out for across this broad spectrum include CVNE, La Rioja Alta, Marqués de Murrieta, and Marqués de Riscal at the most traditional end, as well as modernists such as Artadi, Remírez de Ganuza, Finca Allende, and Roda.

TOP VINTAGES

Only produced in the best years—in reality just two or three times per decade—and with almost two decades of barrel and bottle maturation prior to release, even the youngest available expressions of Viña Tondonia Gran Reserva offer a stunning showcase for aged Rioja. What's more, these wines will continue to evolve beautifully with a longevity to rival Bordeaux—and at a fraction of the price.

The following vintages of Viña Tondonia Gran Reserva red (the house also produces an equally exciting, ageworthy white) are particularly noteworthy:

1995 This complex wine is well balanced, showing both power and elegance. It has well-rounded tannins, good acidity, and shows cherries, spice, and leather. An ethereal wine that could be better than the great 1994.

1994 Full of richness with red cherries, orange peel, and a structured vitality that bodes well for the future.

1987 A compelling, ethereal mix of cherries, mushroom, and smoke flavors, shot through with a lively dash of acidity.

1985 Few wines would be showing such youthful intensity at this age, but this Tondonia is full of harmonious complexity.

1981 Wild strawberries mingle with a creamy texture, giving way to spice, chocolate, and pencil shavings that linger enticingly.

1976 Plenty of tertiary flavors burst out of the glass with a liveliness that belies this wine's age; smooth, sweet-toned, and long.

1970 Aging very comfortably and evenly, with plenty of structure, smooth tannins, and fruit still shining through.

Dream vintage: 1964 A legendary year for Rioja, although all but the very best wines have now faded. This Tondonia remains enticingly ethereal, with delicate waves of fruit, spice, and leather emerging from the glass. Don't pair this with any powerful food—indeed, like fine mature Burgundy, this is a wine that rewards quiet contemplation rather than a crowded dinner table.

VEGA SICILIA (UNICO)

The high, arid Ribera del Duero was best known for its lamb until this estate almost single-handedly forged the region a reputation as a leading source of Spanish fine wine.

Vega Sicilia existed as an unofficial first growth of Spain long before its home of Ribera del Duero had even won recognition as a wine region. With no Denominacion de Origen until 1982, for a long time this was Spain's smartest *vino de mesa*. Established in 1864 by Don Eloy Lecanda y Chaves, Vega Sicilia's roots are distinctly Bordelais. Returning to Spain after training as a winemaker in Bordeaux, Don Eloy brought with him cuttings of Merlot, Cabernet Sauvignon, and Malbec, which he planted alongside the Spanish variety Tinto Fino, a local name for Tempranillo.

It was under the control of Cosme Palacio, a Rioja grower who leased Vega Sicilia while his own region was being ravaged by phylloxera, that the estate really began to build a reputation for excellence. This image endured through a series of twentieth-century ownership changes until Vega Sicilia found stability and fresh investment when it was bought by the Alvarez family in 1982.

The wines from this estate, and especially its top wine Unico, are characterized by a powerful yet not always immediately expressive style that derives in part from low-yielding old vines. In common with the approach seen at traditional Rioja bodegas, Unico historically underwent extensive barrel aging—sixteen years for its 1970 and twenty-three years for its 1968. Today that has shortened to just

At a Glance

ADDRESS
Carretera 122
47359 Valbuena de Duero, Spain
Tel: +34 983 680 147

PEOPLE
Alvarez family (owners)
Javier Ausás (winemaker)

SIZE
A thousand-hectare estate, of which around 270 hectares are planted with vines. In years when Unico is produced, quantities tend to be fewer than seven thousand cases.

KEY WINES
Unico (made only in the best years)
Reserva Especial (a blend of different Unico vintages)
Valbuena (released after five years)

GRAPE VARIETIES
Tinto Fino/Tempranillo (around 80 percent of the Unico blend)
Cabernet Sauvignon (20 percent)
Merlot
Malbec

five years with a similar period of bottle aging. The shift coincides with some critics noting a riper style and softer tannins than in the past. Time will tell whether this more approachable Unico still manages to age as well as its predecessors.

RIBERA DEL DUERO

Upstream from the famous port vineyards across the border in Portugal, Ribera del Duero offers an equally challenging climate where the tenacious vine can thrive. Nevertheless, it is only since 1982 that—thanks in no small part to the international acclaim won by Vega Sicilia—the region has held official Denominacion de Origen status.

As in Rioja, this is Tempranillo (known locally as Tinto Fino) country, with Cabernet Sauvignon, Garnacha, Malbec, and Merlot also permitted.

From the modest twenty-four wineries on the scene when its DO was created, Ribera del Duero has now become a major success story for Spain with over two hundred producers, many of them backed by outside investors. Despite its potential for greatness, however, wine quality remains far from uniform and prices may more closely reflect the region's prestige than the caliber of their product. Other names to look out for include Aalto, Dominio de Pingus, Pesquera, and Téofilo Reyes.

TOP VINTAGES

Only made in the best vintages, Unico today is usually released after ten years' combined barrel and bottle maturation, although this aging period will have varied considerably for older expressions.

The following vintages of Unico are particularly noteworthy:

2004   A voluptuous, explosively expressive character shows off this wine's stylistic shift at its most seductive, while retaining balance.

2002   Savory spice adds an intriguing layer of complexity to this smooth, rich expression.

1996   Dense but silky, even after nearly two decades, this wine is still tightly knit but reveals layers of dark fruit with a savory edge.

1990   Opulent and meaty with huge persistence, this shows off a strong vintage for the region to great effect.

1986   Full of seductive, plummy fruit, this expression of Unico brings intensity, depth, and a delightfully lingering finish.

1983   The purity and freshness of this wine has kept it youthful even after thirty years with a vibrancy that bodes well for the future.

1982   A marked stylistic contrast with the 1983, this offers a much broader and richer expression framed by firm tannins.

1981   Unico's run of exciting years continues with this vintage, which is full of dried herbs and dark berry fruit.

1979   A touch of animal character now adds an extra layer of complexity to this aromatic, earthy wine—decant well in advance of drinking.

1974   This wine's velvety texture and savory, herbal character remains full of excitement and shows no sign of tiring.

1972   Beautifully perfumed with dried flowers, there remains an enticing intensity to this wine that belies its considerable age.

1970   Another vintage that is maturing with real flair and energy, this wine is enormously expressive and full of charm.

1964   As with Rioja, this was a great year for Ribera, with Unico showing off a magnificently seductive, rich, and expressive style.

1962   Faultless, according to Parker, this vintage won a perfect score for its elegant blend of firm structure and stunning complexity.

1953   Showing the sweet, dried fruit character that can be expected with such considerable maturity, but wearing its age very lightly.

Dream vintage: 1942   Made in the middle of World War II, this wine represents a true triumph in the face of considerable adversity. Purity, elegance, and focus remain very much at the fore here, with flavors blossoming on the palate and a long finish.

GRAHAM'S (VINTAGE)

The sweet, opulent Graham's style has seduced many port lovers, but beneath this lies a finely honed structure that ensures its vintage wines thrive into a venerable old age.

The majority of port's biggest names are split between two English firms: The Fladgate Partnership, which owns Taylor's, Fonseca, and Croft, and Symington Family Estates, whose portfolio covers Graham's, Warre's, Dow's, and Cockburn's, as well as ambitious Douro table wines. Graham's was founded in 1820 by textile merchants William and John Graham. The Symington family connection began in 1882, when Andrew James Symington joined the company, became captivated by the Douro, and sparked a family link to this region that remains intact five generations later.

A major step forward for Graham's came with the acquisition in 1890 of Quinta dos Malvedos, which today provides the base for the house's top ports, including its highly regarded single quinta of this name. The same year saw Graham's make an equally significant move in the port trade's headquarters of Vila Nova de Gaia, where the firm built a new lodge to mature and store its wine. These two major investments won Graham's a place among the top port houses in time for a series of great prewar vintages as the category enjoyed something of a heyday.

At a Glance

ADDRESS
Rua Rei Ramiro
514 4400-281 Vila Nova de Gaia,
Portugal
Tel: +351 223 776 484

PEOPLE
Jointly run by Paul, Dominic, John, Rupert, and Charles Symington.

SIZE
Symington Family Estates is the Douro's largest vineyard owner. Graham's holdings cover five "A" grade quintas: dos Malvedos, das Lages, do Vale de Malhadas, da Vila Velha, and do Tua. This house produced about eight thousand six-bottle cases of its 2011 vintage port.

KEY WINES
Vintage styles: Graham's Vintage, Quinta dos Malvedos, Ne Oublie, a range of other mature colheitas, LBV. Nonvintage styles: ten-, twenty, thirty-, and forty-year-old tawny ports, and Six Grapes, a reserve ruby made with fruit from the five "A" grade properties.

GRAPE VARIETIES
A wide range of native varieties, of which the most widely used are: Touriga Franca, Touriga Nacional, Tinta Roriz, Tinta Barroca, Tinta Amarela, Tinta Cão, and Sousão.

The Symington connection revived in 1970, when the family bought Graham's. Among the most notable of many modernizing

investments have been robotic *lagares*, which, the family insists, match the quality of labor-intensive foot treading.

In 2014 the Symingtons' long link to Graham's came full circle with the launch of Ne Oublie, a tawny port laid down in the auspicious year of 1882 when their ancestor started the family's love affair with the Douro.

SINGLE QUINTA

Port lovers in search of alternatives to the region's great but irregular vintage releases could do worse than look at single-quinta ports. These estates invariably form the backbone of a house's vintage port in years when one is declared, but their individual charisma is really allowed to shine through in interim years when this high-quality fruit is often bottled as a single entity.

For fine-wine lovers the single-estate concept is not only familiar from other high-end wine regions, but also offers a revealing insight into their favorite vintage port through one of its key components.

Despite being made in a very similar way to vintage port, these single-quinta styles are designed to be drunk considerably earlier, usually at around eight to ten years old, although top examples will age beyond that. Among the most notable single-quinta ports to look out for are Graham's Quinta dos Malvedos, Warre's Quinta da Cavadinha, Dow's Quinta do Bomfim, Quinta do Vesuvio (another Symington holding), Taylor's Quinta da Vargellas, and Croft's Quinta da Roêda, not forgetting perhaps the most historic, prized port of all: Quinta do Noval's Nacional.

TOP VINTAGES

Each of the great ports is characterized by its own distinctive attributes, upon which is laid the individual style of the vintage. For Graham's that personality is one marked by richness and sweet-fruited complexity, with reassuring backbone.

The following vintages of Graham's vintage port are particularly noteworthy:

2011 The house's characteristic opulence shone through in this top vintage, but is tempered by precision, depth, and a mineral finish.

2007 Voluptuous and full of exotic spice, this was approachable in youth, but conceals a structure to carry it into the long term.

2003 That Graham's sweetness sits within a super-ripe vintage to create an explosive style that hides some of the powerful tannins.

2000 Striking sweetness sits on top of a wine of great density. A bit awkward in youth, it's set to come together and mature beautifully.

1994 A hedonistic port full of sweetness but also complex notes of spice, cigar box character, and leather to excite the drinker.

1985 Dark damson fruit and a smoked meat character lend real substance here, yet there's a dash of violets and deftly dry finish.

1977   Evolved and rich but plenty of tannin and acidity give this a lively kick, bolstered by spicy, nutty notes that linger on the finish.

1970   A great vintage to mark Symington's purchase of Graham's, this offers sweet, ripe fruit with a floral lift, then lingering spice.

1963   A fresh, enticing perfume brings nuts and spice before a beautifully balanced palate comes in, building to a long crescendo.

1955   Viewed by many as an underrated year, Graham's certainly shone with generous fruit, a supple structure, and bittersweet finish.

Dream vintage: 1948   Together with 1945, this is one of the great postwar port vintages. Hot weather in the weeks leading up to harvest created rich, sweet, caramel-edge fruit, but also great intensity that makes the hundred-year mark not impossible for this port.

TAYLOR'S

One of the oldest British-owned port houses, Taylor's has played a formative role in the evolution of one of the world's most beautiful but challenging wine regions.

Port may not fit so effortlessly into a modern era of table wines and informal dining, but quality in the region has never been better. One of the port houses with the longest and finest track records is Taylor's, which has remained independent since its creation in 1692 by English merchant Job Bearsley. His descendants built the business until the Napoleonic Wars of the early nineteenth century saw it pass into the neutral hands of the American-Turkish Joseph Camo for safekeeping. However, it was Joseph Taylor, a London employee, who gave his name to the house upon taking over from Camo as the founding family died out. Having set Taylor's port firmly on the right track, he passed the company on to one of his best customers, Morgan Yeatman, and John Fladgate, another merchant. It was Fladgate who moved to the Douro and guided the business through the phylloxera crisis before Frank Yeatman, Morgan's grandson, and his London-based brother Harry slowly rebuilt Taylor's vineyards and sales in the aftermath.

Frank's son Dick studied viticulture and brought a host of fresh ideas, including planting and fermenting grape varieties separately. After subsidizing the business through postwar austerity, Dick died in

At a Glance

ADDRESS
Rua do Choupelo No. 250
4400-088 Vila Nova de Gaia, Portugal
Tel: +351 223 742 800

PEOPLE
Adrian Bridge (CEO, Fladgate Partnership)
David Guimaraens (chief winemaker)

SIZE
Fruit sourced from across the Douro, but the top ports come from three estates: Quinta de Vargellas, Quinta de Terra Feita, and Quinta do Junco.

KEY WINES
Vintage styles: Taylor's Vintage, Quinta de Vargellas, Quinta de Terra Feita, Vargellas Vinha Velha, LBV.
Tawny styles: Ten-, twenty-, thirty-, and forty-year-old expressions, as well as limited editions Scion, 1863 single harvest, and a series of fifty-year-old single-harvest releases starting with 1964.

GRAPE VARIETIES
A wide selection of native grape varieties, of which some of the most widely used are: Touriga Franca, Touriga Nacional, Tinta Roriz, Tinta Barroca, Tinta Amarela, and Tinta Cão.

1966 and his nephew Alistair Robertson took over. He introduced LBV and a full range of tawny expressions, while guiding Taylor's through Portugal's political turmoil of the 1970s. Today Alistair's son-in-law Adrian Bridge heads a group that includes star players Croft and Fonseca, but Taylor's remains very much the jewel in the crown.

TEMPTING TAWNY

Vintage port may be the flagship for most serious producers, but with this vintages usually being declared no more than three times per decade, some houses have begun to shout more loudly about other top-end expressions. For Taylor's, this means a flurry of very old tawny styles. As well as being one of the few houses to produce a forty-year-old tawny as part of its core range, the house made headlines in 2010

when it released Scion, a single-harvest (*colheita*) tawny from 1855. This was followed by an 1863 release and, thanks to Taylor's acquisition of tawny specialist Wiese & Krohn, the house has now been able to introduce a series of fifty-year-old single-harvest expressions, starting in 2014 with a 1964 tawny.

Other houses have also recognized the excitement that such mature tawny styles can generate. In 2014 Graham's launched 656 decanters of "Ne Oublie," an 1882 single-harvest tawny port; meanwhile Sandeman celebrated its 225th birthday in 2015 by unveiling a 685-bottle release from a single-cask blend containing port up to seventy years old.

TOP VINTAGES

The mountainous Douro is not an easy place to make wine. As such, despite enormous improvements in viticulture, vinification, and the quality of spirit used to fortify these ports, it remains rare to see more than three vintages declared per decade.

The following vintages of Taylor's vintage port are particularly noteworthy:

2011 Some stunning vintage port was made this year, and Taylor's elegant and restrained yet expressive style was no exception.

2009 One of the few major houses to declare a vintage, this is a particularly ripe, dense style with a nevertheless firm structure.

2003 An intense burst of August heat helped to create a blockbuster expression from Taylor's with immediate polished appeal.

2000 A serious, refined expression, full of spicy aromas, peppery dark fruit and the fine tannins that are such a hallmark of this house.

1994 A classic style with rich, purple fruit framed by marked but fine tannins, which made this less accessible in youth than the 1992.

1992   Top marks from Parker with other critics in agreement about the quality of this beautifully balanced, perfumed expression.

1985   Notably delicate compared to many of its peers, this still packs a real punch on the palate, but in a truly elegant framework.

1970   Now at full maturity, this has really blossomed with age into a rich, leather-flecked, mellow style that retains plenty of density.

1963   An enticing nuttiness shows here, intertwined with spice, pepper, sweetness, and still a vibrant hit of ripe fruit.

Dream vintage: 1945   This end-of-World-War-II vintage produced some exceptional celebratory wines in many regions of Europe, the Douro included, and Taylor's is widely regarded to have made one of the finest expressions of all. Pale with age, this retains plenty of power, heady aromas, and great length.

SZEPSY (TOKAJI ASZÚ 6 PUTTONYOS)

As Tokaji battles to regain some of its former international glory, István Szepsy is leading the charge with his inspirational wines and relentless pursuit of fresh ideas.

In a world where so many regions and wines are arguably overhyped, or at least appear to have better mastery of their marketing than their grapes, it is important not to overlook those people and places making exceptional wines in relative obscurity. It is not as though Tokaji lacks pedigree: References to these sweet wines exist as far back as the sixteenth century, it was the first wine region in Europe to be recognized as an official appellation, and it began work on a classification system in 1730—more than 120 years ahead of Bordeaux. During the eighteenth and nineteenth centuries these wines were enjoyed and used as diplomatic weapons by everyone from Napoléon to Queen Victoria, Peter the Great, Emperor Franz Josef, and Thomas Jefferson. Sadly, by the time Hungary emerged from two world wars and the Iron Curtain, the world had moved on and sweet wines were no longer so fashionable. Nevertheless, the region is today full of exciting producers, of whom the widely acknowledged leading light is István Szepsy. Directly descended from the Szepsy who in 1631 is said to have become the first to write down the Tokaji "recipe," his wines set a quality benchmark for the region's modern face. Szepsy is

At a Glance

ADDRESS
Batthyány út 59
3909 Mád, Hungary
Tel: +3647 348349

PEOPLE
Istvan Szepsy (owner and winemaker)

SIZE
Fifty-two hectares of vines across twenty-two vineyards and six regions, but mostly located around the town of Mád. Annual production is about 3,200 cases of dry wine, six hundred cases of sweet wine, and one thousand cases of *szamorodni* (a sherried style).

KEY WINES
Dry styles: Estate Furmint and a range of single-vineyard expressions based on both single-varietal and blended Furmint, Hárslevelű, and Muscat. Also *szamorodni*.
Sweet styles: Late harvest, 6 Puttonyos Aszú, esszencia.

GRAPE VARIETIES
Furmint (65 percent of 6 Puttonyos blend)
Hárslevelű (20 percent)
Muscat Blanc à Petits Grains (15 percent)

also recognized as a pioneer, both in terms of developing dry styles

with a site expression that rivals Burgundy, and also in his work over the years with other top producers such as the Royal Tokaji Wine Company and Királyudvar. While dry styles may represent this region's commercial future, its sweet wines keep alive a link to Tokaji's noble past and Szepsy shows why both deserve far greater attention.

DRY STYLES

For all the thrills of traditional sweet Tokaji, many of the region's top producers have recognized that their survival depends on dry wines. Fortunately these are proving exciting and charismatic styles in their own right, shining a brighter spotlight on the qualities of local

OWNER AND WINEMAKER ISTVÁN SZEPSY.

grapes Furmint and Hárslevelű. Alongside Szepsy, other Tokaji producers to look out for include the Royal Tokaji Company (cofounded by UK wine writer Hugh Johnson), Királyudvar (owned by Anthony Hwang of Domaine Huet in the Loire), Zoltan Demeter, Diznókő (part of the AXA Millésimes portfolio alongside the likes of Château Pichon Baron and Suduiraut), Oremus (owned by Vega Sicilia), and Hétszőlő. With any luck, such a striking collection of high-end foreign investors will eventually help Tokaji to regain some of its lost international prestige.

N.B. Tokaj denotes the region, while Tokaji refers to its wine.

TOP VINTAGES

Tokaj's sweet aszú (pronounced "ossu," and meaning botrytis) wines come in a scale ranging from 3 to 6 puttonyos (named after the *puttony*, or basket, used to carry harvested grapes). Above this comes esszencia, which can reach up to eight hundred grams per liter of residual sugar. The minimum residual sugar level for a 6 puttonyos style is 150 grams per liter but Szepsy goes well beyond this with his own expression weighing in at around 260 grams per liter. The high natural acidity and sugar combined give exceptionally long-lived wines, although the modern industry dates only from the end of communism in 1989.

The following vintages of Szepsy Aszu 6 Puttonyos are particularly noteworthy:

2007 The hot summer gave this wine an even higher sugar content, even by Szepsy's high standards, but there's a complexity to match.

2006 Widely viewed as Szepsy's best vintage yet, this is a rich mix of marmalade, tea, and tobacco in a structured, harmonious package.

2003 Almost perfect conditions brought good levels of botrytis, creating an intensely apricot-flavored wine with plenty of acidity.

2000 "Pure pleasure," sums up Jancis Robinson MW about this winning combination of "gentle texture and explosive sweetness."

Dream vintage: 1999 From the first really good vintage of Tokaj's modern era, even in its youth this wine showed a lingering array of preserved fruit, spice, smoke, and floral notes. Some huge acidity combined with its intense concentration set it up for a lively future as an ambassador for this unfairly overlooked corner of Europe.

BODEGAS CATENA ZAPATA
(NICOLÁS CATENA ZAPATA)

*Producers and fans of Argentine wine have much to thank
the Catena family for, as these pioneers continue to explore
the next step for their country's top-end wines.*

The extraordinary rise of Argentine wine from an almost standing start in the 1990s, and in particular the runaway success of its Malbec, is due in no small part to the efforts of the Catena family. The variety was planted by Nicola Catena in 1902, soon after his arrival in Mendoza as part of a wave of Italian immigrants. While Nicola's son Domingo grew the businesses, it was the third generation in the form of Nicolás Catena whose influence proved most transformative. After seeing his family business struggle through Argentina's economic and political turmoil of the 1960s and 1970s, Nicolás left in the early 1980s to take a post as visiting professor of economics at UC Berkeley. This exposed him to the blossoming Napa Valley wine industry, which was by then attracting international attention. Returning home with new ambition, Nicolás brought in US consultant Paul Hobbs, himself a Malbec novice at that stage, to show that Argentina was capable of more than bulk wine. This goal saw him develop clones better suited to Argentina than the rustic results he was achieving with French cuttings. Raised trellises and improved irrigation were followed by the exploration of higher-altitude sites

and the addition of Cabernet Sauvignon and Chardonnay. The real breakthrough came in 2001, when Catena's 1997 Cabernet/Malbec launched with blind tastings in Europe and the US, attracting favorable comparison with Latour, Solaia, and Opus One. Today Nicolás's daughter Laura is pursuing ever higher quality levels for Malbec and ensuring Argentina retains its place on the world stage.

GOING TO EXTREMES

Argentina's ambitions have risen in tandem with the exploration of ever more extreme vineyard sites. In search of less fertile soil and cooler conditions, the solution has been either to go high or head south. Catena led the way with the former and has now been joined by many other producers in Mendoza's Uco Valley, where vineyards

lie at up to five thousand feet in altitude. Farther north, the heat pushes producers even higher, with Bodega Colomé in Salta having among the loftiest vineyards in the world at around ten thousand feet. For others, the key to finesse has been to head south into the cooler, less arid, apple-growing regions of Patagonia. Here in areas such as Neuquén and Río Negro, producers are not only making fresh, perfumed Malbecs but are also seeing success with other grapes, most notably Pinot Noir. Apart from Catena, other producers to look out for include Bodegas Fin del Mundo, Humberto Canale, and Bodegas

Chacra and Noemia in Patagonia; Terrazas de los Andes, Salentein, Achaval Ferrer, Dominio del Plata, and Viña Cobos in Mendoza; and Bodega El Esteco, El Porvenir de Cafayate, and Michel Torino in the northern valleys.

TOP VINTAGES

Having announced its arrival on the world stage in some style with the inaugural 1997 vintage, Nicolás Catena Zapata is still made from the estate's best plots of Cabernet Sauvignon and Malbec. Produced only in the best years, this wine sees the proportion of Malbec vary from just 5 percent in its first year to around 25 percent in more recent vintages.

The following vintages of Nicolás Catena Zapata are particularly noteworthy:

2010   Hailed as one of the finest versions of this wine to date, critics praised an intensity backed by acidity and striking sense of place.

2008   Malbec played a particularly big role this year at 35 percent of the blend, creating an enticing perfume and a rich but structured style.

2007   Packed full with aromas ranging from graphite to lavender and coffee, this is a powerful style built to last.

2006   Again, that characteristically exotic and alluring perfume marks this wine out, with plenty of complexity in the mouth too.

2005   A very polished and complete wine, full of complexity that draws the drinker in with its floral-tinted black fruit.

2004   Power tempered by elegance saw Parker describe this as "Argentina's equivalent of a great vintage of Lafite-Rothschild."

2001   With maturation, that complex array of flavors has evolved further as beetroot and rhubarb come into play with real vigor.

Dream vintage: 1997   The vintage that did so much to put not only this producer but Argentine wine as a whole on the map. This maiden expression set the tone for Nicolás Catena Zapata's ongoing ability to strike a delicate balance between show-stopping intensity, ripeness, and concentration and more refreshing qualities of lively acidity and elegance that make this wine as much a pleasure to drink as to taste.

PENFOLDS (GRANGE)

Australia's most famous wine represents a triumph of winemaking vision over corporate adversity and in the hands of Peter Gago is achieving greater heights than ever.

The vast majority of the world's great wines are rooted in a single estate or vineyard, but not Penfolds Grange. This slice of Australian history is a multiregional blend that today takes in Barossa Valley, Adelaide Hills, McLaren Vale, Clare Valley, and Penfolds' own Magill Estate on the outskirts of Adelaide.

Although Grange enjoys cult status today, its early history was far less surefooted. Having been sent to Europe in 1949 to learn more about port- and sherry-making, Penfolds' winemaker Max Schubert detoured via Bordeaux where he was inspired instead to make an ageworthy, full-bodied dry red. By 1952 he had unveiled the first commercial release of a wine then known as Grange Hermitage (the second part was dropped in 1989), only to be met by overwhelmingly negative feedback. Although ordered by the head office to abandon his project, Schubert kept making it in secret. As bottle age helped the 1951 and 1955 vintages to win over critics, Grange production "restarted"

in 1960, this time to widespread praise. When Schubert retired in 1975, successor Don Ditter finessed the wine by improving fruit and oak quality. Grange's star rose higher under the stewardship of John Duval from 1987 to 2002, when Peter Gago took over as winemaker. Like his predecessors, Gago has shielded Penfolds as the brand passed between corporate owners. Since 1991, Penfolds has run free recorking clinics around the world, an effective tool for removing poorly stored or counterfeit bottles from a secondary market where enthusiasm for this Australian icon more than vindicates Schubert's bold vision.

MOVING WITH THE TIMES

When he founded his estate in 1844, Dr. Christopher Rawson Penfold's aim was to produce medicinal tonic wine. In time the producer's focus shifted toward the fortified styles that remained the bedrock of Australian winemaking until well into Schubert's day. By the 1920s Penfolds had grown so significantly that its wines accounted for half of the country's annual wine sales.

In recent decades, nonfortified wine styles have come to the fore but Penfolds has stuck to its principle of multiregional blending for both its top wines, Grange and Yattarna, a Chardonnay first made in 1995. If Grange is South Australian through and through with a consistently large chunk of its blend coming from the sun-drenched Barossa, Yattarna has always been more cold-blooded and adventurous in terms of regional inclination. Its inaugural vintage used fruit from Adelaide Hills in South Australia, Henty in Victoria, Tumbarumba in New South Wales, and Derwent River Valley in Tasmania. By the 2010 vintage this blend reflected the wider enthusiasm for Tasmania among Australia's producers, with 96 percent of the fruit sourced from this remote island state. The remaining 4 percent came from Adelaide Hills, another region at the forefront of an exciting new era of elegant wines from the land Down Under.

TOP VINTAGES

In contrast to many estates' top wines, which are often made only in the best years, the multiregional approach used by Grange offers a useful safety net year in, year out. While certain vineyards feature regularly, Grange is nevertheless a tribute to the art of blending.

The following vintages of Grange are particularly noteworthy:

2010 Not many wines could survive seventeen months in new American oak, but this wowed critics with its alluring depth and complexity.

2009 Seductive and spicy, blending sweet vanilla character from the oak with more savory tar character; smooth but muscled.

2008 Some critics questioned whether it was worth its release price, but all agreed this exotic vintage is one of the best yet made.

2006 A dark, highly structured wine whose brooding intensity drew rave reviews but advice to leave this vintage for several years.

2005 Despite its heavy oaking, the fruit is what dominates here with real intensity, seasoned with aniseed and dark chocolate notes.

2004 A seamless, beautifully proportioned wine framed with plenty of ripe tannins and heralded by an intoxicating perfume.

2002 Australian critic James Halliday hailed this textured, black-fruited, licorice-edged wine as "one of the great Granges."

2001 A rare example of a Grange made from 100 percent Barossa Shiraz, it has taken time to harmonize such an opulent array of flavors.

1998 Almost overwhelmingly concentrated in its youth, this is evolving very slowly in a manner set to delight Grange fans.

1996   Another expression whose reviews look set to hot up further as this rich, intense wine relaxes with age to reveal its full charm.

1990   A majestic year for Grange, with its characteristic opulence tempered by just a suggestion of restraint and freshness.

1986   Hailed as a monumental Grange, this has been showing ever more exciting character with age but is still far from finished.

1982   Opulent and lush, this seduced critics across the board, although some felt it tipped over into slightly medicinal territory.

1976   Well-cellared bottles of this wine should still show well, even if youthful exuberance has now given way to more discreet charms.

Dream vintage: 1953   This historic artifact from the very earliest days of Grange's history may not have won over skeptics in its youth, but since then, along with other years such as 1955, has steadily unveiled the quality of which this wine is capable. Even after sixty years it retains a freshness, vitality, and great length.

SUMMARY OF GREAT VINTAGES
AND THOSE TO AVOID

Austria (Riesling)	Great	2007	2006	1999	1997	1995	1990	1986			
	Avoid	1998	1991	1989	1988	1987	1985	1984	1983	1982	
Bordeaux (St-Julien, Pauillac, St-Estèphe)	Great	2010	2009	2008	2005	2003	2000	1996	1995	1990	1989
	Avoid	2013	1993	1992	1991	1984					
Bordeaux (Graves)	Great	2010	2009	2008	2005	2000	1998	1990	1985		
	Avoid	2013	1992	1991	1984						
Bordeaux (Pomerol, St-Emilion)	Great	2012	2010	2009	2008	2006	2005	2003	2001	2000	1998
	Avoid	1993	1992	1991	1987	1984					
Bordeaux (Margaux)	Great	2010	2009	2008	2005	2000	1990	1986	1983		
	Avoid	2013	1993	1992	1991	1987	1984				
Côte de Nuits	Great	2013	2012	2011	2010	2009	2005	2003	2002	1999	1995
	Avoid	1994	1992	1987	1986	1984	1983	1982			
Côte de Beaune (Reds)	Great	2012	2011	2010	2009	2005	1999	1990			
	Avoid	2007	2006	2004	2001	2000	1998	1994	1993	1992	1991
Côte de Beaune (Whites)	Great	2013	2012	2011	2010	2009	2008	2007	2006	2005	2004
	Avoid	1994	1993	1991	1988	1987	1986	1984			
Rhône (Côte-Rotie, Hermitage)	Great	2012	2011	2010	2009	2006	2003	1999	1998	1997	1995
	Avoid	2008	2002	1993	1992	1986	1984				
Rhône (Châteauneuf-du-Pape)	Great	2012	2010	2009	2007	2006	2005	2003	2001	2000	1999
	Avoid	2002	1997	1996	1992	1991	1987	1986	1984	1982	
Germany (Riesling)	Great	2012	2011	2009	2007	2005	2004	2002	2001	1998	1996
	Avoid	2000	1981	1982							
Piedmont (Barbaresco)	Great	2012	2011	2010	2009	2008	2007	2006	2005	2004	2001
	Avoid	2002	1994	1992	1991	1984	1983				
Piedmont (Barolo)	Great	2011	2010	2009	2008	2007	2006	2005	2004	2003	2001
	Avoid	2002	1994	1992	1991	1984	1983				
Tuscany (Brunello di Montalcino)	Great	2010	2009	2008	2007	2006	2005	2004	2001	1999	1997
	Avoid	2002	1986	1984							
Tuscany (Chianti Classico)	Great	2013	2012	2010	2009	2008	2007	2006	2005	2001	1999
	Avoid	2003	1986	1984							
Port (Vintage)	Great	2011	2009	2008	2007	2003	2000	1994	1992	1991	1985
	Avoid	2001	1999	1998	1996	1995	1993	1990	1989	1988	1987
USA California (North Coast Cabernet)	Great	2014	2013	2012	2010	2009	2008	2007	2006	2005	2004
	Avoid	2011	2000	1988	1983						
USA California (North Coast Chardonnay)	Great	2014	2013	2012	2011	2010	2009	2007	2005	2004	2003
	Avoid	1989	1987								
USA Oregon (Willamette Valley)	Great	2012	2011	2008	2002	1999	1994	1990	1983		
	Avoid	1995	1987	1984							
Argentina	Great	2013	2012	2011	2010	2009	2008	2007	2006	2005	2004
	Avoid										
Australia	Great	2013	2012	2010	2006	2005	2004	2003	2002	2001	1998
	Avoid	2011	1983								

Source: Robert Parker's *Wine Advocate*.

1986   1985   1982

1995   1990   1989   1983   1982

1990

1987   1986   1984   1983   1982
2002   1996   1995

1991   1990   1989   1988   1985

1998   1995   1990   1989

1995   1989   1988

2000   1999   1998   1997   1996   1990   1989   1988   1985   1982

2000   1999   1998   1997   1996   1993   1990   1989   1988   1986   1985   1982

1995   1993   1990   1988   1985   1982

1997   1990   1988   1985   1982

1983

1986   1984

2003   2002   2001   1997   1996   1995   1994   1993   1992   1991   1990   1987   1986   1985   1984

2002   2001   1997   1995   1993   1992   1990   1986

1996   1994   1986

NOTES

32   *"Many French sommeliers"*: Michael Steinberger, "A Turn of the Corkscrew," *Slate*, January 2, 2008, http://www.slate.com/articles/life/drink/2008/01/a_turn_of_the_corkscrew.html.

32   *the word "sommelier"*: David Johnson, "A Historical Perspective of the Art of the Sommelier," *Hearsight*, http://hearsight.com/articles/d.johnson/sommelier3.html.

32   *old Provençal*: "Sommelier," *Wikipedia*, https://en.wikipedia.org/wiki/Sommelier.

32   *"official charged with"*: "sommelier," *Merriam-Webster*, https://www.merriam-webster.com/dictionary/sommelier.

33   *"We are expected to provide a positive"*: Rajat Parr and Jordan Mackay, *Secrets of the Sommelier: How to Think and Drink Like the World's Top Wine Professionals* (Berkeley, CA: Ten Speed Press, 2010), p. 14.

CREDITS

52–53 © Deepix 54 © Lacy Kiernan 55–57 Courtesy of Château Ausone 58 Per Karlsson—BKWine.com/Alamy Stock Photo 60 © Lacy Kiernan 61 © Studio Twin Photographie—Hervé Lefebvre 62–63 © Guillaume de Laubier 64–69 © Domaine Clarence Dillon 71 PersimmonPictures.com/Alamy Stock Photo 73 © Lacy Kiernan 75, top Adam Eastland/Alamy Stock Photo 75, bottom Olivier Roux/Sagaphoto.com/Alamy Stock Photo 76 © Lacy Kiernan 77 Courtesy of Château Léoville Las Cases 79 © Lacy Kiernan 80 Olivier Roux/Sagaphoto.com/Alamy Stock Photo 82 © Lacy Kiernan 83 © Guillaume de Laubier 84 © Michael Coode 85 © Deepix 88 © Lacy Kiernan 90 Tim Graham/Alamy Stock Photo 92 © Lacy Kiernan 94, top © Château Pichon Baron/photo A. Benoit (Deepix) 94–95 © Château Pichon Baron/photo Vinexia.FR 97–98 Courtesy of Château Pichon Longueville Comtesse de Lalande 99–100 © G. Uféras/Château d'Yquem 101 © Lacy Kiernan 104 Per Karlsson, BKWine 2/Alamy Stock Photo 105 © Lacy Kiernan 109–11 © Jean Chevaldonné 115–16 © Lacy Kiernan 118 © Elisabeth Andanson/Sygma via Getty Images 120 Courtesy of Domaine Dujac 122–31 © Lacy Kiernan 133–34 Courtesy of Domaine Méo-Camuzet 138 © Lacy Kiernan 139–42 Courtesy of Domaine Armand Rousseau

144–46 Courtesy of Louis Roederer **148** Richard Semik/Alamy Stock Photo **150** © Lacy Kiernan **151** © Thierry Des Ouches **152** Krug Clos du Mesnil © Alexis Jacquin **153–57** © Lacy Kiernan **160, top** © Serge Chapuis **160, bottom** © Philippe Martineau **161–65** © Lacy Kiernan **168, top** Per Karlsson—BKWine.com/ Alamy Stock Photo **168, bottom** Per Karlsson, BKWine 2/Alamy Stock Photo **169** © Lacy Kiernan **172–73** Courtesy of F. E. Trimbach **176–77** Courtesy of Château Montelena **180** © Debra Peterson **181** Courtesy of Hanzell Vineyards **183–85** Courtesy of Harlan Estate **189** Courtesy of Hundred Acre **192, top** © Kelly McManus/ Courtesy of Kistler Vineyards **192, bottom** © David Wakely/Courtesy of Kistler Vineyards **193** © Kelly McManus/Courtesy of Kistler Vineyards **197** © Lacy Kiernan **200** Courtesy of Heidi Nigen/Ridge Vineyards **201** Courtesy of Ridge Vineyards **205–8** © Lacy Kiernan **210** Thomas Heinser/Courtesy of Spottswoode Estate Vineyard & Winery **211** Courtesy of Spottswoode Estate Vineyard & Winery **214** Courtesy of Stag's Leap Wine Cellars LLC **215** © Lacy Kiernan **216** © Gilles Bassignac/Gamma-Rapho via Getty Images **221** © Lacy Kiernan **224** Courtesy of Allegrini **225** © Lacy Kiernan **227** Manfred Glueck/Alamy Stock Photo **228** © Lacy Kiernan **231** Philippe Martineau/Le Pictorium/Alamy Stock Photo **231** Map Courtesy of Gaja **234** © Lacy Kiernan **235–36** Courtesy of Bruno Giacosa **237–39** Courtesy of Tenuta San Guido **242** Julian Eales/ Alamy Stock Photo **243–47** © Lacy Kiernan **250–51** Courtesy of Graham's Port/Symington Family Estates **254–55** Courtesy of Taylor's Port **258–59** Courtesy of the Szepsy Winery **261–62** Courtesy of Catena Zapata **266** © Lacy Kiernan

INDEX